D1602906

# THE GROUP OF 77

## EVOLUTION, STRUCTURE, ORGANIZATION

*by*

KARL P. SAUVANT

OCEANA PUBLICATIONS, INC.
New York • London • Rome

DR. KARL P. SAUVANT is currently Transnational Corporations Affairs Officer, Centre on Transnational Corporations, United Nations. He has previously been with the United Nations Department of Economic and Social Affairs; the Multinational Enterprise Unit, the Wharton School, University of Pennsylvania, and the Foreign Policy Research Institute. Current address: Rm. BR-1008, Centre on Transnational Corporations, United Nations, c/o Box 20, Grand Central P.O., New York, N.Y. 10017.

**Library of Congress Cataloging in Publication Data**
Sauvant, Karl P.
  The Group of 77.
  Includes index.
  1. Group of 77.  2. Underdeveloped areas--
Commerce.  I. Title.
HF1413.S315    1981        338.91'09172'4        81-3998
ISBN 0-379-00964-1                               AACR2

Manufactured in the United States of America

*.. our diversity exists in the context of one
common and overriding experience. What we have
in common is that we are all, in relation to the
developed world, dependent — not interdependent —
nations. Each of our economies has developed as a
by-product and a subsidiary of development in the
industrialized North, and is externally oriented.
We are not the prime movers of our own destiny.
We are ashamed to admit it; but economically we are
dependencies — semi-colonies at best — not
sovereign States.... The object is to complete
the liberation of the Third World countries from
external domination. That is the basic meaning of
the New International Economic Order. And unity is
our instrument — our only instrument — of liberation.*

*Mwalimu Julius K. Nyerere*

# TABLE OF CONTENTS

# LIST OF FIGURES

# LIST OF TABLES

# FOREWORD

The Group of 77 came into being at the first session of the United Nations Conference on Trade and Development in 1964. In spite of all the Group's imperfections—some of which can be ameliorated while others are inherent in its very nature—the developing countries would not have been able to function without it.

Not being institutionalized, the Group of 77 constitutes itself whenever the need arises for any particular set of negotiations. Nonetheless, the Group has become consolidated and its existence is no longer questioned. Although the logic for its need may not always be clear to some outsiders, every member country will stay in the Group for as long as it considers it to be in its interest. And the Group will continue to exist as long as it is needed to fulfill its indispensable role. For it is certain that, without the Group of 77, the world would have done little, if anything, to modify its previous attitudes and actions on development matters.

There is a clear awareness within the Group of 77 that, as far as actions are concerned, little progress has been made. Achievements have been limited to isolated cases of international co-operation, such as the Generalized System of Preferences and the Common Fund for commodities. Moreover, it is equally clear that the compromise solutions on these issues, agreed upon after long and difficult negotiations, would not have materialized without the Group of 77.

The accumulated mistakes of the main developed countries resulted in major upheavals—wrongly presented as the energy crisis— at the beginning of the 1970's. This gave the Group of 77 the unique opportunity, at the Sixth Special Session of the United Nations General Assembly, to launch the idea of the New International Economic Order. This initiative galvanized the Group of 77 anew and permeated all subsequent international discussions on development issues. One of the high points of these discussions was the Seventh Special Session of the United Nations General Assembly at which a consensus between the North and the South was reached. On the other hand, the Paris Conference on International Economic Co-operation (in which the Group of 77 acted through the Group of 19) was, although worthwhile, on the whole an inconclusive effort to make progress.

Since then, the North-South dialogue has returned to the United Nations. There, the Group of 77 has again taken the initiative by proposing global negotiations on international economic co-operation for development. So far, however, delaying tactics have prevented the dialogue from advancing. The inertia of the main developed countries, together with their inability to reconcile common long-term objectives with short-term constraints, is largely responsible for the present stalemate. An unprecedented lack of vision, with serious risks for *all* the peoples of the world, continues to prevent the adoption of urgently needed improvements and the establishment of the New International Economic Order.

Bearing in mind the ever increasing number of specialized multilateral economic meetings (both within and outside the United Nations) and especially the importance and complexity of the global negotiations, there is an increasing need to establish a small and competent technical team to support the Group of 77 in its negotiations. Such a technical supporting team would be directly responsible to the chairperson of the Group of 77, but would not imply an attempt to institutionalize the Group. However, it could play an important role in assuring the negotiating preparedness of the Group as a whole and hence make a valuable contribution towards achieving more satisfactory results from the negotiations themselves.

In realizing its own broad potential, the Group of 77 has given increasing attention to the idea of individual and collective self-reliance and has provided new impetus to economic co-operation among developing countries. This is another challenge of vast proportions, and it is one with good prospects for success. The diversity among developing countries provides them with immense opportunities for mutually beneficial exchanges. What was thought by some as a weakness of the developing countries—that is, the disparities existing in their stages of development, a situation often used with divisive intentions—could be seen as a source of present and future strength for the Group of 77 as a whole.

It is clear in retrospect that, although the Group of 77 has made tactical mistakes, its course has been, from the outset, the right one. It has been a course not only for the benefit of the developing countries, but rather for the benefit of the world community as a whole. The concept of the New International Economic Order represents the only innovative and challenging blueprint for a new world order that has been offered by any group of countries. Through it, the Group of 77—whether in New York, Geneva or elsewhere—has become an important moral and political force in international economic relations.

The Group of 77 is therefore confident that it can continue to play an important role for its members and for the world community. Nevertheless, it is obvious that the world requires decisive contributions from the North as well. What I hope is that the confluence of these forces will not come too late to bring about a peaceful, just, and prosperous world. The Group of 77 is aware that this is a difficult undertaking because it requires profound structural changes. By remaining united, the Group will be able to take upon itself greater responsibilities. In the end, the solidarity of the international community passes through the solidarity of the Third World.

Given the importance of the Group of 77, this book by Karl P. Sauvant fills a gap in the literature on North-South relations. Its thorough coverage and penetrating analysis of the evolution, structure and organization of the Group of 77 make it an important reference book. It is a publication which should be read by all those concerned with the negotiation of the New International Economic Order.


New York
January 1981                                      Manuel Pérez-Guerrero

# PREFACE

Since its inception in 1964, the Group of 77 (which now actually has 122 members) has served as the principal organ of the Third World for articulating and promoting its collective economic interest. In the performance of this function, the Group has shaped large parts of the international economic programme of the Third World and hence the substantial content of the international development discussions.

Most of these discussions and, therefore, the activities of the Group of 77 take place in the framework of the United Nations system. There, the Third World succeeded, at the 1974 Sixth Special Session of the United Nations General Assembly, in making the development task a priority item on the international agenda. The adoption of the "Declaration and Programme of Action on the Establishment of a New International Economic Order" by that Session marked the universal recognition that development ought to be one of the principal purposes to be served by the international economic system.

If this is to be done efficiently, the mechanisms and structures of the existing order have to be changed accordingly: an order has to be created that is maximally conducive to development. In the negotiations undertaken in the pursuit of this objective, the Group of 77 represents the collective economic interest of the Third World in all global negotiations with the developed countries. North-South negotiations about the international economic system in general and its impact on the development process of the Third World in particular are thus unthinkable without the Group of 77.

In spite of the obvious importance of the Group of 77 and its remarkable ability to maintain its unity, no detailed examination of the functioning of the Group has as yet been attempted. There are many reasons for this. To begin with, the Group of 77 has neither permanent institutions nor even a constitution. In addition, the Group is multi-central in character, with each of the centres having developed independently in response to different circumstances and with communication among the various centres being often imperfect. The informality of most of the Group's arrangments also reflects the need to maintain a high degree of organizational flexibility in order to be able to absorb new developments and to accommodate the diverging special interests of its individual members. Finally, most of the individual countries are very reluctant to commit themselves to any rules that might restrict the sovereign right of each to independent action.

Nevertheless, in response to new needs and through the observance of precedents, generally accepted patterns of conducting the affairs of the Group of 77 have evolved and organizational structures have been created. Some are formally recognized as being permanent; others are periodically and predictably revived; and yet others have acquired an implicit status by remaining unchallenged. Together they represent the formal and informal institutional infrastructure of the Group of 77.

The purpose of this book is, therefore, to show how the capacity of the Group of 77 for joint action developed, how the Group organized itself, and how it functions today. In Part I, the origin of the Group, its purposes and objectives, its membership, and its decision-making procedures are analysed. Part II, then, deals with the structure of the Group of 77 and examines its organization at the main centres in which it is (or was) active: The United Nations Conference on Trade and Development (UNCTAD) in Geneva, the United Nations Industrial Development Organization (UNIDO) in Vienna, the International Monetary Fund (IMF) and the World Bank in Washington (the Group of 24), the Conference on International Economic Co-operation in Paris (the Group of 19), and the United Nations in New York. If the following text contributes to a greater understanding of the Group of 77 and if it succeeds in capturing the diversity of ways in which the Group functions in the global development negotiations, this book will have served its purpose.

This manuscript was written while I was also preparing a collection of the documents of the Group of 77 spanning the period 1963-1980; it is, therefore, based mainly on documentary research. However, the analysis of an institution of which informality is a salient feature and in which few records are kept can only be done with the generous support of persons affiliated with the institution. I am thus very conscious of my good fortune of having been able to benefit from the insights and help of Mohamed Ben Redjeb, Marin Buhoará, Miodrag M. Cabrić, Wilbert-Kumalija Chagula, Liliana de Silva, Ahmed Ghezal, Enrique G. ter Horst, Roy E. Mattar, Nicolás Rigoberto Monge López, Mian Quadrud-Din, Douglas A.C. Saunders, Veena Sikri, Gustavo Silva Aranda, and Atmono Suryo. Manuel Pérez-Guerrero, apart from greatly furthering my understanding of the Group of 77, also kindly agreed to write the foreword. To Miguel Rodriguez-Mendoza I owe a special debt: his continuous support and incisive criticisms have been invaluable. I am also indebted to a number of officials, who wish to remain anonymous, from the secretariats of UNCTAD, UNIDO, the IMF, and the United Nations in New York for their clarifications and criticisms. And, finally, I greatly appreciate the careful editing that Vishwas Govitrikar gave to the manuscript. To all of them: thank you very much.

Naturally, any errors, omissions or misinterpretations that may have occurred are my responsibility alone. And, of course, nothing in this volume necessarily represents the views of the institution with which I am affiliated.

New York, January 1981                                    Karl P. Sauvant

# PART I
# THE EVOLUTION OF THE GROUP OF 77

# The Evolution of the Group of 77

## A. The Origin

In December 1961, the General Assembly of the United Nations designated the 1960s as the "United Nations Development Decade".[1] At the same time, it also adopted a resolution on "International Trade as the Primary Instrument for Economic Development",[2] in which the Secretary-General of the United Nations was asked to consult governments on the advisability of holding an international conference on international trade problems. These resolutions led to the United Nations Conference on Trade and Development (UNCTAD); their underlying developmental model—trade as the motor of development—shaped the outlook and approach of the new institution.

After obtaining favourable reactions from most governments and strong support from a developing countries' "Conference on the Problems of Economic Development" held in Cairo in July 1962,[3] the United Nations General Assembly decided to convene the first session of UNCTAD.[4] A Preparatory Committee was established to consider the agenda of the conference and to prepare the necessary documentation.

During the deliberations of the Preparatory Committee—in identifying the relevant issues and problems, endeavouring to list proposals for action, and indicating lines along which solutions might be sought —the divergence of the interests of the developing from those of the developed countries began to emerge sharply. The distinctive interests of the Third World manifested themselves at the closing of the second session of the Preparatory Committee (21 May to 29 June 1963), when the representatives of the developing countries submitted a "Joint Statement" to the Committee in which they summarized the views, needs and aspirations of the Third World with regard to the impending UNCTAD session.[5] Later that year, this Statement was submitted to the General Assembly, as a "Joint Declaration", on behalf of 75 developing countries which were members of the United Nations.[6] This Declaration was the prelude to the establishment of the Group of 77.

UNCTAD I met in Geneva between the 23rd of March and the 16th of June 1964. It was the first major North-South conference on development questions. During the negotiations at that conference, economic interests clearly crystalized along geo-political-group lines and the developing countries emerged as a group that was beginning to

1

find its own identity (see Table 1 - all tables are contained in Annex I of this volume). The "Joint Declaration of the Seventy-Seven", adopted on 15 June 1964, referred to UNCTAD I as "an event of historic significance"; it continued:

> The developing countries regard their own unity, the unity of the seventy-five, as the outstanding feature of this Conference. This unity has sprung out of the fact that facing the basic problems of development they have a common interest in a new policy for international trade and development. They believe that it is this unity that has given clarity and coherence to the discussions of this Conference. Their solidarity has been tested in the course of the Conference and they have emerged from it with even greater unity and strength.

> The developing countries have a strong conviction that there is a vital need to maintain, and further strengthen, this unity in the years ahead. It is an indispensable instrument for securing the adoption of new attitudes and new approaches in the international economic field. This unity is also an instrument for enlarging the area of co-operative endeavour in the international field and for securing mutually beneficent relationships with the rest of the world. Finally, it is a necessary means for co-operation amongst the developing countries themselves.

> The seventy-five developing countries, on the occasion of this declaration, pledge themselves to maintain, foster and strengthen this unity in the future. Towards this end they shall adopt all possible means to increase the contacts and consultations amongst themselves so as to determine common objectives and formulate joint programmes of action in international economic co-operation. They consider that measures for consolidating the unity achieved by the seventy-five countries during the Conference and the specific arrangements for contacts and consultations should be studied by government representatives during the nineteenth session of the United Nations General Assembly.[7]

Although the recommendations adopted by UNCTAD I were to a large extent inspired by the conceptual work undertaken in the preceding decade by the Economic Commission for Latin America — whose Executive Secretary, Raúl Prebisch, became the Secretary-General of UNCTAD I and stayed in that post as one of the principal promoters of Third World unity until 1969[8] — the conference was nonetheless a new departure: for the first time, the Third World *as a whole* had participated in the elaboration of a comprehensive set of measures.[9] Accordingly, "new" was the theme of the "Joint Declaration of the Seventy-Seven": UNCTAD I was recognized as a significant step towards "creating a new and just world economic order"; the basic premises of the "new order" were seen to involve "a new international division of labour" and "a new framework of international trade"; and the adoption of "a new and dynamic international policy for trade and development" was expected to facilitate the formulation of "new policies by the Governments of both

2

developed and developing countries in the context of a new awareness of the needs of developing countries". Finally, a "new machinery" was considered necessary to serve as an institutional focal point for the continuation of the work initiated by the conference.

This machinery was established later that year, when the General Assembly decided to institutionalize UNCTAD as an organ of the General Assembly.[10] UNCTAD remained the main forum for global development discussions for the next decade and—guided by the expectations voiced in 1964—it became the focal point of the activities of the Group of 77 which, by the fall of 1980, counted 122 members[11] (see Table 1). (United Nations membership totalled 154.) During that period, the Group of 77 became an integral part of UNCTAD, was one of the most important agents for the socialization of the developing countries in matters relating to international political economy, and established itself firmly in all major relevant parts of the United Nations system as the Third World's principal organ for the articulation and aggregation of its collective economic interest and for its representation in the negotiations with the developed countries.[12]

## B. Purpose and Objectives

No-one has formulated the political point of departure of the Third World more succinctly than Mwalimu Julius K. Nyerere when he said in his address to the Fourth Ministerial Meeting of the Group of 77 in Arusha, in February 1979:

> What we have in common is that we are all, in relation to the developed world, dependent - not interdependent - nations. Each of our economies has developed as a by-product and a subsidiary of development in the industrialized North, and it is externally oriented. We are not the prime movers of our own destiny. We are ashamed to admit it, but economically we are dependencies - semi-colonies at best - not sovereign States.[13]

(The speech is reprinted in Annex II-B.) The objective is, therefore, quite naturally, "to complete the liberation of the Third World countries from external domination".[14]

Until the early 1970s, the Group of 77 thought to achieve this objective through improvements of the system, the high-points being UNCTAD II (New Delhi, 1968) and UNCTAD III (Santiago, 1972) and the preparatory First (Algiers, 1967) and Second (Lima, 1971) Ministerial Meetings of the Group of 77, as well as UNIDO I (Vienna, 1971) and the adoption of the international development strategy for the Second United Nations Development Decade (1970). A number of

3

changes were in fact made (witness, for instance, the Generalized System of Preferences), but many other negotiations (for instance in the commodity sector) hardly made any progress and no drastic improvements took place. On the contrary, the gap between North and South widened, especially for the least developed among the developing countries.

The limitations of the approach taken by UNCTAD and the Group of 77 naturally took time to become apparent. In addition, until the end of the 1960s, neither developed nor developing countries had fully realized the importance of economic development as a necessary complement to political independence. The development issue was regarded as "low politics", left to the technical ministries of planning, economics, commerce, finance, and development. Attempts to politicize the issue therefore failed. The most prominent among them was the "Charter of Algiers", adopted by the First Ministerial Meeting of the Group of 77 in October 1967 in preparation of UNCTAD II. The intention of this first comprehensive declaration and programme of action of the Group of 77 was to give a new impetus to the North-South negotiations. For this purpose, the Ministerial Meeting even decided to send high-level "goodwill missions" to a number of developed countries (both those with centrally-planned and those with market economies) to inform key governments about the conclusions of the meeting and to persuade them of the need for accelerated progress.[15]

At the beginning of the 1970s, however, several developments converged to produce a change in attitudes: the political decolonization process had largely run its course and the political independence of most of the new states had been consolidated; the political-military pressures of the Cold War were subsiding; the regional and international development efforts had shown disappointing results; and doubts had begun to be voiced about the prevailing development model.[16] As a result, more attention could be given to other important matters. For the developing countries, this meant that questions of economic development began to receive greater attention and they became increasingly aware that the institutions of the international economic system had been established by the developed market economies to serve primarily their own purposes.[17] Since, in the process, the interests, needs and special conditions of the developing countries had largely been ignored, they remained in poverty and dependency. Hence, fundamental changes in the international economic system were required to establish a framework conducive to development and to create the economic basis of independence. In fact, the system itself had come under serious strain with the

4

breakdown of the Bretton Woods system, the food and oil crises, payments imbalances, a general surge of inflation, world recessions, increasing protectionism, rising environmental concerns, and the spectre of the scarcity of raw materials. When the economic tranquility of the 1960s gave way to the turbulence of the 1970s, international economic matters could no longer be ignored.

The non-aligned movement offered the framework for this recognition to grow and, within a few years, development questions became "high politics": they were elevated to the level of heads of state or government and were made a priority item on their agenda. Between 1970 and 1973, the non-aligned movement evolved into a pressure group for the re-organization of the international economic system.[18] Since the Non-Aligned Countries considered themselves to be playing a catalytic role within the Group of 77,[19] the politicization of the development issue had an important effect on the manner in which this issue was perceived, presented and pursued within North-South negotiations. Thus, the political clout and pressure of the Non-Aligned Countries, coupled with OPEC's forceful actions, led to the Sixth Special Session of the United Nations General Assembly which adopted, on 1 May 1974, the "Declaration and Programme of Action on the Establishment of a New International Economic Order".[20] Hence, almost exactly one decade after the first session of UNCTAD, and after years of debates about improvements in the international economic system, the call for a new beginning was again taken up - this time, however, with a view to a structural re-organization of the world economy. The establishment of the New International Economic Order (NIEO) has since been the main objective of the Third World. The concrete changes that the Group of 77 proposes in order to achieve this objective are spelled out in detail in the "Arusha Programme for Collective Self-Reliance and Framework for Negotiations," adopted by the Fourth Ministerial Meeting of the Group of 77 in Arusha, in February 1979. Given the importance of this document for the content of the current international development discussion, it is reprinted in full in Annex II-B.

While the Non-Aligned Countries played a key role in making the development issue a priority item on the international agenda, the Group of 77 has become the principal organ of the Third World through which the concrete actions required for the establishment of the NIEO are negotiated within the framework of the United Nations system. This objective dominated UNCTAD IV (Nairobi, 1976) and UNCTAD V (Manila, 1979) and the preparatory Third (Manila, 1976) and Fourth (Arusha, 1979) Ministerial Meetings of the Group of 77;

5

UNIDO II (Lima, 1975) and UNIDO III (New Delhi, 1980) and the preparatory meetings of the Group of 77 in Vienna (1974), Algiers (1975) and Havana (1979); the regional preparatory meetings convened for each of these UNCTAD and UNIDO conferences by the African, Arab (for UNIDO only), Asian, and Latin American members of the Group of 77; the 1976 Mexico City Conference on Economic Co-operation among Developing Countries; the 1975-1977 Paris Conference on International Economic Co-operation, in which the Group of 77 acted through the Group of 19; and a series of ministerial-level meetings of the Group of 77 (including meetings of ministers for foreign affairs) in preparation for sessions of the United Nations General Assembly. It also entered into the discussions in the IMF and the World Bank, where the Group of 77 has been acting through the Group of 24 since 1972.

There is still a considerable gap between the declaration of a new order and the action programmes formulated to establish it in the major areas of North-South interactions: commodities and trade, money and finance, R and D and technology, industrialization and transnational enterprises, and food and agriculture. In fact, an analysis of the contents of the present NIEO programme shows that, although a number of additional problems have been identified, many of the concrete proposals under discussion have remained the same since 1964—even if the emphasis on some of them, e.g., proposals concerning technology, has grown. This is a clear indication of the slow progress made in the past. Now, however, these proposals are aimed at creating new economic structures; and, to a greater extent than in the past, it has come to be recognized that the various dimensions of North-South interactions are interrelated and hence have to be approached in a comprehensive and integrated manner. Over time, the gap between objectives and concrete proposals may be closed through the elaboration of new policies or possibly even through changes in the underlying development model. For the time being, however, this model continues to assume that development is best served by a very close association of the developing with the developed countries.

A conceptual change may however be in the offing with the concept of individual and collective self-reliance. In contradistinction to the prevailing associative development strategy with its orientation towards the world market and its heavy reliance on linkages with the developed countries for stimulating industrialization, self-reliance seeks greater selectivity in traditional linkages, accompanied by a greater mobilization of domestic and Third World resources and a

6

greater reliance on domestic and Third World markets. It is these markets, rather than those in the developed world, which are now expected to provide the principal stimulus for economic development.

The concept of self-reliance was introduced into the international development discussion by the Non-Aligned Countries in 1970, which were also responsible for most of the practical follow-up that has been undertaken so far in this area.[21] Although self-reliance can be strengthened by international measures,[22] it requires primarily a strengthening of linkages among developing countries. For this reason, the Group of 77—which, as was pointed out above, concentrates almost exclusively on North-South negotiations within the system of the United Nations—has been slow in incorporating self-reliance into its own programme.

The first effort was made at the 1976 Third Ministerial Meeting of the Group of 77, during which a resolution on economic co-operation among developing countries was adopted.[23] Through this resolution, which links the work of the Group of 77 with that of the Non-Aligned Countries (whose pioneering merits in this area are recognized in the resolution), it was decided to convene a meeting in Mexico City during the month of September 1976 to prepare a detailed programme on economic co-operation. Originally, it was planned to hold this meeting at the level of an intergovernmental working group; but at the subsequent UNCTAD IV session it was decided to hold it at the highest possible level.[24] Hence, the Conference on Economic Co-operation among Developing Countries was convened in Mexico City from the 13th to the 22nd of September 1976, to date the only major conference of the Group of 77 that was not closely and directly related to an important impending activity within the United Nations system.

The full integration of this approach into the Group's conceptual main stream came, however, only during the 1979 Arusha Fourth Ministerial Meeting in preparation of UNCTAD V, an event signalled by the very title of the final declaration of that meeting, the "Arusha Programme for Collective Self-Reliance and Framework for Negotiations". As this title indicates, the declaration consists of two parts: a programme for self-reliance (even if this is formulated only in terms of economic co-operation among developing countries) and a programme for North-South negotiations. Thus, a shift in the United Nations-orientation of the Group may be taking place and the Group of 77 (together with, or in addition to, the Non-Aligned Countries) may make greater efforts towards stronger South-South co-operation.

That such a re-orientation is, in fact, occurring seems to be corroborated by the actions taken by the Arusha Ministerial Meeting:

it strongly endorsed the recommendations of the Mexico City Conference regarding an institutional follow-up for economic co-operation among developing countries. As a consequence, a (regionally prepared) first meeting of Governmental Experts of Developing Countries on Economic Co-operation among Developing Countries was convened for March-April 1980. This inter-regional gathering, in turn, was fully supported by a March 1980 Ministerial Meeting of the Group of 77 in New York, during which economic co-operation among developing countries was a special item on the agenda and which decided to set up an open-ended *ad hoc* group "with the task of elaborating appropriate action-oriented recommendations for the early and effective implementation of the objectives of economic co-operation among developing countries".[25] This task was begun by the "*Ad-hoc* Intergovernmental Group of the Group of 77 on Economic Co-operation among Developing Countries in Continuation of the Ministerial Meeting of the Group of 77 Held in New York in March 1980" in a session in Vienna in June 1980. Its conclusions and recommendations were considered a useful basis for further discussions by the 1980 Meeting of Ministers for Foreign Affairs of the Group of 77. Deliberating shortly after the 1980 Eleventh Special Session of the General Assembly, the failure of that Session led the Ministers to stress that economic co-operation among developing countries is "an indispensable element both of the accelerated development of developing countries and of strengthening their negotiating power in their relations with the rest of the world".[26] The Ministers decided, therefore, to convene a high-level conference on economic co-operation among developing countries for 1981, to expedite the implementation of various programmes and decisions relating to this subject matter.

A re-orientation towards South-South co-operation is facilitated by the extremely slow pace of progress in North-South negotiations and the frustrations created thereby, as well as the recognition of the limits of the prevailing associative development model. It is also facilitated by the bi-dimensional nature - recognized explicitly in the statement quoted in the last paragraph - of the self-reliance approach. One dimension, as described above, involves bringing about changes in the patterns of interaction between North and South which allow a more equitable sharing of the benefits of and control over international economic activities by developed and developing countries.

Besides being a part of the necessary structural change, self-reliance is also an instrument for achieving it: it increases the individual and collective bargaining strength of the developing countries and, especially where it allows joint action, creates the countervailing power that is needed to negotiate the desired changes in the international system. In this respect, self-reliance means strengthening the joint-action capacity of the Third World. An awareness of the weakness of each individual developing country in isolation was, in fact, the genesis of the Group of 77. In this sense, then, the Group of 77 "is a kind of trade union of the poor", which is kept together by "a unity of nationalisms" and "a unity of opposition" - not by "the ideals of human brotherhood, or human equality, or love for each other" or, for that matter, a common ideology.[27] The unity of the Group of 77 is based on a shared historical experience, a shared continuing economic dependence, and a shared set of needs and aspirations.

Still, since the Group is by no means homogeneous, group cohesiveness is not an easy matter to maintain. The immediate interests and specific negotiating priorities of many of its 122 members —this great number in itself makes it difficult to achieve consensus— are different from those of the others. The individual countries differ vastly from one another with respect to their cultural, ideological, political, and economic systems. No strong unifying institutional force exists: the Group of 77 has no long-term leadership, regular staff, headquarters, secretariat or, for that matter, any other permanent institution. In fact, the office of the co-ordinator rotates on an annual basis in New York and Vienna and on a three-monthly basis in Geneva. And although countries like Algeria, Argentina, Brazil, Egypt, India, Indonesia, Jamaica, Mexico, Nigeria, Pakistan, the Philippines, Sri Lanka, Venezuela, and Yugoslavia often play an important role in many issues, none of them dominates the Group. Very important also are great differences in the level of economic development, especially between the Latin American Group on the one hand and the African Group on the other. This cleavage is accentuated further by the exclusion of most Latin American countries from the preferential schemes of the Lomé Convention. The individual weight of some countries can also complicate matters, especially when these countries are specially cultivated by developed countries and when occasions for separate bilateral deals arise. Similar complications can be created by the continuation of strong traditional links of some developing with some developed states—e.g., of some Central American countries with the United States or some African countries with France. Some of the special interests of the members of the Group have, in fact, led to the formation of informal sub-groups - of, for example, the most-seriously-affected, the least developed, the newly-industrialized, and, of course, the oil-producing.[28] While the success of OPEC was welcomed by most developing countries, especially since it strengthened the bargaining power of the Third World as a whole, the balance-of-payments burden of the increased oil price has introduced considerable strains into the Group of 77 (and, for that matter, into the non-aligned movement). But since there exists no alternative for the oil-importing developing countries, this experience, however painful, is not likely to endanger the unity of the Group of 77.[29]

In the face of these factors it is a formidable task indeed to maintain the cohesiveness of the Group. But so far, the strength of the common interests, the capacity to maintain consensus through acceptable trade-offs among the developing countries themselves, the recognition that separate deals bring only marginal and temporary concessions, and the resistance of the developed countries to enter into a broad range of detailed negotiations have succeeded in overriding the pressures towards disunity. The maintenance and strengthening of the unity of the Group of 77 is, in fact, a vital precondition for achieving the desired changes in the international economic system. To return to Nyerere's analogy and his evaluation of OPEC's "historic action" in 1973:

> But since then OPEC has learned, and we have learned once again, that however powerful it is, a single trade union which only covers one section of a total enterprise cannot change the fundamental relationship between employers and employees. ...For the reality is that the unity of even the most powerful of the subgroups within the Third World is not sufficient to allow its members to become full actors, rather than reactors, in the world economic system. The unity of the entire Third World is necessary for the achievement of the fundamental change in the present world economic arrangements.[30]

## C. Membership

UNCTAD's group system was one of the most important factors in the consolidation of the Group of 77 as an effective interest group because it introduced certain institutional pressures for co-ordination and co-operation. From an organizational viewpoint, the origin of the Group of 77 can be found in this group system.

### 1. The Group System in the United Nations

The group system as such was not invented by UNCTAD, although nowhere else has it been formalized and practised to the same extent. The principal purpose of this system is to obtain an equitable geographical distribution of seats in non-plenary organs of the United Nations system[31] and hence to ensure the proper representation of all members in order to strengthen the legitimacy of the institution as a whole.[32] Originally, therefore, the main function of the regional groups was administrative in nature, namely, to decide on the candidates for the seats reserved for them.[33] This function was, in fact, the basis for the formal recognition of the regional groups through the "Rules of Procedure of the General Assembly" during its Twelfth Regular Session in 1957. Noting "the considerable increase in the membership of the United Nations" and taking into account the principle "that the General Committee should be so constituted as to ensure its representative character on the basis of a balanced geographical distribution among its members", the General Assembly confirmed the practice established with regard to the regional distribution of the principal officers of the seven Main Committees of the General Assembly and decided that the 13 Vice-Presidents of the General Committee be elected, according to a certain key, from the following five groups: Asian and African States (later separated into two groups), Eastern European States, Latin American States, Western European and Other States, and permanent members of the Security Council.[34] These groups (see Tables 2-7 for membership) remained the official regional groups in the United Nations in New York and their main function continued to be the allocation of seats. Since the Arab states (see Table 8) represent a grouping of common interests of their own, they have increasingly met separately since the beginning of the 1970s without, however, being recognized as a regional group under the rules of procedure (see Table 9).[35]

Given the original function of the regional groups, the number of seats allocated to each is naturally of great concern as it affects the influence of a group in a given organ. An important decision of the Preparatory Committee for UNCTAD I was thus concerned with the composition of the General Committee, i.e., of that body which assists the president in the general conduct of the business of the Conference and which ensures the co-ordination of its work. The formula that was finally agreed upon for UNCTAD recognized four groups.[36] They were formally institutionalized when General Assembly resolution 1995 (XIX) established UNCTAD as an organ of the Assembly and, for the purpose of electing the members of the Trade and Development Board (the standing committee of the conference[37]) on the basis of the principle of equitable geographical distribution, four lists of states were drawn up and annexed to that resolution: the African and Asian countries and Yugoslavia (List A); the Western European countries and Australia, Canada, Cyprus, Japan, New Zealand, and the United States (List B);[38] the Latin American countries (List C); and the Eastern European countries (List D).[39] The separate category of the permanent members of the Security Council was dropped as not being relevant to the development problem.[40] The lists of states are reviewed periodically, especially in the light of changes in the membership of UNCTAD. Every country that accedes to UNCTAD is assigned to one of the groups, essentially on the basis of its geographical location (see Table 10).

When membership in the Trade and Development Board was subsequently increased and finally thrown open to all members of UNCTAD,[41] the principle of equitable geographical distribution continued to be applied, on the basis of the four lists, to the election of the 12 members of the Bureau of the Board and the 7 members of the Bureaux of its Main Committees.[42] Furthermore, a pre-determined cycle for the rotation of groups in the election of the president and rapporteur of the Board (see Table 11) and the chairperson and rapporteur of each of the main committees was established.[43] A key reflecting the numerical strength of the various groups - 3 (Group of 77): 2 (Group B): 1(Group D) - has emerged to govern the composition of many formal and informal bodies and the rotation of officers, with a special allowance (usually in the form of the post of a vice-president in the quota of Group A) being made for China. This applies, for instance, to the Bureaux of the Trade and Development Board and its Main Committees and to the rotation of the president of the Board.

## 2. *The Formation of Interest Groups*

Although primarily administrative in origin, the four UNCTAD groups soon acquired a political character as well. This was facilitated by the fact that the geographical lines that guided the establishment of the groups had already been adjusted to a certain extent[44] to existing or emerging group identification and, most importantly, to the configuration of interests vis-à-vis the development issue. Hence, only a few adjustments were needed for the groups to coalesce into distinct and cohesive interest groups. The most important of them was, of course, the merger, for inter-group negotiation purposes, of Groups A and C - and the emergence of the Group of 77.[45] The Group of 77 in Geneva is thus made up of regional groups, not of individual countries. For election purposes and for the definition of their own regional interests, the regional groups continue to act separately; for inter-group negotiation purposes, they act in unison. It is this strong substantive orientation that distinguishes the Group of 77 in Geneva from the Group of 77 in New York; at the latter location, the constituting members of the Group are not the regional groups but the individual countries.[46] Group B, whose membership (apart from Cyprus, Malta and the Western European mini-states) is now identical with that of the OECD, drew an immediate consequence from the developments and made the OECD its *de facto* secretariat. A similar step was taken by Group D, for which the Council for Mutual Economic Assistance has becomed the organizational focus.

As a result—and this had already begun in 1964—negotiations within UNCTAD are carried out among well-defined geographically-prescribed political-economy groups, each representing its own interests. The group system reflects the fact that there are different group interests in the world community that cannot be ignored. By the same token, decisions by majority do not resolve an issue in a community of sovereign nation-states, because countries, as a rule, do not accept decisions to which they have not agreed voluntarily. This, in turn, leads to the need for negotiations. A consensus is first negotiated within each group on every item on UNCTAD's agenda. As a rule, a spokesperson is then designated to present the common position in negotiations with other groups and a high degree of group discipline generally prevails. Unforeseen changes in positions require, of course, new substantive intra-group discussions.[47] Although this procedure makes decision-making very cumbersome, it is nevertheless a system through which the interests of all states are taken into account, a precondition for achieving consensus in diplomatic negotiations.

From UNCTAD, the system of negotiations through groups spread, with some delay, to other organs of the United Nations and, today, permeates virtually all considerations of economic matters. In UNIDO, in particular, whose main focus is industrialization, group negotiations are now as well-defined and pervasive as in UNCTAD.[48] The result has been that the proceedings in these bodies have moved from discussions to negotiations.

In the General Assembly and its subsidiary bodies in New York, the developing countries observe a division of labour that results from the range of subject matters to be covered. In political matters, the Non-Aligned Countries take a leading role (which is reflected, as Table 12 shows, in the increasing frequency of their meetings), in economic ones the Group of 77;[49] initiatives of individual countries remain, however, quite frequent in both areas. Neither group is a regional group in the sense of the Rules of Procedure of the General Assembly, but each plays a key role in the elaboration of common policies, more so on economic questions than on political ones. As will be discussed in greater detail below, the politicization of the development issue (especially since the Sixth Special Session of the General Assembly, in which the Group of 77 acted on the basis of a common draft) has led to greater efforts at harmonizing positions and acting in unison in the United Nations in New York. The number of meetings of the Group—

in New York as well as in Geneva—has therefore increased considerably (see Table 12 as well as the Chronology of Meetings of the Group of 77 in Annex III of this volume). The Geneva model has influenced practices in New York in that Japan and the United States (which are not members of the Western European and Other States Group) as well as the Holy See and Switzerland (which are only observers to that Group) participate fully in the deliberations of the Western European and Other States Group when it meets in the context of the Second Committee of the General Assembly, i.e., as the "Vinci Group".[50] But otherwise the meetings of this Group, as well as those of the other regional groups, continue to deal mainly with the allocation of posts. The shift of the focus of the development discussions to the global negotiations in the General Assembly and the accompanying need for day-to-day co-ordination can, however, be expected to lead to a greater substantive orientation of all regional groups in New York. This process has, in fact, already begun.

## 3. *Membership Criteria of the Group of 77*

From an organizational point of view, the Group of 77 in Geneva thus emerged from a merger of the developing countries which were members of Groups A and C, i.e., the developing countries located in the geographical regions of Africa and Asia (A) and Latin America (C). All new members of UNCTAD were assigned to a regional group according to the same geographical criterion; and since in almost all cases those assigned to Groups A and C were clearly developing countries, they automatically became members of the Group of 77 as well. There was no need for special membership criteria; when a new country joined UNCTAD, its name was simply added to the list of those already participating in the Group of 77.

The need for special criteria arose, however, when countries from outside the region—Malta (Group B) and Romania (Group D)—sought membership.[51] In view of these two applications, the 1976 Manila Third Ministerial Meeting of the Group of 77 decided:

(a) The countries in question should agree to participate in the work and positions of the Group of 77 in all forums and not only on specific topics and aspects of international relations;

(b) The fact of continuing to belong to the "B" or "D" lists would not constitute a problem, provided that the country in question did not aspire to elective offices;[and]

(c) The initiatives of developing countries members of the Group of 77 which do not belong to any of the three regional groups should be endorsed and channelled through any one of them.[52]

Although these provisions were adopted mainly in reference to

Romania, they do indicate the basic membership criteria for the Group of 77 in UNCTAD.[53]

Developing countries located within the geographical regions of Africa, Asia and Latin America can thus become members of the Group of 77 in UNCTAD only through membership in a regional group. Hence a developing country desiring membership has to direct its request to the regional group of the geographical region to which it belongs. At the same time it has to indicate its willingness to support the objectives of this regional group and of the Group of 77 and to accept the conditions of its membership. However, "while its geographical location entitles it to membership of the regional group concerned, it cannot claim membership of that regional group as a matter of right".[54] Rather, the regional group has to decide by consensus on the admission. If regional membership is granted, this is sufficient to make the country a member of the group as a whole.[55] These procedures govern the normal situation and a border-line case can be resolved by accepting the country in question as a member of a particular region - as was the case of Malta which became a member of the Asian Group and, through it, of the Group of 77 as a whole.[56]

The procedures for admission also allow that,

> in exceptional circumstances, the Group of 77 may consider the application of a developing country located outside the three geographical regions for membership of the Group provided the developing country concerned has shown over a sufficient period of time that it has an identity of interests with the Group of 77 and has consistently supported the positions of the Group in all fora.[57]

In such a case, a written application has to be submitted directly to the Group of 77 and, as under the normal procedure, the willingness to support the objectives of the Group of 77 and to accept the conditions of membership has to be stated. If one regional group then decides to *sponsor* the applicant (without granting *membership* to the regional group), such sponsorship is sufficient to make the applicant a non-regional member of the group as a whole who can participate in all its plenary meetings.[58] As the criteria spelled out for Romania indicate, however, its proposals have to be channelled through a regional group and it cannot seek or accept seats allocated to the members of the regional groups that constitute the Group of 77.[59] Finally, non-regional members cannot block a consensus of the Group of 77, which continues to be based on the consensus of the three regional groups.

The 1976 Third Ministerial Meeting accepted Romania[60] on the basis of these special criteria as a full member of the Group of 77 in UNCTAD. Romania, a Latin country, is at a level of development similar to that of some Latin American countries and has, in the past, very often co-operated closely on substantive issues with the Group of 77 in general and the Latin American Group in particular; she has, for example, co-sponsored many resolutions with the Group. It was for these reasons, in fact, that the Latin American Group sponsored Romania's membership. Subsequently, Romania has worked out what one could describe as an associative status with that Group. It takes part in the deliberations of the Latin American Group (in Geneva and Vienna) whenever substantive matters concerning the Group of 77 as a whole are discussed; when Latin American or election questions are on the agenda, Romania does not attend. In New York, where the regional groups deal almost entirely with election questions only, Romania participates fully in the substantive work of the Group of 77 as a whole.

It can be expected that actual recourse to these procedures will remain limited. Applications from non-regional members are very likely to remain rare. And for the remaining colonies the procedure will most probably be a mere formality and their membership in the Group of 77, as in the past, will be virtually automatic upon their accession to UNCTAD.[61] But the procedure underlines the importance of the regional groups as the constituent parts of the Group of 77, and it signifies a further step in the evolution of the Group away from its administrative origin in the framework of the United Nations system and towards an independent role as the Third World's principal negotiating body for matters of collective economic interests.

### D. Decision-Making

Majority votes seldom resolve controversial issues among sovereign states. The rules of procedure for the first three Ministerial Meetings in relation to UNCTAD specified, therefore: "All decisions of the Meeting shall be taken without a vote", a provision that was changed, for the Fourth Ministerial Meeting, to "All decisions of the Meeting shall be taken by consensus".[62] (The rules of procedure of the Fourth Ministerial Meeting are reprinted on Annex II-C.) Since votes are therefore not taken at any level,[63] the task becomes one of achieving consensus and recognizing it when it has been reached.

The consensus-formation process is one of negotiations. In Geneva, it begins in the regional groups. They normally convene before meetings of the Group of 77 as a whole, to define their positions. The first round of negotiations takes place, therefore, among the countries of a region, most of which have specific interests that are often more or less at variance with one another. The main operating principle during these negotiations is *quid pro quo*. Countries

16

sponsoring special projects of little interest to others exchange support for each other's special projects. The result is an aggregation of proposals, frequently in the form of package deals. Of course, if concrete diverging interests are at stake, this method of resolving conflicts does not work. In those cases, the group members can either "split the difference"—i.e., all sides give a little in the interest of a common position—or they arrive at a maximum common denominator—i.e., the specific demands of the various interested parties are added together to a maximum proposal.

When the Group of 77 meets in plenary, the second round of negotiations begins, this time among the three regions. (In New York, where the regional groups seldom meet to discuss substantive questions, this is the first round of negotiations.) Again, compromises have to be found that are acceptable to all, even if these should require renewed consultations within the regional groups. Since formal records are not kept, discussions are open and frank. As a rule, the consensus-formation process is very time-consuming and the resulting positions are not likely to be very flexible.

Negotiations continue until consensus is reached. Consensus does not require that, if a roll-call were taken, all countries would vote in the same manner. Rather, to quote from a passage on "Decision-Making by Consensus" adopted by the Non-Aligned Countries at their 1979 Havana summit conference, "consensus has a certain indefinable quality" which "presupposes understanding of and respect for different points of view including disagreement and implies mutual accommodation on the basis of which agreement can emerge by a sincere process of adjustment among member nations..."[64] Or, to quote the definition of consensus used by the Paris Conference on International Economic Co-operation, "decisions and recommendations are adopted when the Chair has established that no member delegation has made any objections".[65] In other words, consensus exists when no state has taken formal exception to the course of action that is being proposed.

The third round of negotiations, then, takes place between the Group of 77 and Groups B and D as well as China. The other groups have, of course, their own internal consensus-formation process for formulating their positions. To maintain group solidarity, the "hard liners" of each group are frequently delegated to negotiate with the other groups, i.e., those delegations that support the most far-reaching claims or are least willing to make concessions. The rigidity of the positions from which the negotiations often start, the importance of maintaining the unity of the group, and a certain reluctance to endanger internal compromises that have been agreed upon earlier

17

after painstaking negotiations are often serious obstacles to finding the best solution to a given problem. The tendency is therefore to seek compromises that are frequently very vague or represent only partial solutions. This, in turn, means that the same issue is likely to be taken up again in the future.

Unsatisfactory as this procedure may be, it is based on the realization that consensus-formation among sovereign states is a necessary, though difficult and time-consuming, task. On the other hand, interest-aggregation at the group level may facilitate consensus-formation on many occasions by reducing the number of interests that, in the end, have to be reconciled with each other. For the developing countries, furthermore, a united stand is often an important bargaining asset in itself and, in any event, protects them from being played off against each other.

## FOOTNOTES OF PART I

[1]General Assembly resolution 1710 (XVI) of 19 December 1961.

[2]General Assembly resolution 1707 (XVI) of 19 December 1961.

[3]For the text of the "Cairo Declaration of Developing Countries", see Odette Jankowitsch and Karl P. Sauvant, eds., *The Third World without Superpowers: The Collected Documents of the Non-Aligned Countries* (Dobbs Ferry, N.Y.: Oceana, 1978), vol. I, pp. 72-75, hereinafter cited as Jankowitsch and Sauvant. This meeting was the first attempt of the developing countries to co-ordinate their international development policies in the United Nations.

[4]See Economic and Social Council resolution 917 (XXXIV) of 3 August 1962 and General Assembly resolution 1785 (XVII) of 8 December 1962.

[5]Of the 32 members of the Preparatory Committee, 19 were developing countries (including Yugoslavia which, from the beginning, played a key role in the Group of 77). Seventeen of the nineteen supported the "Joint Statement". The other two, El Salvador and Uruguay, did so only when the "Joint Statement" became the "Joint Declaration".

[6]Contained in Karl P. Sauvant, ed., *The Third World without Superpowers,* 2nd Ser., *The Collected Documents of the Group of 77* (Dobbs Ferry, N.Y.: Oceana, 1981), 6 vols., hereinafter cited as Sauvant. (The documents of the Group of 77 referred to below, as well as those of the United Nations meetings for which they were an input, are contained in these volumes; no specific reference is, therefore, made to them each time they are mentioned.) In 1963, 76 developing countries were members of the United Nations. Except for Cuba and the Ivory Coast, all developing countries, along with New Zealand, co-sponsored the Joint Declaration. Cuba was ostracized by the Latin American Group and hence was not accepted as a co-sponsor of the resolution. (The principle of co-sponsorship requires that every sponsor of a given resolution has to accept any new co-sponsor.)

[7]*Ibid.,* document I.C.1.a. (Since this volume was written when the collection of documents was still under preparation, no page numbers can be given for the quotes.) At the time of UNCTAD I, 77 developing countries were members of the United Nations. Of these, the Ivory Coast again did not join at that time and Cuba remained excluded until the 1971 Second Ministerial Meeting. Two others, the Republic of Korea and the Republic of Viet-Nam (which were not members of the United Nations

but were the only other developing countries at UNCTAD I), did join after being accepted for membership by the Asian Group, so that 77 countries supported the "Joint Declaration of the Seventy-Seven". Since, however, the original membership of the Group was 75 - see the 1963 "Joint Declaration" - the resolution continued to refer to seventy-five countries. It was only with UNCTAD I, that the Group acquired its present name.

[8]Prebisch actively encouraged the developing countries during the preparations for UNCTAD I, the session itself, and the subsequent years to co-operate and to strengthen their unity in the framework of the Group of 77. His successor, Manuel Pérez-Guerrero, continued this policy.

[9]The resolution on the First United Nations Development Decade did not spell out a strategy.

[10]Through resolution 1995 (XIX), contained in Sauvant. For membership, principal functions, organization, etc. of UNCTAD, see that resolution.

[11]Including the Palestine Liberation Organization, the only non-state member of the Group of 77.

[12]The literature on the Group of 77 is still very scarce. One of the best analyses is still contained in Branislav Gosovic, *UNCTAD: Conflict and Compromise. The Third World's Quest for an Equitable World Economic Order through the United Nations* (Leiden: Sijthoff, 1972). For a recent perceptive analysis of the Group of 77 and the non-aligned movement and their role in the main international economic conferences dealing with the New International Economic Order, see Robert A. Mortimer, *The Third World Coalition in International Politics* (New York: Praeger, 1980).

[13]*Infra*, p. 133.

[14]*Ibid.*, p. 134.

[15]See, Co-ordinating Committee, "Ministerial Mission" and First Ministerial Meeting of the Group of 77, "Charter of Algiers", Part III, in Sauvant, documents II.B.3 and II.D.7, respectively.

[16]For an elaboration, see Karl P. Sauvant, "The Origins of the NIEO Discussions", in Karl P. Sauvant, ed., *Changing Priorities on the International Agenda: The New International Economic Order* (Elmsford, N.Y.: Pergamon, 1981).

[17]Apart from the Latin American states, only the following developing countries took part in the Bretton Woods Conference: Egypt, Ethiopia, India, Iran, Iraq, Liberia, and the Philippines.

[18]See Odette Jankowitsch and Karl P. Sauvant, "The Initiating Role of the Non-Aligned Countries", in *ibid*. This observation should not be taken to slight the political purpose and function of the non-aligned movement; it is intended only to point out that the movement had also acquired an equally important economic function and that this change proved to be of crucial importance for making the development issue a priority item on the international agenda.

[19]See, e.g., the "Final Communiqué" adopted at the 1978 Havana meeting of the Co-ordinating Bureau of the Non-Aligned Countries at the Ministerial Level, reprinted in Jankowitsch and Sauvant, vol. V.

[20]General Assembly resolutions 3201 (S-VI) and 3202 (S-VI). Together with the "Charter of Economic Rights and Duties of States", adopted 12 December 1974 by the Twenty-Ninth Regular Session of the General Assembly as resolution 3281 (XXIX), and resolution 3362 (S-VII), entitled "Development and International Economic Co-operation", adopted on 16 September 1975 by the Seventh Special Session of the General Assembly, these resolutions (which are contained in Sauvant) lay the foundations of the programme for the New International Economic Order. For an exposition of this programme, see Karl P. Sauvant, "The NIEO Programme: Reasons, Proposals and Progress", and for its criticism, Rüdiger von Wechmar, "The Position of the Industrialized Countries", both in Sauvant, *Changing Priorities on the International Agenda*.

[21]Especially in the framework of the "Action Programme for Economic Co-operation", adopted by the 1972 Georgetown Third Conference of Ministers of Foreign Affairs of Non-Aligned Countries, as a consequence of which Co-ordinator Countries were designated for 18 fields of activity. Important also are a number of the follow-up activities to the Conference of Developing Countries on Raw Materials, which was held in Dakar from the 4th to the 8th of February 1975; although the Dakar Conference was convened by the Non-Aligned Countries, it was explicitly designed to include all developing countries. For the relevant documents, see Jankowitsch and Sauvant.

[22]The establishment, within UNCTAD and in pursuance of a resolution adopted at UNCTAD IV, of a Committee on Economic Co-operation among Developing Countries in 1976 and the increased emphasis given since UNCTAD V to this approach are efforts in this direction.

[23]See Sauvant, document IV.D.7.

[24]See, Main Documents of the Group of 77 at UNCTAD IV, "Statement Regarding the Forthcoming Conference on Economic Co-operation among the Developing Countries", *ibid.*, document IV.E.1.

[25]See, Ministerial Meeting of the Group of 77, "Communiqué", *ibid.*, document X.C.1.a.

[26]Ministers for Foreign Affairs of the Group of 77, Fourth Meeting, "Declaration", *ibid.*, document X.B.4.a.

[27]Nyerere, *infra*, pp. 123, 122.

[28]Producers' associations other than OPEC have not acquired a political significance of their own.

[29]In other words, the oil-importing developing countries have nothing to gain from turning against OPEC since this would not affect the price of oil. Maintaining solidarity, on the other hand, combined with some pressure, could lead to some concessions by the OPEC countries (be it in the form of aid, special price arrangements, or both) and it strengthens the bargaining power of the oil-importing developing countries in their negotiations with the North.

[30]Nyerere, *infra*, p. 133.

[31]Not, however, its only purpose. The group system also plays an important role in the management of the Assembly and its committees. Thus, when the President of the General Assembly has to contact the member countries, this is done through the regional groups. For a review of the history of the group system in the UN, see Thomas Hovet, *Bloc Politics in the United Nations* (Cambridge, Harvard Univeristy Press, 1960).

[32]Actually, the results of this system are not always equitable. On the decision of the Eighteenth Regular Session of the General Assembly, the Presidency of the General Assembly, for instance, rotates among the regional groups; this arrangement gives the small Eastern European Group (11 members) greater representation than, for example, the large African States Group (50 members). On the other hand, if (as it was customary in the 1950s) the President were to be determined by voting, candidates from the Eastern European Group or, for that matter, the Western European and Other States Group, would stand little chance of being elected today.

[33]On the basis of a gentlemen's agreement, the candidates of one group are accepted by the other groups. An exception was Portugal before the dissolution of its colonial empire: the African countries, and hence the Group of 77, voted down its candidacy. As a consequence, the developed countries did not nominate Portugal again.

[34]See General Assembly resolution 1192 (XII) on Rules 31 and 38. The Rules were amended further by the Eighteenth Regular Session of the General Assembly in 1963 which increased the number of Vice-Presidents and introduced the regional key into the election of the non-permanent members of the Security Council and the members of the Economic and Social Council; see General Assembly resolutions 1990 (XVIII) and 1991 (XVIII). In a 1971 revision of Rule 145 concerning the election of the members of the Economic and Social Council (General Assembly resolution 2847 (XXVI)), Africa and Asia were, for the first time, listed as separate groups, reflecting thereby the rapid increase of membership and the development of regional identifica- tions. This practice was confirmed in 1978 with the revision of Rule 31 concerning the election of members of the General Committee (General Assembly resolution 33/138). Today, only Rule 142 still speaks of the Afro-Asian States Group; but since it is understood that each of the two regions has a fixed quota, the Afro-Asian Group as a whole does not meet any longer.

Actually, the resolutions did not speak about "regional groups" but rather about elections "according to the following pattern", with the regions and the number of seats allocated to them being listed. It was only when the "Conclusions of the Special Committee on the Rationalization of the Procedures and Organization of the General Assembly" were annexed to the rules of procedure of the General Assembly by resolution 2837 (XXVI) of 17 December 1971 that the concept "regional groups" was mentioned for the first (and only) time in the Rules of Procedure of the General Assembly.

³⁵Although the Arab states meet in reference to most committees of the General Assembly (as well as in reference to intra-Group relations), most of their meetings concern political questions relating to the Arab region. The Arab Group has not yet submitted resolutions in its name.

³⁶See, "Report of the Preparatory Committee (Third Session)" in UNCTAD, *Proceedings of the United Nations Conference on Trade and Development*, vol. VIII, *Miscellaneous Documents, List of Participants* (New York: United Nations, 1964), p. 57.

³⁷General Assembly resolution 1995 (XIX), contained in Sauvant. In addition to the exclusive responsibilities assigned to it by this resolution, the Trade and Development Board, a permanent organ of the Conference, carries out the functions of the Conference in inter-sessional periods.

³⁸The Preparatory Committee had called this group "Western European countries, United States and Commonwealth countries not falling into other categories listed"; it did not contain Japan which, at that time, still figured among the African and Asian countries.

³⁹The distribution of the 55 seats of the Board was, respectively, 22, 18, 9, and 6.

⁴⁰Resolution 1995 (XIX) stated, however, that continuing representation of the principal trading states (which were not specified) on the Board was desirable.

⁴¹On the recommendation of UNCTAD III, membership in the Board was increased to 68 countries and on the recommendation of UNCTAD IV, membership was thrown open to all members of the Conference.

⁴²The Bureau of the Board consists of the president, ten vice-presidents, and one rapporteur. Four seats are allocated to Group A, four to Group B, two to Group C, and two to Group D. The Bureau of each of the Main Committees of the Board consists of the chairperson, five vice-chairpersons, and one rapporteur. Four seats are allocated to Groups A and C combined, two to Group B, and one to Group D. See, respectively, UNCTAD, *Rules of Procedure of the Trade and Development Board* (Geneva: UNCTAD, 1973), as amended, and UNCTAD, *Rules of Procedure of the Main Committees of the Traded and Development Board* (Geneva: UNCTAD, 1979).

⁴³For the cycle of rotation of the groups in the election of the chairperson and rapporteur of each of the Main Committees, see Annex I of the rules of procedure of the Main Committees.

⁴⁴The most notable deviation from the geographical principle in the establishment of the groups was, of course, List B which put together most (though not all) developed countries regardless of their geographical location. The shift of Japan (noted in footnote ³⁸) from List A to B is indicative.

⁴⁵Since Cyprus had aligned itself from the beginning with the Group of 77, it continued to participate fully in the substantive work of that Group, although it remains, for election purposes, in Group B (in New York, Cyprus belongs to the Asian Group). Conversely, Israel, Mongolia and South Africa were not included in the Group of 77 and China, from the beginning (i.e., first Taiwan), played a separate role. Political considerations determine, of course, whom the Group of 77 nominate for office when deciding separately as Groups A and C; the candidature of these countries was never advanced. Since, as noted in footnote ³³, the candidates advanced by a group are not challenged by the plenary, these countries can participate in non-plenary bodies as observers only (unless they are accepted, for election purposes, by other groups and included in their quota; this has been done, for instance, with Cuba, whose candidature was occasionally advanced by the Eastern European States Group when Cuba was ostracized from the Asian Group). In recent years, China has been treated increasingly as a *de facto* regional group for substantive purposes in Geneva; but it remains allocated, for election purposes, to Group A in Geneva and to the Asian States Group in New York. Yugoslavia, finally, a key member of the Group of 77, belongs to the Eastern European Group in New York for election purposes. Since Yugoslavia had been an active founding member of the non-aligned movement in 1961 and had strong ties to a number of Third World countries (especially India), it was accepted as a member of Group A in Geneva in 1964.

⁴⁶Thus, Cuba became a member of the Group of 77 in 1971, but it remained excluded from the deliberations of the Latin American regional group in New York until 1975.

⁴⁷In which case the African and Asian members of Group A meet separately.

⁴⁸At the 1971 Special International Conference of UNIDO (UNIDO I), the Group

of 77 still acted on an *ad hoc* basis and without the cohesiveness characteristic of its actions in UNCTAD; at the 1975 Second General Conference of UNIDO and especially at the 1980 Third General Conference, on the other hand, the Group acted as a single body.

[49]Some political questions, however, affect the work of the Group of 77, particularly those pertaining to the PLO, Israel and South Africa. In addition, the Group of 77 has become very active in questions pertaining to the New International Information Order.

[50]The Vinci Group (now without Malta) - i.e., the OECD members and the Holy See - began to meet under the name of the "Enlarged Western European and Other States Group" for informal exchanges of views on substantive questions, without, however, taking any formal decisions. Since the meetings of this group (which are called on the request of any member) began on the initiative of Piero Vinci, the Permanent Representative of Italy to the United Nations, it became known as the "Vinci Group". In the first years, the Group met to deal with political matters only; but since about 1977, the economic counsellors of the members of the Group began to meet in reference to the Second Committee of the General Assembly, which deals with economic matters. (On occasion, the Group also met in reference to the Third and Fifth Committees, i.e., on humanitarian and cultural matters as well as administrative and budgetary questions.) Beginning with the work of the Committee of the Whole and the preparations for the global negotiations (see below), the Vinci Group was convened more regularly and with increasing frequency (when need arose, several times a week), especially in reference to important economic negotiations in the United Nations. Meetings on political matters, on the other hand, decreased in number, although a separate caucus, the Barton Group, has emerged in reference to the disarmament question.

In the light of the need for constant intensive preparations for the economic negotiations under way since 1978, most members of the Vinci Group, led by the United States and Australia, urged that it go beyond informal exchanges of views and actively co-ordinate the economic policies of its members, thus becoming, in effect, a negotiating group similar to Group B in Geneva. Other states, led by the Nordic countries and France, however, preferred to avoid the impression that the Group of 77 is confronted with a solid front of the OECD countries. Hence, they urged the continuation of the present informal arrangements. Nevertheless, in March 1980 it was decided, *inter alia*, to rotate the chair of the Group every two months in alphabetical English order; to hold meetings at more regular intervals; to rotate the place of meetings (which, in the past, had been, for practical reasons, the Canadian Mission) among the missions of the Group's most important members; and to improve the exchange of information among the participating states, especially through the advanced circulation of texts to be presented by individual members in United Nations meetings on economic matters. At the present time, the actual policy co-ordination of the developed market economies takes place in the "Group on North-South Economic Issues" which meets under the guidance of the OECD Executive Committee in Special Session.

[51]Apart from general political considerations, membership in the Group of 77 was also sought, at least at one time, for the sake of economic benefits. Thus, when the Generalized System of Preferences was discussed, the Group of 77 asserted that it considered the members of the Group to be prospective beneficiaries of the system (and therefore entitled to preferential treatment in the markets of all preference-giving countries) and that no member of the Group of 77 should be excluded from the system at any time. See, UNCTAD, "Report of the Trade and Development Board on Its Fourth Special Session Held at the Palais des Nations, Geneva, on 12 and 13 October 1970", TD/B/330 of 14 October 1970, Annex I.

[52]Third Ministerial Meeting of the Group of 77, "Resolutions and Decisions: Admission of New Members", in Sauvant, document IV.D.7.

[53]With the same decision, a working group was established to study and make recommendations on rules and procedures for the admission of new members. The report was ready in time for UNCTAD IV, but was not discussed there by the Group of 77 (see, Working Group on Membership, "Report on Procedures for the Admission of New Members to the Group of 77 and on Membership in the Group", in *ibid.*). Nevertheless, the report reflects the discussions that had taken place during SELA's 1976 First Extraordinary Meeting in preparation for the Third Ministerial Meeting;

and it drew heavily on work done in preparation for the 1976 Third Ministerial Meeting of the Asian Group of the Group of 77 (see "Jakarta Declaration, Programme of Action, Joint Communiqué, and Report of the Third Ministerial Meeting of the Asian Group of the Group of 77", in *ibid.*, document IV.B.2.a.). Even though not formally endorsed, the report can be taken as representing a broad view within the Group of 77 since the Working Group on Membership was composed of representatives of all regional groups.

[54]Working Group on Membership, in *ibid.*, document IV.F.3.a.

[55]Already during the preparations for the Second Ministerial Meeting of the Group of 77, the Ministerial Meeting of the Asian Group of the Group of 77 had affirmed, in its "Bangkok Declaration 1971", that "Any country applying for membership must be sponsored by the regional sub-group to which it belongs. The decision of a sub-group on such questions must be respected by the other sub-groups." (In *ibid.*, document III.C.2.a.)

[56]Malta had submitted its application for membership to the 1976 Jakarta Third Ministerial Meeting of the Asian Group of the Group of 77. The matter was, however, left pending until the Manila Third Ministerial Meeting of the Group of 77 itself, during which the Asian Group accepted Malta as a member. (Malta had also received the support of the Non-Aligned Countries which recommended to the Group of 77 that it grant membership to the country.) For election purposes, Malta remains in Group B (and the equivalent groups elsewhere), but it does not participate in the substantive work of this Group. Instead, Malta participates fully in the substantive work of the Group of 77 and in that of the Asian Group whenever substantive matters are being discussed.

[57]Working Group on Membership, in *ibid.*, document IV.F.3.a.

[58]In a sense, Cuba was, in New York, the first non-regional member. Although Cuba had been admitted to the Group of 77 during the 1971 Second Ministerial Meeting (sponsored by the African and Asian Groups and not opposed by the Latin American Group), it continued to be excluded from the deliberations of the Latin American States Group in New York until 1975.

[59]The relevant provision (b) of the Manila decision on membership (quoted above) could imply that the countries in question can not seek or accept office on behalf of the groups to which they used to belong exclusively. Subsequent practice clearly has failed to support this interpretation. However, the question of whether or not Malta and Romania can take up official representative office in the Group of 77 is still unresolved. A precedent may, however, have been set by the Ministerial Meeting of the Group of 77 on Science and Technology for Development, held in Bucharest on the 16th and 17th August 1979. Romania, as the host country, chaired this meeting. (The declaration that resulted from it is contained in United Nations document A/CONF.81/8 of 18 August 1979.) In addition, representatives of Malta have already been the spokespersons of the Group of 77 on specific questions at UNCTAD V. Nevertheless, if there should be a clash of opinions at any point in the future in this matter, provision (b) could possibly be utilized to prevent the two countries from holding offices in the Group of 77.

The same decision also specified that Malta and Romania should, in effect, request as soon as possible a re-classification of their group listings in UNCTAD (and, by implication, in the other centres of the Group of 77), i.e., leave Groups B and D and join the appropriate regional groups of the developing countries. However, since the Group of 77 has not insisted on the implementation of this stipulation, both Malta and Romania remain, for election purposes, in their original groups. Apart from the question of the regional association of Romania (see *infra*), one of the reasons for this lack of action is certainly that the regional groups of the developing countries did not want to increase the number of countries that are competing for the limited number of posts allocated to them.

[60]Romania's association with the Group of 77 dates back to UNCTAD I. At that time, Romania took its first steps towards an independent foreign policy and began to co-operate with the developing countries, among other things by co-sponsoring resolutions. After UNCTAD II, it declared itself to be a developing country and began actively to seek membership in the Group of 77. An official request to that end was submitted to the co-ordinator of the Group of 77 at UNCTAD III. The Latin American Group discussed this request at UNCTAD III favourably, but since the other regional groups did not pronounce themselves on the issue, there was no

decision on the application. When the (open-ended) Preparatory Committee was established in Geneva to prepare the 1976 Third Ministerial Meeting, Romania (and Malta) expressed interest in participating in the preparatory work. The Group of 77 in Geneva agreed provisionally that this could be done on an *ad hoc* basis (and this was then extended to other meetings of the Group of 77 as well, including those in New York), a fact that was explicitly mentioned in the Preparatory Committee's "Progress Report, as at 22 December 1975, on the Work of the Preparatory Committee and Annexes" (contained in Sauvant, document IV.A.1.). On the strength of this participation, and in order to continue this work, the two countries received invitations to Manila. At the same time, Romania again officially wrote to the co-ordinator of the Group of 77 in Geneva to submit its application for membership. The African regional meeting in preparation for the Third Ministerial Meeting was unable, for lack of time, to consider the matter but, at the Senior Officials Meeting, expressed itself strongly against the notion of non-regional membership (see, Senior Officials Meeting, "Report and Annexes", in Sauvant, document IV.C.4.). The Asian regional meeting considered the question but did not reach a consensus; it did, however, agree to support fully Malta's membership in the Group of 77 as a non-regional member and, for that purpose, elaborated guidelines for membership which, in the end, were relevant also to Romania. The Latin American regional meeting, finally, elaborated criteria of membership (those that were finally incorporated in the Ministerial Meeting's decision on the "Admission of New Members", quoted above) and indicated its willingness to work out an arrangement on that basis. When the question was discussed at the Ministerial Meeting, the compromise was reached that, in exceptional cases, *membership* in a regional group is not a precondition for membership in the Group of 77 in UNCTAD, provided that a region *sponsors* the applicant and the Latin American criteria are applied. On this basis, the Latin American Group sponsored Romania and the country became a member of the Group of 77. The detailed procedures of co-operation between Romania and the Latin American Group were worked out later.

[61]Normally, the Group of 77 in Geneva decides on membership in the Group. Since membership in UNCTAD is not specified as a pre-condition, it is conceivable that countries accede to the Group of 77 before entering UNCTAD, or even without becoming members of that organization. The Palestine Liberation Organization, for instance, is neither a member of UNCTAD nor the United Nations.

[62]See, respectively, First Ministerial Meeting of the Group of 77, "Rules of Procedure", in Sauvant, document II.D.2, and Fourth Ministerial Meeting of the Group of 77, "Rules of Procedure", *infra*, p. 212.

[63]However, votes may occasionally be taken in the regional groups in New York, especially in the Latin American Group, when it is decided which countries should be nominated for the posts allocated to the Group.

[64]Sixth Conference of Heads of State or Government of Non-Aligned Countries, "Decision Regarding Methods of Strengthening Unity, Solidarity and Co-operation among Non-Aligned Countries", in Jankowitsch and Sauvant, vol. V.

[65]Conference on International Economic Co-operation, First and Second Preparatory Meeting, "Final Declaration and Related Documents", in Sauvant, document XII.B.1. The informal text of the Draft Convention on the Law of the Sea (A/CONF.62/WP.10/Rev.3* of 22 September 1980, article 161) defines consensus as "the absence of any formal objection".

# PART II
# STRUCTURE AND ORGANIZATION

## Structure and Organization

The group system was certainly important for the development of group identifications and the emergence of the Group of 77. But it provided only an organizational basis. It had to be married to a political will for solidarity and united action to transform the Group of 77 into an effective and dynamic negotiating body whose expertise and bargaining strength would be taken seriously in North-South relations. In the following, the emergence of the organizational infrastructure of the Group of 77 for its joint action capacity in the main centres of its activities will be examined.

Until the mid-1970s, UNCTAD was the unchallenged institutional focal point of the Group of 77. But since the beginning of the 1970s, following a directive of the Charter of Algiers that "Informal co-ordinating groups of the Group of 77 should be established at all headquarters of the various United Nations specialized agencies,"[1] the Group began to constitute itself, with more or less permanence and institutional infrastructure (and, depending on the delegations present at a given forum, a varying number of active members), in several other fora. As a result, the Group of 77 has become a multi-central organization whose main foci are UNCTAD,[2] the Industrial Development Organization (UNIDO), the International Monetary Fund/World Bank, and the United Nations in New York (see Figure 1). In addition, the Group has constituted itself at the Food and Agriculture Organization of the United Nations in Rome, the United Nations Educational, Scientific and Cultural Organization in Paris, the International Atomic Energy Agency in Vienna, the United Nations Evironment Programme in Nairobi, and, since 1975, at virtually all global United Nations conferences. In these fora, however, the Group of 77 has not (yet) acquired the organizational sophistication and permanence that characterize its presence at the main foci of its activities. In the case of the global conferences, in any event, its work is entirely of an *ad hoc* nature.[3] Nevertheless, the concerns of the Group of 77 now influence nearly all considerations of international economic issues in the United Nations system.

There have been, furthermore, two major occasions on which the Group of 77 has become active outside the framework of the United Nations. One of them was the 1976 Mexico Conference on Economic Co-operation among Developing Countries which has already been discussed. Although, as was noted, this conference was not held in direct relation to an impending event within the United Nations, it

27

# FIGURE 1
## The multi-central structure of the Group of 77

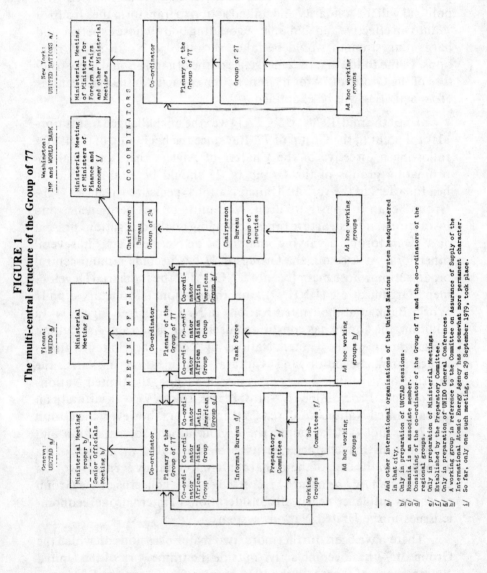

a/ And other international organizations of the United Nations system headquartered
   in that city.
b/ Only in preparation of UNCTAD sessions.
c/ Romania is an associate member.
d/ Consisting of the co-ordinator of the Group of 77 and the co-ordinators of the
   regional groups.
e/ Only in preparation of Ministerial Meetings.
f/ Established by the Preparatory Committee.
g/ Only in preparation of UNIDO General Conferences.
h/ A working group in reference to the Committee on Assurance of Supply of the
   International Atomic Energy Agency has a somewhat more permanent character.
i/ So far, only one such meeting, on 29 September 1979, took place.

28

signalled the increasing emphasis of the developing countries on economic co-operation among themselves and was thus of a piece with the rest of the Group's activities.

The other occasion was the Conference on International Economic Co-operation which was held in Paris during 1975-1977 and in which the Group of 77 acted through the Group of 19. Since this conference represented an experiment in negotiating the major North-South issues in a forum of restricted membership outside the United Nations system, it will be considered separately below.

Although the procedures of the Group of 77 are essentially based on precedent, the Group has maintained a high degree of organizational flexibility. The patterns that will be described below are therefore not rigid but subject to evolution. This flexibility, the informality of many of the Group's arrangements, the careful observance of equal regional representation, the openness of all non-plenary organs to all members of the Group, and the rule that decisions are to be taken by consensus are the principal sources of strength of the Group of 77 and have been the basis of its great capacity to grow and to absorb new developments.

## A. The Group of 77 in UNCTAD

In the 1964 Joint Declaration of the Seventy-Seven, adopted at the closure of UNCTAD I, the developing countries celebrated "their own unity...as the outstanding feature of this Conference" and they expressed their "strong conviction that there is a vital need to maintain, and further strengthen, this unity in the years ahead". For this purpose, they pledged themselves to "adopt all possible means to increase the contacts and consultations amongst themselves so as to determine common objectives and formulate joint programmes of action in international economic co-operation".[4] It took, however, some time for this pledge to be translated into reality and for the developing countries to reach, through the Group of 77, "an operative stage which.. [enabled] them to act as an effective and convincing negotiating force".[5] Only with the commencement of the preparations for UNCTAD II during the Fall of 1966 did organized co-operation among the members of the Group of 77 begin and only then did the Group become "a technically able and prepared unit for negotiations".[6]

In September 1966, the Trade and Development Board approved the provisional agenda for UNCTAD II. At the same time, the Group of 31 decided to call a ministerial meeting of the Group of 77 to prepare for UNCTAD II and to establish a Co-ordinating Committee to prepare for the ministerial meeting.[7] The Group of 31 consisted of the 31 developing countries (12 from Africa, 10 from Asia, 9 from Latin America) that were members of the Trade and Development Board.[8] Because the Board met regularly twice a year, these were the only developing countries that maintained regular contact among themselves and co-operated actively on economic matters.

Recognizing the usefulness of preparing UNCTAD sessions by ministerial-level gatherings, the 1967 Algiers First Ministerial Meeting of the Group of 77 in relation to UNCTAD provided, in the "Charter of Algiers", that the Group of 77 meet at the ministerial level "as often as this may be deemed necessary, and in any case always prior to the convening of sessions of the United Nations Conference on Trade and Development". The Charter continued:

> In all matters relating to preparations for ministerial meetings of developing countries, and during the intervals between these ministerial meetings, and for the formulation of joint positions on issues within the purview of UNCTAD, the competent authority of the Group of 77 is the Group of 31 developing countries.[9]

The Charter of Algiers thus recognized and formally endorsed the role that the Group of 31 had played *de facto* since UNCTAD I and gave it an official mandate to act on behalf of the Group of 77 (to which it continued to report). The Group of 31 also created the Preparatory Committee for the Second Ministerial Meeting and hence initiated the preparations of the developing countries for UNCTAD III.[10] When membership on the Board was first expanded (1972) and then made open-ended (1976), the Group of 31 dissolved, or, more precisely, expanded to encompass the membership of the entire Group of 77. By that time, the Group of 77 had begun meeting regularly as a whole, had become sufficiently institutionalized to absorb the tasks of the Group of 31, and had also begun to assert itself increasingly as the only body qualified to make major decisions on behalf of all developing countries.

The decision to hold preparatory meetings of the Group of 77 for UNCTAD I marked the creation of a distinct sequence of preparations for UNCTAD sessions. The sequence as it has now been established is schematically presented in Figure 2. In its thoroughness it was to become a model for the Group of 77 in other fora.

## 1. *The Preparatory Committee*

When an UNCTAD session (held now every three years) approaches, the Group of 77 in Geneva establishes a Preparatory Committee to prepare for the Ministerial Meeting of the Group of 77 preceding that session. Its core membership consists of ten countries

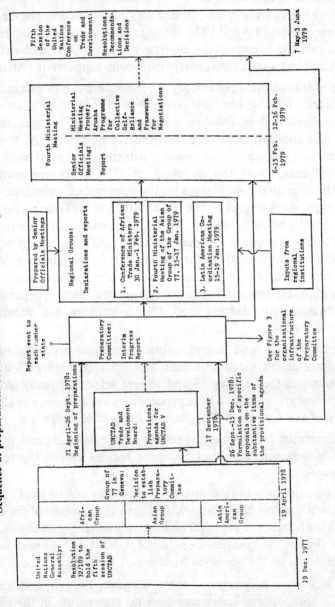

**FIGURE 2**

**Sequence of preparations for a session of UNCTAD, exemplified for UNCTAD V**

Fifth Session of the United Nations Conference on Trade and Development: Resolutions, Recommendations and Decisions

7 May–3 June 1979

Fourth Ministerial Meeting

Ministerial Meeting Proper: Arusha Programme for Collective Self-Reliance and Framework for Negotiations

12–16 Feb. 1979

Senior Officials Meeting: Report

6–15 Feb. 1979

Prepared by Senior Officials Meetings

Regional Groups: Declarations and reports

1. Conference of African Trade Ministers 30 Jan.–1 Feb. 1979
2. Fourth Ministerial Meeting of the Asian Group of the Group of 77, 15–17 Jan. 1979
3. Latin American Co-ordination Meeting 15–19 Jan. 1979

Inputs from regional institutions

Report sent to each member state

Preparatory Committee: Interim Progress Report

See Figure 3 for the organizational infrastructure of the Preparatory Committee

21 April–26 Sept. 1978: Beginning of preparations

UNCTAD Trade and Development Board: Provisional agenda for UNCTAD V

17 September 1978

26 Sept.–15 Dec. 1978: Formulation of specific proposals on the substantive items of the provisional agenda

Group of 77 in Geneva: Decision to establish Preparatory Committee

African Group

Asian American Group

Latin American Group

19 April 1978

United Nations General Assembly: Resolution 32/189 to hold the fifth session of UNCTAD

19 Dec. 1977

31

from each of the three regions (see Tables 13 and 14);[11] but since proceedings are open to all members of the Group, this core membership indicates only special interest—and special responsibilities—on the part of the countries involved.[12] The same principle—core membership on the basis of equal regional distribution, but admission to sessions for all other members—applies to virtually all other non-plenary bodies of the Group of 77. In the case of the Fourth Ministerial Meeting, the Preparatory Committee was established by the Group of 77 at a meeting on 19 April 1978, during which it was also decided that its Bureau should consist of the chairperson (Asia), a vice-chairperson (Latin America) and a vice-chairperson-cum-rapporteur (Africa).[13]

The work of the Preparatory Committee evolves essentially in three stages. During the first stage, the Preparatory Committee organizes itself and establishes a sub-committee on organizational matters and sub-committees on substantive questions. At the same time, the chairpersons of the existing working groups as well as the Secretary-General and the directors of UNCTAD are invited to present the principal policy issues for the upcoming Conference. In the second stage, work begins on the formulation of the Group's positions on the items to be included in UNCTAD's provisional agenda. Once the provisional agenda is adopted by UNCTAD, the actual position papers and recommendations for the Ministerial Meeting are drafted. Hence, the Preparatory Committee has two major functions: (1) to consider all questions relating to the administration and organization of the Ministerial Meeting and (2) to prepare the substantive documents for it.

Administrative and organizational questions are handled by a Sub-Committee on Organizational Matters (see Figures 3 and 4), whose members (see Tables 13 and 15) are selected equally from the three regional groups (but whose proceedings are also open to all other members of the Group of 77). Among its specific tasks are:

— to determine, if this has not yet been done, the date and venue of the Ministerial Meeting (the venue rotates among the regional groups);

— to issue invitations (the invitations are sent out by the President of the preceding Ministerial Meeting to all members of the Group of 77, a number of regional and international organizations, and the former Secretaries-General of UNCTAD as well as the Presidents of the previous Ministerial Meetings);

— to decide on languages (Arabic, English, French, and Spanish have been official languages for oral statements in the plenary sessions from the beginning; Arabic as a working language, i.e., a

## FIGURE 3
## The organizational infrastructure of the Preparatory Committee for the 1979 Fourth Ministerial Meeting*

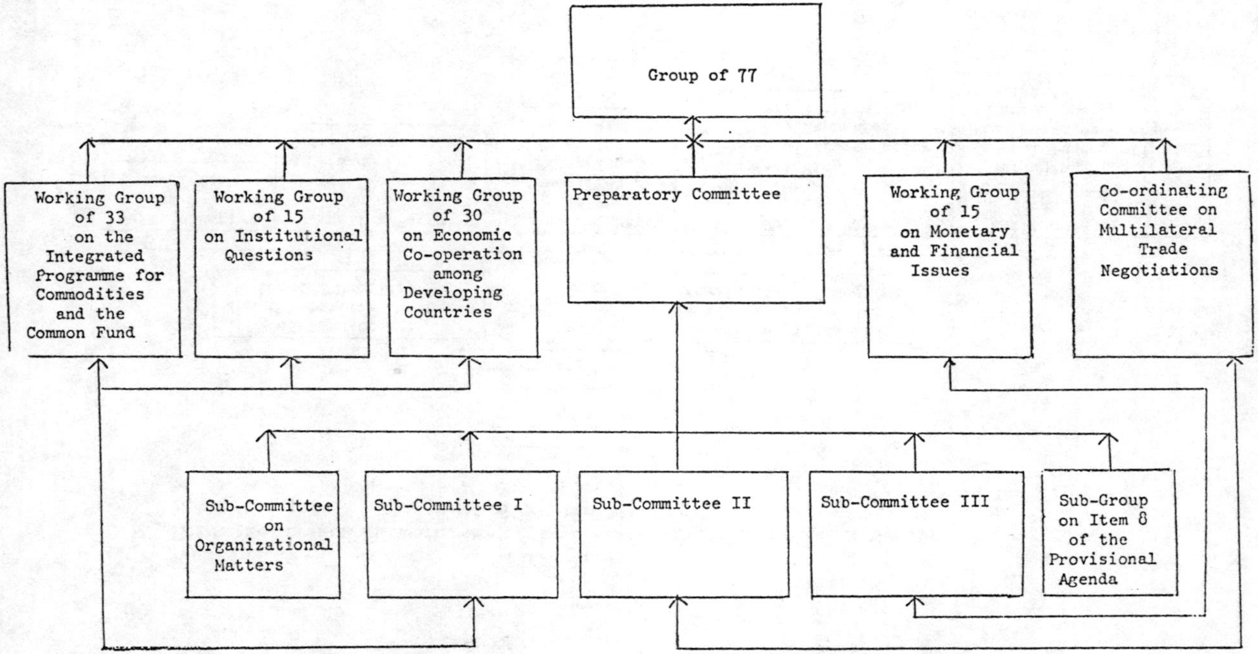

* The Working Groups are those in existence at the time of the Preparatory Committee.

33

# FIGURE 4
## The organizational infrastructure of the Co-ordinating Committee for the 1967 First Ministerial Meeting

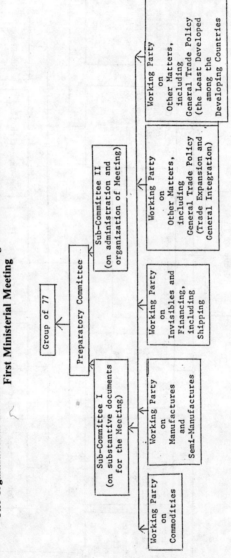

34

language in which documents are published, was only added on the decision of the 1976 Third Ministerial Meeting);

— to prepare the rules of procedure (the rules of procedure were adopted by the First Ministerial Meeting and those governing the subsequent meetings were based on them);[14] and

— to organize the work of the ministerial meeting.

As a general principle, precedents set by previous Ministerial Meetings are followed on organizational matters.

The main task of the Preparatory Committee, however, is to produce the basic documents required for the Ministerial Meeting and to draft the agenda. Since most of the substantive items on the agenda of the UNCTAD sessions are fairly clear—and have not changed very much, except for priorities, since UNCTAD I—the general preparatory work can begin before UNCTAD's provisional agenda is adopted. The formulation of specific proposals for the report of the Committee, however, begins as a rule only after this agenda has been agreed upon and it usually follows the order of the substantive items of the provisional agenda. The actual work is done by Sub-Committees. Each of these has a chairperson and a vice-chairperson-cum-rapporteur, its core members are determined on the basis of equal geographical representation (see Figures 3 and 4 and Tables 13 and 15), and its gatherings are open to all members of the Group of 77. They can establish their own Working Parties (see Table 16) and may draw on existing Working Groups (see Table 17)—the composition of both of these is also based on equal geographical representation—and they receive some assistance from the UNCTAD Secretariat.

The precise organizational infrastructure of the Preparatory Committee is flexible, but it has clearly become increasingly elaborate, reflecting the expansion of UNCTAD's agenda and the intensification of the work of the Group of 77. Thus, for instance, the Preparatory Committee for the 1967 First Ministerial Meeting had one substantive sub-committee which, in turn, established five working parties (see Figure 4). The Preparatory Committee for the 1979 Fourth Ministerial Meeting, on the other hand, had four substantive sub-committees and could draw on five existing Working Groups (see Figure 3).[15]

The Working Groups are not created by the Preparatory Committee. Rather, they are established by the Group of 77 (and report to it) whenever specific tasks (especially on-going negotiations) require special attention. The need for them reflects the increasing technicality of the subject matters with which UNCTAD deals. At the end of 1980, nine such Working Groups were in existence (see Table

17), each with a core membership that is based on equal geographical distribution,[16] but all open-ended. These Working Groups have acquired a certain status owing to their continuity and have become (even if they may have been—or are—dormant for certain periods) standing committees of the Group of 77. (Working groups are also created on an *ad hoc* basis, whenever need arises.[17]) It is in the Working Groups that the members of the Group of 77 clarify their interests, formulate positions and prepare for negotiations. Frequently, the spokespersons of the Working Groups also conduct—at a similar informal level—negotiations with the representatives of Groups B and D and China, before plenary sessions are seized with an issue. Naturally, the Preparatory Committee has to draw on the expertise of these Working Groups when drafting the documentation for the Ministerial Meeting.

This documentation takes the form of a report of the Preparatory Committee to the Ministerial Meeting. It is a substantial document[18] which contains, for each of the substantive items on UNCTAD's agenda, a review of the particular issues, an analysis of current trends, and an evaluation of the progress made since the last session of UNCTAD. It also deals with problems and obstacles encountered in the pursuit of particular objectives and discusses new factors that may call for a modification of some tactics or objectives. It may also identify differences in views and approaches among the developing countries (and, for that matter, the developed countries). Finally, alternative suggestions for further action are spelled out. Hence, the report is not a declaratory paper or a vague call for action; rather it is an operative document that spells out specific solutions to concrete problems.

Thus, the Preparatory Committee has to do the groundwork for the formulation of a joint programme and agreed common negotiating objectives on all substantive questions within the purview of UNCTAD. Although the report is a working document and not binding upon any government, many of its proposals are usually incorporated, often verbatim, into the final document of the Ministerial Meeting and hence become part of the official programme of the Group of 77.

The report of the Preparatory Committee is submitted directly to the Ministerial Meeting. However, it is also made available to the three regional groups to facilitate the proceedings of *their* preparatory meetings.

## 2. *The Regional Groups*

Given the crucial role of the regional groups—as pointed out earlier, they are the constituent parts of the group as a whole in Geneva and their importance is reflected in the strict regional distribution of seats that can be observed in all the activities of the Group of 77—these regional meetings make an important input into the Ministerial Meeting. They take place a few months before the Ministerial Meeting and formulate the regions' positions on the substantive items on UNCTAD's agenda. The regional groups receive the technical support of the United Nations regional commissions and sometimes of other regional institutions.

The Asian Group has the weakest common institutional infra-structure. There is no intergovernmental organization—comparable, for instance, to the Organization for African Unity (OAU)—that could provide organizational unity. Instead, the region is fragmented into several sub-regional groups, among which the Association of South East Asian Nations and the League of Arab States (which, moreover, extends into the African region) are most prominent. In addition, a number of individual countries have an important weight of their own, most notably India, Indonesia, Pakistan, the Philippines, Sri Lanka, and Yugoslavia. The Economic and Social Commission for Asia and the Pacific attempts to play a certain co-ordinating role. But since the Arab States belong to the Economic Commission for Western Asia, it does not cover the entire region, which limits its usefulness greatly. A substantial part of the co-ordinating work of the Asian Group takes place, therefore, during meetings of the Group of 77 as a whole or during the negotiations with Groups B and D and China.

In Africa, the Economic Commission for Africa has traditionally occupied, in close institutional co-operation with the OAU, a position of leadership. This position it continues to occupy, although the OAU is assuming a more prominent role and the Conference of Trade Ministers of OAU Member Countries appears to be emerging as the principal forum of the region for matters related to UNCTAD.

The Latin American Group has the best institutional support. It can draw on the Economic Commission for Latin America (ECLA), which has traditionally been one of the strongest of the United Nations regional commissions. Under its first Executive Secretary (1948-1962), Raúl Prebisch, its contributions to the international development discussions were among the most significant of those that came from developing countries. Much of the programme of UNCTAD and the Group of 77 arose out of ECLA's work. ECLA had close ties with the Special Committee on Latin American Co-ordination (CECLA) which was established in 1963 for the specific purpose of co-ordinating the position of the Latin American states attending

UNCTAD I and of promoting greater understanding with the other developing countries.[19] CECLA, a ministerial-level body, became the Latin American forum for questions relating to UNCTAD and exercised great influence in formulating the position of the Latin American Group. In 1975, CECLA was superseded by the Latin American Economic System (SELA) which, with the help of a permanent secretariat (but also a much broader mandate), is now the institutional focal point of the Latin American Group. In fact, SELA's permanent secretariat soon assumed the function of providing technical support (including the drafting of relevant documents) to the Latin American Group of the Group of 77, a development that was confirmed by the region's preparatory meeting for UNCTAD V.[20]

Thus, the regional groups of the Group of 77 have, on the whole, considerable institutional support in preparing their positions. In addition, as already indicated, they benefit from the work of the Preparatory Committee. Too, they can draw on the expertise of their representatives in the various international bodies in which the Group of 77 is active and where the regional groups meet whenever need arises. The thorough preparation of the declarations or reports of the regional groups, combined with the weight of the regional groups in the Group as a whole, gives these pronouncements a significant role in shaping the final document of the Ministerial Meeting.

The Ministerial Meeting begins therefore with four basic texts: the report of the Preparatory Committee and three regional declarations or reports.[21] Obviously, considerable work and extensive negotiations are still required before an authoritative text of the Group of 77 as a whole can be adopted. This is the task of the Ministerial Meeting.

## 3. *The Ministerial Meeting*

The Ministerial Meeting is the supreme organ of the Group of 77. Its basic terms of reference were laid down in the 1967 Charter of Algiers, adopted by the first meeting of the Group of 77 at the ministerial level: "The Group of 77 should meet at the ministerial level...in order to harmonize the positions of developing countries and to formulate joint programmes of action in all matters related to trade and development".[22] In harmonizing the positions of the developing countries, outlining the strategies to be pursued, and adopting specific positions and proposals, the Ministerial Meeting also arbitrates among the regional groups, provides over-all political guidance, sets negotiating priorities, and, in the process, reaffirms the unity of the Group of 77. The agreements reached at a Ministerial Meeting govern the policy of the Group until the next meeting at the ministerial level.

The Ministerial Meetings, in turn, have undergone considerable changes in their organizational infrastructure and mode of operation (see Figure 5). Each Ministerial Meeting[23] elects a President, who, in accordance with established practice, comes from the country hosting the meeting and, with one exception (Arusha), is the minister for foreign affairs of that country. In accordance with the principle of rotation, the role of host country (and hence the post of President) rotates among the regions (see Table 18). The terms of office of the Presidents end with the termination of the Ministerial Meetings, i.e., they are not, as in the case of the Non-Aligned Countries, Presidents-in-Office until the next Ministerial Meeting. The functions of the President-in-Office (after the Ministerial Meetings) are performed by the co-ordinators of the Group of 77 at the various centres where the Group of 77 has constituted itself.

The President is supported by 10 Vice-Presidents and one Rapporteur-General.[24] (The post of the Rapporteur-General also rotates among the regions.) During the first two Ministerial Meetings, these officers formed the Bureau (see Table 19). The posts of the Bureau were allocated to each region strictly on the basis of equitable geographical distribution—Africa 5, Asia 4, Latin America 3—with the distribution of the seats of the developing countries on the Trade and Development Board serving as a guideline (see Table 20). Although this key was still operative for the "inner" Bureau at the 1976 Ministerial Meeting, all three regions have been represented equally since then, with special allowance being made for the host country. At the same time, the mode of operation of the Ministerial Meeting has changed, as will be discussed below.

The actual drafting work of the Ministerial Meeting is carried out in committees, which are free to set up as many working groups as they think necessary. Their task is to prepare a "declaration" (or "charter")[25] and a "programme of action" (or "framework for negotiations").

The declaration is a political pronouncement. It provides the general framework for the final document of the Ministerial Meeting. It is a non-technical document which outlines the main issues facing the developing countries, presents the case of the Third World, and identifies the crucial objectives on which actions are urgently needed and on which negotiations should therefore focus. It is intended "to create maximum psychological impact on world public opinion".[26]

Since the beginning, the task of preparing the declaration (taking into account the corresponding provisions in the declarations or reports of the regional groups and the report of the Preparatory

39

# FIGURE 5
## The structure of the Ministerial Meeting, 1967-1979

| Ministerial Meeting | 1967 Algiers | 1971 Lima | 1976 Manila | 1979 Arusha |
|---|---|---|---|---|
| Ministerial Meeting proper | Bureau<br><br>Drafting Committee (to prepare the declaration)<br><br>4 Main Committees of the Whole (to prepare the programme of action) | Bureau<br><br>Working Group (to prepare the declaration)<br><br>4 Main Committees of the Whole (to prepare the programme of action) | Bureau<br><br>Co-ordination Committee (to prepare the declaration)<br><br>4 Main Committees of the Whole (to prepare the programme of action) | Bureau<br><br>Drafting Group (to prepare the declaration)<br><br>3 Working Groups of the Whole (to prepare the programme of action) |
| Senior Officials Meeting | - | The meeting as a whole dealt with organizational matters | Drafting Group (to draft the declaration)<br><br>4 Working Groups of the Whole (to draft the programme of action) | |

Committee) has been entrusted to a separate committee. It was originally called the Drafting Committee (according to rule 5 of the rules of procedure), but has since been referred to by different names at each Ministerial Meeting (see Figure 5). Its membership has always been selected on the basis of geographical distribution. Traditionally, this committee has also dealt with general items on UNCTAD's agenda,[27] the institutional arrangements of UNCTAD, and questions relating to the organization of the Group of 77. It is, in other words, the political-economy committee of the Ministerial Conference.

The drafting of the main parts of the programme of action, on the other hand, is always entrusted to three or four technical committees of the whole (see Figure 5).[28] Like the Preparatory Committee and the regional meetings, these technical committees concentrate on the principal substantive items on the agenda of the forthcoming UNCTAD session. As the basis of their work they take those parts of the reports of the Preparatory Committee and the declarations or reports of the regional meetings that fall within their respective terms of reference. Their main task is to synthesize these texts into a coherent draft. Where no major disagreements exist, whole passages may be accepted verbatim. As the proposals under discussion have grown more detailed and as concrete interests have been increasingly at stake, differences have tended to increase and it has become all the more important to find trade-offs acceptable to all. Where disagreements persist—and the regional groups regularly caucus separately—they are left for the ministers to decide. Thus the sessions of the committees are typically drafting and negotiating sessions in which there is not much room for general debate.

The result of the work of the committees is a comprehensive[29] programme of action, supported by all countries. It embodies the consensus of the members of the Group of 77 on all substantive items to be discussed at the UNCTAD session. It also spells out specific proposals for action and sets agreed priorities. It is a technical document that becomes, after being adopted by the Ministerial Meeting, the basis of negotiations with the other groups at the UNCTAD sessions. Passages that are acceptable to Groups B and D as well as to China may well find their way into UNCTAD's resolutions, recommendations or decisions.

Originally, the entire work was undertaken by the Drafting Committee and the four Main Committees of the whole. But since the 1971 Lima Meeting, an increasing part of the preparations has been undertaken by the Senior Officials Meeting. The Ministerial Meeting, therefore, is actually held in two parts (which were initially two

41

separate time-periods but overlapped considerably at the 1979 Arusha Meeting): the Senior Officials Meeting and the Ministerial Meeting proper. By the time of the 1979 Arusha Meeting, the Senior Officials Meeting has ascended to a central position in the Ministerial Meeting, with its own rules of procedure and a sizable bureau (see Table 21), and had become responsible for the entire preparation of the final document (see Figure 5).

When the Group of 31 initiated the preparations for the Second Ministerial Meeting, it also decided that the Meeting be preceded by a preparatory meeting of high officials. When the officials met, they dealt almost exclusively with organizational matters relating to the Ministerial Meeting, completing, in a sense, the work of the Preparatory Committee.[30] The substantive work continued to be done in the committees of the Ministerial Meeting proper. The next Ministerial Meeting marked a turning point for the Senior Officials Meeting. The officials were entrusted with a large part of the substantive work and, for that purpose, adopted rules of procedure (identical with those of the 1971 Lima Meeting). They also established a Drafting Group to begin work on the declaration and created four Working Groups of the Whole to draft the programme of action. The materials prepared by the five groups were submitted to the parallel bodies of the Ministerial Meeting proper: the preliminary draft text of the declaration[31] was passed on to the Co-ordination Committee and the elements for the programme of action were passed on to the four Main Committees of the Ministerial Meeting proper.[32] These, in turn, prepared the final draft of the texts (which were largely left intact) for adoption by the ministers.

At the 1979 Arusha Meeting, the process that had been transferring the substantive work to the Senior Officials Meeting was brought to completion. The reports of the senior officials were submitted to the closing plenary session of the Ministerial Meeting proper and were adopted at the same session (as amended) for inclusion in the final document of the Ministerial Meeting.

The rules of procedure reflect this change. The Senior Officials Meeting gave itself rules of procedure in Arusha that differed from those of the Ministerial Meeting proper. Apart from the differences that reflect differences in status (e.g., "chairman" instead of "president", "working group" instead of "committee"), and the omission of a reference to a "Final Document" (which remained, of course, the responsibility of the ministers), the main differences concerned the organizational infrastructure: while the Senior Officials Meeting "shall" establish working groups and a drafting group, the Ministerial Meeting proper now merely "may" create sub-bodies of this kind. In a

42

sense, the old rules of procedure of the Ministerial Meeting proper became those of the Senior Officials Meeting.

It is consistent with this evolution that the 1979 Ministerial Meeting proper omitted, for the first time, to establish a Drafting Committee or Main Committees. Its Bureau consisted therefore only of its president, its ten vice presidents, the rapporteur-general, the regional co-ordinators and the chairperson of the Senior Officials Meeting (in an *ex officio* capacity).[33] The last two categories had not been represented in the Bureaux at earlier Ministerial Meetings. Their inclusion showed the increasing importance that is accorded to the regional groups and the Senior Officials Meeting. The Arusha Bureau of the Senior Officials Meeting, on the other hand, consisted of its chairperson, its six vice-chairpersons, a rapporteur-general, the co-ordinators of the regional groups and, in addition, the chairpersons, vice-chairpersons and rapporteurs of its Working Groups and the chairperson and vice-chairperson of the Drafting Group (see Table 21). The Bureau of the Senior Officials Meeting has thus become a working bureau and assumed the function of a steering committee of the Ministerial Meeting. Geographical distribution remains, of course, the determining factor in its composition. But as in the case of the Bureau of the Ministerial Meeting proper, there has been a shift to *equal* regional representation, a shift reflecting the fact that the practice of taking decisions by consensus has become so firmly established that *equitable* representation is no longer considered to be crucial.

Thus, the substantive and organizational work of the Ministerial Meeting has shifted entirely to the Senior Officials Meeting which, of course, operates under the directives of the ministers. With the ascent of this body to prominence, the Ministerial Meeting proper acquired primarily ceremonial functions, although it continues to provide overall direction and remains the final arbiter among the regional groups. The equal representation of the regions and the inclusion of the regional co-ordinators in its Bureau facilitate these tasks.[34]

### 4. *Follow-up*

As mentioned earlier, the 1967 First Ministerial Meeting decided to send high-level "goodwill missions" to countries belonging to Groups B and D. Their task consisted of informing the respective governments about the conclusions of the Meeting "so as to contribute to the creation of the best possible conditions for negotiations on the programme of action at the second session of the Conference".[35] At the next Ministerial Meeting, the member states of the Group of 77 were asked to instruct their national ambassadors to publicize the conclusions of the Meeting and promote the case of the developing countries. On both occasions, furthermore, a delegation of high-ranking officials of the Ministerial Meeting was charged with presenting the final document to the General Assembly and the Secretary-General of the United Nations.

Since then, such special efforts have no longer been considered necessary. Instead, the President of the host country is requested to present the final document to UNCTAD's next session and the President of the Ministerial Meeting is requested to present the final document to UNCTAD's next session and the President of the Ministerial Meeting is requested to give the widest possible publicity to it. The document is issued immediately by UNCTAD and circulated to all its member countries as being of obvious relevance to the substantive items on the provisional agenda of the next session of UNCTAD. If a session of the Trade and Development Board intervenes between the end of the Ministerial Meeting and the next UNCTAD session, it may be used to discover how Groups B and D as well as China react; and pre-negotiations on specific proposals, which are put in the form of draft resolutions, may begin immediately.[36] Most negotiations, however, take place at the respective UNCTAD sessions themselves. And, of course, the subsequent work of the Trade and Development Board consists to a large extent of the implementation of the resolutions adopted at these sessions.

Since all developing countries meet again at the UNCTAD session, this gives the Ministerial Meeting the opportunity to establish *ad hoc* working groups on matters considered urgent and to request them to report their conclusions to the Group of 77 at the UNCTAD session for discussion and possible action. At the session, the members of the Group of 77 as well as the members of its regional groups often meet separately as part of the normal process of negotiation among themselves and with other groups. Virtually all these activities are directed towards drafting the resolutions, recommendations and decisions of UNCTAD; occasionally, however, formal documents of the Group of 77 are also issued.

5. *The Regular Organizational Infrastructure of the Group of 77 in Geneva and the Question of a Permanent Machinery*

a. *The Regular Infrastructure*

The preparations for UNCTAD sessions represent the most important set of activities of the Group of 77 because the results of the Ministerial Meetings constitute the Group's common platform until the next gathering at the same level. These activities, as we have seen, are well-structured and follow a firmly established sequence. The greatest amount of work, however, has to be accomplished in the periods between Ministerial Meetings, in the constant negotiations between UNCTAD sessions. The Group of 77 and its regional groups meet, therefore, quite frequently to prepare themselves for these inter-sessional negotiations (see Tables 9 and 12). In fact, the growing intensity of the North-South negotiations is reflected in the dramatic increase in the number of inter-sessional meetings of the Group of 77 and its various sub-groups: it more than trebled from under 200 meetings in 1974 to cover 600 in 1979 (see Table 12).

As in the case of preparations for Ministerial Meetings, the regions play a key role. Virtually all matters are first examined by them. The regions' positions, in turn, are harmonized in *ad hoc* plenary meetings of the Group of 77 which are held whenever need arises and in particular just before or during important international negotiations of interest to the Group. The plenary itself (whose decisions are at times recorded in informal notes) can draw on regular Working Groups (see the discussion above) which lend it continuing technical assistance for specific questions of particular interest to the Third World. It can also set up *ad hoc* working groups or committees to prepare for official meetings of the Group of 77 (such as the Ministerial Meetings), to examine particular questions, to conduct consultations or negotiations with other groups, and to prepare draft materials for specific purposes.

Once the Group of 77 has identified the items on the agenda of the Trade and Development Board that are of special interest to it, the Working Groups undertake a substantial part of the preparatory work. It is possible that in the future they will be supplemented in this function by *ad hoc* task forces for areas in which Working Groups do not exist.[37] The preparatory work consists mainly of analysing the latest developments, formulating negotiating positions, and drafting statements, resolutions and decisions. The identification of particular priority items in a general statement by the co-ordinator at the opening meeting of a session of the Trade and Development Board then serves to draw the attention of the other groups to the areas of primary interest to the Group of 77 and thus helps to focus the ensuing negotiations. This mechanism of co-ordination tends to increase the participation of members of the Group of 77 in the preparatory work because more countries have to assume responsibilities; and it facilitates and directs special substantive inputs and requests for assistance from individual countries or other institutions.

In this context, the UNCTAD Secretariat plays an important

role. Its support begins with the provision of a range of administrative services such as reproduction and distribution, conference rooms and conference services, and translation and interpretation into the four languages of the Group. UNCTAD also provides advice and resources for research, and may draft background materials, reports, position papers, and resolutions. In fact, the Group of 77 frequently adopts proposals of the UNCTAD Secretariat as its own positions and can thus capitalize on the entire preparatory work undertaken in this respect. A liaison officer in the office of the Secretary-General of UNCTAD co-ordinates the activities of the Group of 77 and the Secretariat - and, at times, even those of the individual members of the Group. To a certain extent, therefore, the UNCTAD Secretariat performs a number of the functions of a secretariat for the Group of 77 in Geneva.[38]

Naturally, the support system of the Group of 77 also includes the secretariats of the various regional organizations of the Third World[39] and the relevant expert groups of the Non-Aligned Countries.[40] It can also draw on the expertise and infrastructure of the countries that act as host countries for specific meetings and, occasionally, those individual members of the Group that make contributions to specific projects. But support from these sources is more the exception than the rule. To the extent that it is forthcoming, it is of limited importance in the day-to-day negotiations of the Group of 77.

The management of the Group of 77 in Geneva is in the hands of the regional co-ordinators[41] and the co-ordinator of the Group of 77 as a whole. Since 1968, the office of the co-ordinator of the Group as a whole rotates on a quarterly basis amongst the three regions (see Table 22).[42] This arrangement ensures that the burden of work is shifted relatively frequently while, at the same time, more countries are given the opportunity to represent the Third World than would otherwise be the case. On the other hand, the lack of continuity associated with these frequent changes can be an obstacle to efficient negotiations. The co-ordinator country for the Group as a whole is determined by each region on the basis of alphabetical order, provided that there is no objection to a particular country[43] and that the country accepts this responsibility (which, in turn, may depend on its resources).[44] The plenary then accepts the designated country as a matter of course.

Co-ordinators can be very influential because they can take initiatives and hence precipitate actions and guide them. They can call meetings, define and structure the work that has to be done, suggest the establishment of *ad hoc* working groups, take an active role in co-ordination (locally as well as with other centres of the Group of 77), and the like. The co-ordinators of the Group of 77 are the Group's official spokespersons at its various centres, its chief negotiators in ongoing negotiations, and chairpersons of plenary meetings during which issues of concern to the Group as a whole are discussed.[45] One of the most important tasks in this context is the formulation of consensus because it reflects the decisions taken by the Group. The co-ordinator has the right of first refusal to chair meetings on specific subject-matters and *ad hoc* working groups, although this right is routinely relinquished in favour of a person who has become—on the basis of technical expertise, past work or special interests—the recognized spokesperson of the Group of 77 on the issue in question.

The Group's co-ordinator works in very close co-operation with the regional co-ordinators, who are normally consulted before the plenary is convened and before any action is taken. The four co-ordinators therefore meet frequently. In effect, they exercise the function of an informal bureau because as a group they make many decisions—especially those of an organizational nature such as allocating new questions to a Working Group—without calling the plenary into session.

The plenary, the regional groups, the working groups, and the co-ordinators represent the regular organizational infrastructure of the Group of 77 in Geneva. Many countries have felt, however, that this infrastructure is inadequate for the proper execution of the support and management function of the Group of 77.[46] From the First Ministerial Meeting onwards, therefore, repeated efforts have been made to provide the Group with a more satisfactory permanent machinery and an institutional focal point.

b. *Efforts to Establish a Permanent Machinery*

Initially, these efforts aimed at creating a standing committee by institutionalizing the Co-ordinating Committee, i.e., the organ that prepared the 1967 Ministerial Meeting. Thus, in its "Reference Document" the Co-ordinating Committee (after noting that the Group of 31 normally met only twice a year) suggested that "a permanent body to carry out the administrative and current business of UNCTAD should be established...in Geneva."[47] It was expected that, apart from carrying out the routine work of the Group of 77, this body would make recommendations to the Group of 31 as well as to the plenary concerning all matters in the purview of UNCTAD. The Ministerial Meeting, however, did not accept the suggestion and merely extended the mandate of the Co-ordinating Committee until the 1968 New Delhi session of UNCTAD.[48] The Group of 31 continued to carry the main burden of work.[49]

Efforts were renewed again during the Second Ministerial Meeting, but from now on they shifted towards setting up a secretariat for the Group of 77. More specifically, the ministers found it desirable to "establish in Geneva a small 'Service Bureau' for purposes of documentation and archives for the work of the Group of 77" and to "consider the possibility of establishing appropriate arrangements to prepare whatever documentation may be necessary for the Group's participation in the work of all bodies within the permanent machinery of UNCTAD".[50] Although studies of each of these proposals were to be undertaken in time for the forthcoming UNCTAD session, no final action was taken in Santiago and the proposals were not pursued further.

The Third Ministerial Meeting saw another revival of the push for a permanent machinery. The main initiative came from the Asian Group of the Group of 77[51] which recommended[52] the creation of an Interim Committee to serve between Ministerial Meetings and the establishment of an international secretariat for the Group of 77, both to be located in Geneva. It was proposed that the Interim Committee have a broad mandate and a relatively strong position and be headed by the representative of the country that hosted the last Ministerial Meeting.[53]

The Ministerial Meeting adopted two decisions[54] on these proposals, but both remained without consequences. The decision on the proposal regarding the Interim Committee merely provided that it be studied further, but no actual follow-up took place. As to the secretariat, provisions were made for a working group to undertake a comprehensive study of the subject, to be made available before the 1976 Nairobi session of UNCTAD. Such a working group was, in fact, convened and it did report to the Group of 77 at Nairobi.[55] The working group discussed the objectives and tasks of a secretariat and a number of alternative approaches by which these objectives and tasks could be accomplished. One of these approaches—which ranged from the continuation of the existing informal arrangements to the establishment of a full-fledged independent secretariat—foresaw the creation of an intermission servicing secretariat in the form of a co-ordinating committee consisting of the co-ordinator of the Group of 77 in Geneva and the co-ordinators of the regional groups, assisted by one senior official from each region who would be appointed for at least one year as secretary of each regional group and as co-ordinating secretary for the co-ordinating committee.

The report of the working group was not discussed in Nairobi. However, since unofficial support had been expressed for the creation of an intermission servicing secretariat, the Group of 77 took up the question again in Geneva and, in September 1976, decided to establish, in principle, such a machinery. The implementation of the decision was left to the regional co-ordinators and the regional groups—but they never carried this assignment through.

This left the matter for the Fourth Ministerial Meeting. But before this Meeting took place, a separate initiative had been taken by the Group of 77 in New York.

At the First Meeting of Ministers for Foreign Affairs of the Group of 77, held in September 1977 in New York, it was proposed that a technical support machinery be set up and the Group of 77 in New York was requested to conduct a detailed examination of this proposal with the purpose of making specific recommendations. In April of the next year, Jamaica, at that time the co-ordinator country of the Group of 77 in New York, circulated an informal paper on the matter, for discussion by the Group of 27 in New York. Subsequently, the 1978 Second Meeting of Ministers for Foreign Affairs requested further action. Thus, when the 1979 Ministerial Meeting in preparation of UNCTAD V took place, there was a broad sentiment in favour of having the Group of 77 in New York examine the question of a technical support machinery. This sentiment was not shared by the Geneva centre of the Group[56] and, as a compromise, the work on this issue was divided between Geneva and New York. A decision was taken to charge a working group, the "Committee of 21" with the task of "studying the desirability or otherwise"[57] of establishing a technical support machinery. Reflecting the greater role that the Group of 77 in New York had acquired in the meantime, the Committee of 21 was explicitly advised to consult with representatives of the New York Group and to submit its report to the Fall 1979 Meeting of Ministers for Foreign Affairs of the Group of 77 at the United Nations headquarters, this being the next ministerial-level meeting planned. Although the Committee of 21 agreed that "there was an urgent need to strengthen the technical support available to the Group of 77 and the mechanics for co-ordination",[58] it could not reach consensus on whether or not the establishment of a special technical support machinery was, indeed, required. The continued divergence of opinion is reflected in the report in that one section argued for the setting up of such a machinery while the other argued against it. The final decision was hence left to the ministers for foreign affairs of the Group of 77 who met in New York in September 1979 and whose political orientation, some countries hoped, would make them more favourably inclined towards a support machinery. But the foreign ministers, after an intense discussion that reflected the established divergence of opinion in this matter, merely requested the Group of 27 in New York to examine this question further and to report to the Group of 77 for appropriate decisions before the end of January 1980.[59] The final decision was, however, left to the Fall 1980 Meeting of the Ministers for Foreign Affairs. Strong opposition by a number of delegations prevented, however, agreement on even a modest strengthening of the present arrangements. The Group of 27 was, therefore, requested to continue its deliberations on this matter, "with a view to ensuring that appropriate decisions are taken prior to the commencement of global negotiations".[60]

On the face of it, this latest effort looks like any of the preceding ones: those opposing a greater institutionalization of the Group succeeded in blocking any action and each concrete proposal failed, in the end to be implemented. However, since a number of accompanying factors have changed, the fate of this latest initiative may be different after all. Now, the developing countries in New York have joined the movement towards strengthening the organizational infrastructure of the Group of 77. And bringing the discussions to New York placed them in a context in which the need for an improved organizational infrastructure is more sharply perceptible than in Geneva. In New York, the Group of 77 does not have, to the extent it does in Geneva, the support of the United Nations secretariat for its technical work. Furthermore, the regional groups in New York (as discussed above) are mainly concerned not with substantive issues but with electoral matters. As a result, the co-ordinator country has to carry the main burden of the work which is not, as in Geneva, shifted every three months from one country to the next, but rather rotates on an annual basis. The proposed global negotiations and the associated imperative for greater co-ordination of all centres of the Group of 77, the increasing range and complexity of the negotiations, the need to prepare a considerable amount of technical material, and the growing number of meetings will make this burden heavier yet.

Even if these factors should not lead to agreement on a full-fledged secretariat, they may well produce an interim solution in the form of an *ad hoc* technical support group.[61] Such a group—consisting, maybe, of not more than five experts who are hired for their technical competence and whose financing is shared by the members of the Group of 77 on the basis of a pre-determined key—could be created by a formal decision of the Group of 77 in response to a concrete and well-defined task, in this case to assist the co-ordinator of the Group of 77 in New York in the global negotiations.

The idea of such a technical support group has already been tested successfully during the Paris Conference on International Economic Co-operation. There, the support team was disbanded upon the closure of the conference, when the Group of 19 (the participating developing countries negotiating on behalf of the Group of 77) also ceased to exist. But the life of a similar body in New York would probably be of a longer duration because the global negotiations can not be expected to terminate within a short period of time. Hence, if an *ad hoc* technical group were, in fact, created in New York, it may well become the nucleus of a secretariat for the Group of 77.

c. *The Current Debate about Strengthening the Organizational Infrastructrure of the Group of 77*

Thus, the history of efforts to establish a permanent machinery has so far left the issue unresolved. While there is a widespread feeling that the organizational infrastructure of the Group of 77 must be strengthened, those who would prefer to do this by establishing a secretariat have not yet convinced those who would prefer to improve the existing framework of the merits of a more permanent body. The arguments of both sides have largely remained unchanged and ineffective since the beginning.

The proponents of greater institutionalization underline that Groups B and D have strong organizational focal points in the secretariats of, respectively, the Organisation for Economic Co-operation and Development and the Council for Mutual Economic Assistance. Based as they are on strong national civil services, which can be mobilized when need arises, these secretariats play a key role in preparing all strategic, substantive and procedural aspects of the work of their groups; they accumulate knowledge on the various questions under discussion and hence can narrow down issues at stake to precise negotiation points; and they also ensure a much more effective backstopping and follow-up of negotiations than the fragmented support system of the Group of 77. In fact, even the single most important component of this support system, the UNCTAD Secretariat (and, for that matter, other international secretariats), can offer only limited support because it has to take into account the interests of all its members, i.e., it has to service Groups B and D as well.[62] In the actual negotiations, furthermore, an international secretariat tends to take a mediating role; to the extent that the Group of 77 links its position to that of an international secretariat, therefore, it may be drawn into compromises that are not entirely in its interest.

This situation is further exacerbated by the fact that only a few of the Group's members have adequate resources for their diplomatic missions in Geneva which, after all, have to conduct the negotiations. Most are under-staffed and unspecialized (and without significant support from their capitals), and a number of countries are not represented in Geneva at all. Thus, in 1980 only 70 of the 122 members of the Group of 77 had missions in Geneva (with Asia and especially Africa inadequately represented)[63] against a virtually full representation of Groups B and D (see Table 23); many of these missions were also accredited to other international organizations headquartered in Geneva (and even to the FAO and UNIDO) and, moreover, had to fulfill regular diplomatic and consular functions. Over two fifths of all missions had to accomplish their tasks with a professional staff of five or fewer persons and only 7 per cent of them had a staff of 16 or more (compared with, respectively, 19 and 31 per cent for Group B and 33 and 11 per cent for Group D) (see Table 24). This staff had to cover, in 1979, a total of 2,083 official meetings in UNCTAD alone (see Table 25) (many of them running concurrently), as well as a total number of 1,098 plenary and regional group meetings of the Group of 77 (see Table 9). And it had to deal with an enormous number of documents: from January to November 1979, UNCTAD alone produced over 12,000 pages of documents, apart from summary records and nearly 2,000 pages of in-session documents related to UNCTAD V.

An additional problem is the high turn-over rate among the highest representatives of the developing countries: in 1980, one third of their permanent representatives had been accredited in Geneva for one year or less and two-thirds for three years or less (see Table 26).[64] This discontinuity (which can also be observed at other levels) is especially unfortunate because critical technical expertise and experience in negotiations are scarce to begin with and if the few most qualified persons leave, the learning process for individuals and the Group of 77 as a whole starts over again, with greatly disruptive effects for intra-group and inter-group negotiations.[65]

These differences have, moreover, to be seen against the background of the multi-central character of the Group of 77 with its possibilities of differing approaches and emphases, the time-consuming process of decision-making by consensus among a large number of states, and the need for geographical distribution and rotation of main offices.

In the light of all these factors, it has seemed to a large number of countries that the establishment of a permanent machinery would strengthen the self-reliant negotiating capacity of the Group of 77. It would do so by improving the Group's technical and organizational preparedness (including, in particular, that of countries with limited resources) for encounters with other groups, by contributing to greater co-ordination among the various centres of the Group, and by encouraging a clear and consistent general strategic design that would guide the day-to-day work of the Group of 77 at its various centres and ensure the systematic follow-up of negotiated agreements. A permanent machinery has come to seem all the more important in view of the expected increase in the range, volume and complexity of the negotiations facing the developing countries. Furthermore, since the developing countries have resolved to increase their individual and collective self-reliance, they will need an institutional focal point to orchestrate the required effort.

Those who oppose setting up a permanent machinery grant that the present arrangements are imperfect, but maintain that their informal character ensures the flexibility that the Group needs to accommodate the diversity of views, questions and situations confronting it. A secretariat, in this view, would bring several major disadvantages with it. For one thing, an attempt to establish such a secretariat would give rise to divisive questions regarding its location and financing.[66] For another, the secretariat would essentially serve only one centre of the Group, and it is unlikely that even a sizable institution—not to mention one consisting, say, of ten professionals— could provide substantive expertise and technical services of a quality comparable to that currently available to the Group from a number of international organizations. Furthermore, such a secretariat might evolve into a supra-national agency constraining the freedom of action of member governments in one fashion or another. This is a matter of particular concern both to countries which fear the domination of such a secretariat (and hence of the Group of 77) by other, more powerful, countries and to those whose own technical and administrative resources are adequate for their own preparations for negotiations and hence secure for them a privileged and influential position in the Group. Finally, it is possible that a central and permanent institution like the proposed secretariat would disturb the Third-World balance of influence between the Group of 77 and the non-aligned movement by making the former more effective and prominent than the latter—a point that naturally worries some major Non-Aligned Countries.

For these reasons, the opponents of a permanent machinery prefer to seek a strengthening of the negotiating capacity of the Group of 77 through greater local and international co-ordination and a fuller utilization of the existing machinery. This could be achieved, for instance, through closer contacts among the various centres of the Group (an increase in the exchange of information, documents, proposals and the like) and a greater utilization of the services offered by other organizations.

Some steps to reinforce the present system have been taken. Although no formal arrangements exist for co-ordination among the various centres of the Group of 77, the co-ordinators of the New York and Geneva Groups, in particular, have met on several occasions for consultation.[67] With the beginning, in Spring 1978, of comprehensive negotiations in the United Nations in New York on the entire range of development questions—first in the context of the Committee of the Whole, then in the framework of the global negotiations[68] —the need for co-ordination has increased further and acquired strategic significance. Consultations between the Group of 77 in New York and the Group in Geneva have since intensified and also expanded to include the other major centre.[69]

The first formal meeting of the co-ordinators of the main centres of the Group of 77 took place in Geneva on 14 February 1980. Invited— and attending—were the co-ordinators from those centres in which the Group of 77 operated on a regular basis and had recognized co-ordinators: Geneva, New York, Paris, Rome, and Vienna. The chairperson of the Group of 24 in Washington was also invited, but did not attend. Questions of interest to the Group of 77 as a whole, *viz.*, the global round of negotiations, the New International Development Strategy, the forthcoming ministerial meeting in New York, and prospects for improving co-ordination among the various centres of the Group were discussed. A second such meeting took place in Geneva on 24 July 1980, attended by the co-ordinators from Geneva, New York, Rome and Vienna as well as by the chairperson of the Deputies of the Group of 24 in Washington. It reviewed the preparations for the impending Eleventh Special Session of the United Nations General Assembly, especially those concerning the New International Development Strategy for the Third United Nations Development Decade and the launching of the global negotiations; considered an intensification of economic co-operation among developing countries; and discussed ways and means of improving the co-ordination among the various centres of the Group. Consensus was reached that the co-ordinators should meet regularly during January and July of each year[70] in order to strengthen the cohesion of the Group of 77 as a whole.

If this conclusion were implemented, communication, co-ordination and co-operation among the various centres of the Group of 77 may, indeed, improve. But whether even this improvement will be sufficient to match the organizational and technical preparedness of the developed countries remains to be seen.

## B. *The Group of 77 in UNIDO*

### 1. *The Emergence of the Group*

One of the recommendations of UNCTAD I had been that the United Nations create a specialized agency for industrial development.

In 1965, the General Assembly took action and adopted a resolution establishing, within the United Nations system, an autonomous organization for the promotion of industrial development.[71] On 1 January 1967, UNIDO was set up in Vienna. At its first major international conference, the "International Symposium on Industrial Development", held in Athens from the 29th of November to the 20th of December 1967, the Group of 77 did not act qua Group of 77.[72] At that time, the number of permanent missions accredited to UNIDO was very low so that no substantial (and certainly no representative) group of delegates could be assembled. Besides, the preparations for the conference had taken place before the Group of 77 had organized itself at the Algiers Ministerial Meeting and had encouraged co-operation outside UNCTAD.

At the 1971 Vienna Special International Conference of UNIDO (UNIDO I), however, the group system began to emerge in UNIDO as well. Since the preparatory time for this Conference was relatively short,[73] separate regional meetings were not organized.[74] Instead, the developing countries represented in Vienna decided, at a meeting on the 7th and 8th of January 1971 (and with an eye to the preparatory process for UNCTAD sessions), to constitute themselves as the Group of 77 in Vienna.[75] At the same time, a Standing Committee of Nine[76] was created to draft a common position paper of the Group of 77 dealing with all items on the agenda of the Conference. After a number of sessions of the Standing Committee and the plenary, a position paper was adopted by the Group of 77 during a plenary meeting on the 29th and 30th of April 1971. It served later as the basis for the draft resolution presented by the Group of 77 to the Special Conference.

At the Conference itself, the Group of 77 acted largely in unison. However, it had not yet established itself as the sole negotiating agent of the Third World: the regional groups as well as individual countries made their own statements and observations and introduced their own draft resolutions—a practice that also characterized the actions of Group B. Still, although most groups had not yet found the same degree of cohesion as in UNCTAD,[77] the conference was clearly marked by the group-negotiations process familiar from Geneva.

This process was completed at the time of the Second General Conference of UNIDO. The developing countries' position for this conference was prepared by meetings of the regional groups, the results of which were synthesized by the First Ministerial Meeting of the Group of 77 in Preparation for UNIDO II.[78] A number of questions that could not be resolved on that occasion were subsequently discussed by a Drafting Group in its capacity as preparatory committee for the Second Ministerial Meeting of the Group of 77 in preparation for UNIDO II. This meeting took place in Algiers in February 1975 and adopted the "Declaration and Plan of Action on Industrial Development and Co-operation".[79] This document became the basis of negotiations at the Second General Conference of UNIDO in Lima in March 1975 and was then adopted, as amended, by it.[80]

While the group system as such was firmly established at the time of UNIDO II, the Group of 77 in Vienna was still operating largely on an *ad hoc* basis. Only several years later did it begin to function in a sustained and more structured manner. The catalyst was the negotiation of a constitution for UNIDO.

On the insistence of the developing countries, the Lima Declaration and Plan of Action, as adopted by UNIDO II, had called for the conversion of UNIDO into a specialized agency of the United Nations. The 1975 Seventh Special Session of the General Assembly endorsed this proposal and established an intergovernmental committee of the whole to draw up the constitution of the agency. After a number of meetings held by the committee, the first session of the United Nations Conference on the Establishment of the United Nations Industrial Development Organization as a Specialized Agency was convened in February 1978 to consider a draft constitution. The conference failed to reach agreement. Greatly concerned about these developments, the Group of 77 in Vienna appointed an open-ended "Task Force of the Group of 77 in Vienna" on 2 October 1978. It consisted of seven core members (two from each region plus one (Romania) from Europe - see Table 27) and chaired by the co-ordinator. The Task Force undertook co-ordination work for the final round of negotiations.[81] At the second session of the Conference in 1979, agreement was finally reached on the text of a constitution for UNIDO.[82] For UNIDO, the work of the Task Force had borne the desired fruit. In addition, the Group of 77 had established itself in Vienna as a negotiating body capable of speaking and negotiating for all developing countries.

When UNIDO's constitution was adopted, the preparations for UNIDO III (scheduled for January and February 1980) had already begun. Hence it was only natural that the Task Force—which had just demonstrated its usefulness—should undertake this work as well. In fact, this had already been anticipated when the Task Force had been set up.

Taking into consideration the regional declarations and other relevant materials, the Task Force accordingly prepared a draft declaration for the 1979 Havana Third Ministerial Meeting. At the Meeting, this draft was merged with a draft prepared by the host country, Cuba, to become the "Havana Declaration of the Group of 77" in preparation for UNIDO III.[83] The Ministerial Meeting further directed the Group of 77 in Vienna to prepare the draft of a programme of action for the implementation of the Havana Declaration, to be submitted to the Group of 77 prior to the Third General Conference of UNIDO in New Delhi in January and February 1980. Such a draft was prepared (by the Task Force) and, after it had been amended[84] in New Delhi, was submitted, together with the Havana Declaration, to the Third General Conference as the position of the Group of 77. Since no consensus could be reached during the negotiations at the conference, these documents were adopted, against the votes of Group B, as the "New Delhi Declaration and Plan of Action on Industrialization of Developing Countries and International Co-operation for Their Industrial Development". Given the grave disagreements in evidence at New Delhi, it was decided to annex the statements and position papers of Groups B and D to the report of the Conference.

## 2. *Current Organization*

The pattern of preparation for UNIDO's General Conferences has thus become similar to that for UNCTAD's sessions, even if it is less structured, refined and thorough. Once the Industrial Development Board adopts the provisional agenda for the next General Conference and the agenda is endorsed by the General Assembly, it is sent to the capitals, where preparations begin for regional meetings. Some of these regional meetings are carried out in the framework of regional commissions of the United Nations and, therefore, are attended by those developed countries that are members of the regional commissions in question.[85] From the first conference in relation to UNIDO in 1967, the Arab states, apart from taking part in the preparatory meetings of the African and Asian regions, met separately as well to agree on a common position of their own. The Arab states do not, however, form a regional group that has an official standing under the rules of procedure of the Industrial Development Board, nor do they constitute a separate group at the Ministerial Meetings.[86]

The regional documents are the building blocks for the work of the Task Force of the Group of 77 in Vienna, which acts under the guidance of the plenary and which carries the heaviest burden of the preparatory work. In contradistinction to UNCTAD, however, the main work of the Task Force is undertaken *after* the regional meetings have taken place. And since the input of some of the regional meetings is co-determined by developed countries, attention is also given to relevant documents of other centres of the Group of 77, especially to those of Geneva and New York. The Task Force synthesizes these materials into a document that becomes the basis of discussion for the Ministerial Meeting. In a sense, then, the Task Force also fulfills some of the functions of the Senior Officials Meeting described in the context of UNCTAD.

The absence of a full-fledged formal preparatory committee reflects the fact that the organizational infrastructure of the Group of 77 in UNIDO is, compared to that in UNCTAD, relatively weak. In Geneva, the Group of 77 can draw on strong support from the UNCTAD Secretariat (which even has a liaison office for the Group of 77); it has its own permanent working groups for a number of issues; and it maintains diplomatic missions that are relatively well-staffed. In Vienna, these features of the Geneva centre are either less well-developed or absent. Thus, there is no liaison office with UNIDO which could provide administrative support nor are there any permanent working groups. The tradition of acting in unison, as remarked earlier, is also not as firmly established as at Geneva. In addition, only 37 of the 122 members of the Group of 77 had Permanent Missions in Vienna in 1980, compared to 25 out of 27 for Group B (see Table 23). Two-thirds of these were also accredited as embassies to the Government of Austria (as well as to the governments of other countries) and had normal diplomatic and consular duties to fulfill. (These bilateral relations are often considered to be more important than relations with UNIDO.) Over two-thirds of these missions worked with a professional staff of five persons or less (see Table 24) and over two-thirds had permanent representatives who had been accredited for three years or less (see Table 26). The African countries, in particular, are under-represented in Vienna.

On the other hand, the Task Force has become a firmly established institution. Its broad mandate to prepare all issues to be dealt with by the Group of 77 has given it the function of a steering and permanent drafting committee of the Group of 77 in Vienna which prepares most of the work of the plenary and, on occasion, even takes the initiative on some issues. The core membership of the Task Force has not changed and its stability and continuity is enhanced by the uninterrupted participation of key individuals. Although nowhere specified, the Task Force is chaired by the co-ordinators of the Group of 77 in Vienna, regardless of whether or not they belong to its core members. Since it is open-ended, it has the flexibility required to pay adequate attention to the interests of countries that pursue distinct policies of their own and to accommodate them within a common approach (*de facto*, however, mostly only the core members meet). At the same time, its limited size makes it an effective working group that provides the necessary structure to the Group of 77 as a whole.[87]

Such an organizational structure is particularly important because the regional groups are not as active as in Geneva and focus
much of their attention on electoral questions. As elsewhere, the
regional groups observe the principle of equitable geographical
representation. Thus, for instance, the offices of the Bureau of the
Industrial Development Board (one president, three vice-presidents,
one rapporteur) are subject to rotation among the four groups - which
are almost identical with those in UNCTAD - according to a pre-
determined five-year cycle (see Table 28).[88]

The regional groups also take turns in designating, usually early
January of each year, on the basis of their own procedures,[89] the co-
ordinator for the Group as a whole. The co-ordinator is then elected by
consensus by the plenary of the Group of 77. Although the first co-
ordinator was chosen in 1971, this function only assumed importance
with the emergence of the Group of 77 as a more organized body
during the preparations for UNIDO II in 1974/75 (see Table 29). As in
other centres in which the Group of 77 is active, the co-ordinators
(assisted by the regional co-ordinators) are the spokespersons of the
Group of 77 in Vienna. They can establish *ad hoc* working groups;[90]
they chair meetings of the plenary, the Task Force and the *ad hoc*
working groups;[91] and they are the main negotiators of the developing
countries. The position of the co-ordinators in Vienna is particularly
delicate because in summing up decisions of the plenary, they need to
take the under-representation of the Group in Vienna into account.
The under-representation in Vienna also makes co-ordination with the
Groups in New York and Geneva important. Still, in spite of the
special problems raised by poor representation, the Group in Vienna
plays the leading role in defining the position of the Third World in all
areas within the competence of UNIDO.[92]

## C. The Group of 77 in the IMF and the World Bank

By August 1971, when the inconvertibility of the US dollar into
gold was made official, the need for a thorough review and reform of
the international monetary system had become obvious. To obtain the
necessary advice, the Board of Governors of the International
Monetary Fund decided, on 26 July 1972, to establish a "Committee
on Reform of the International Monetary System and Related Issues"
(the "Committee of 20").

The most important developed countries were well-prepared to
make their inputs into the deliberations of the Committee of 20. Since
about 1964, the finance ministers and central bank governors of the ten
main industrialized members of the IMF had begun to meet regularly

outside the framework of the IMF as the "Group of 10",[93] first primarily in relation to the General Arrangements to Borrow (which arrangements had been concluded with the Fund in 1962) and then to discuss questions of international liquidity in general. Soon the deputies of the members of the Group of 10 also began to meet to prepare the deliberations of the ministers. (In cases where such meetings took place on the premises of the IMF, meeting facilities and some technical services were provided by the IMF.) Eventually, the Group of 10 expanded its agenda to include all important international monetary issues and became the locus for much of the decision-making on international monetary questions. When the Committee of 20 was established, therefore, it was quite clear that the Group of 10 would co-ordinate its activities with those of the new committee and, if possible, shape the recommendations of the Committee.

## 1. *The Genesis of the Group of 24*

Not surprisingly, the Group of 77 found it "entirely unacceptable that vital decisions about the future of the international monetary system which are of concern to the entire world community are sought to be taken by a limited group of countries outside the framework of the International Monetary Fund".[94] Consequently, "with a view to ensuring full participation of the developing countries in searching for a solution to the present international monetary crisis and to safeguard the interests of the developing countries," the Group of 77 invited, at its 1971 Lima Second Ministerial Meeting, the President of the Ministerial Meeting "to consult with the Governments of the Group of 77 to consider the establishment of an intergovernmental group" to perform the following functions:

(a) Keep under review the course of the international monetary situation, take due cognizance of the studies entrusted to the Executive Directors of IMF at the recent meeting of the Board of Governors, and keep the countries members of the Group of 77 informed;

(b) Evaluate events in the monetary field, as well as any decisions which might be taken by a single country or group of countries whithin the framework of IMF, relating to the interests of the developing countries; [and]

(c) Recommend within the field of its competence to the Governments of the Group of 77 co-ordinated positions in the third session of the United Nations Conference on Trade and Development, as well as in other forums, and consider any other action as might be necessary, including the convening of a world monetary conference within the framework of the United Nations.[95]

Pursuant to a subsequent request to the President of the Second Ministerial Meeting, the Group of 77 met in Geneva on 21 January

1972 and agreed that the establishment of the intergovernmental group was, indeed, desirable. It was decided that the group should consist of 24 members - hence the "Group of 24" - with each region appointing, in a manner determined by itself, 8 members from among its ministers of finance or economy or its governors of central banks.[96] (Any other member of the Group of 77 may, however, participate as observer in all meetings of the Group and its organs, and a number of them often do.) The membership of the Group has not changed since the beginning (see Table 30) and even the participation of individuals has remained relatively stable.[97] In addition, it was agreed that the Group would also meet at the level of deputies (senior afficials from governments or central banks with extensive experience in financial and monetary matters) who are the deputies of the members of the group at the ministerial level. Invited - but not as members - are those nine Executive Directors of the IMF[98] who are appointed or elected exclusively by the developing countries and, since the establishment of the Development Committee, also those nine Executive Directors of the World Bank who are elected exclusively by the developing countries.[99]

At the ministerial level, the Group was given a Bureau consisting of a chairperson and two vice-chairpersons from different regions. Since 1974, the chair of the Group of 24 has rotated annually among the three regions (see Table 31).[100] At the level of deputies, the Group selected a chairperson, and two vice-chairpersons who, together, constitute the Bureau of the Group of Deputies. As in the case of the Group of 10, the chairperson of the Group of Deputies acts as rapporteur for the ministerial meetings. The establishment of working parties, as well as the frequency and timing of meetings, was left to the discretion of the members of the Group. In practice (with the exception of the constituting meeting), the ministers of the Group of 24 have always met immediately before (and at the same place as) the sessions of the Committee of 20 and, later, before those of the Interim Committee. The Deputies, who have to undertake the substantive preparations and therefore carry the major burden of the work of the Group, meet before the ministers; but they may also gather in the interim, depending on the workload of the Group.[101] At both levels of the Group of 24, decisions are reached by consensus, although there are no formal rules of procedure.

After a preparatory meeting of the Deputies in Geneva on 31 January 1972 and their first regular meeting in Caracas from the 3rd to the 5th of April 1972, the Intergovernmental Group of 24 on International Monetary Affairs held its inaugural session at the ministerial level in Caracas on the 6th and 7th of April 1972. In a communiqué[102] issued at the end of the meeting, the Group reaffirmed the terms of reference given to it by the 1971 Lima Ministerial Meeting of the Group of 77 and emphasized in particular that "the most important task facing it at this moment is to provide for fundamental improvements in the decision-making process regarding international monetary issues".[103] This priority reflected the desire of the developing countries to create an effective institutional counterpart to the Group of 10 (on whose structure that of the Group of 24 was patterned) in order to influence decision-making on international monetary and financial matters while negotiating options were still open. The formation of the Group of 24 allowed the members of the Group of 77 to co-ordinate their policies and proposals in the IMF, thus improving their bargaining position by adopting a common approach and ensuring a systematic consideration of the interests of the Third World in on-going negotiations. It also strengthened the role of the nine Directors on the Board of Executive Directors of the IMF (and, later, those on the Board of the World Bank) who are exclusively appointed or elected by developing countries, the informal "Group of 9", [104] by providing them with political backing as well as practical assistance in their day-to-day work.

## 2. Broadening the Mandate

Originally, the work of the Group of 77 was geared towards the Committee of 20. When this Committee concluded its work in June 1974 and submitted its final report together with an "Outline of Reform"[105] to the Board of Governors of the Fund, one of its recommendations for immediate action was that an "Interim Committee of the Board of Governors of the International Monetary Fund on the International Monetary System" be established. This Committee, pending the creation of a permanent and representative Council of the Fund, was to have an advisory role "in supervising the management and adaptation of the monetary system, overseeing the continuing operation of the adjustment process, and dealing with sudden disturbances which might threaten the system".[106] Another recommendation for immediate action concerned the establishment of a "Joint Ministerial Committee of the Boards of Governors of the Bank and the Fund on the Transfer of Real Resources to Developing Countries". This "Development Committee" would maintain an overview of the development process, advise and report to the World Bank and to the Fund on all aspects of the transfer of real resources, and make suggestions regarding the implementation of its conclusions.

These recommendations were implemented without delay when the 1974 Annual Meetings of the Fund and the Bank established the

Interim Committee, whose membership structure corresponds to that of the Fund's Executive Board, and the Development Committee, whose structure is similar to that of the Interim Committee. The Group of 24, which had played a key role in the creation of the Development Committee (and whose support for the Committee was later to be decisive for its continuing existence) henceforth directed its activities towards influencing the deliberations of these two committees (whose agenda items tend to determine those of the Group of 24), with a view to influencing the decision-making of the IMF and the World Bank.[107] At the same time, the Group of 24 broadened its mandate to include in it, in addition to international monetary matters, questions of international development finance as well.

It was not without some discussion that the Group of 24 proceeded with its work after the Committee of 20 had completed its task. At the seventh meeting of the Group in June 1974, the question arose as to whether or not the Group of 24 should be dissolved. Apart from the argument that such a decision could only be taken by the Group of 77, the point was made that the reform of the international monetary system had not yet been completed and that, therefore, a continuing representation of the interests of the developing countries was necessary. It emerged as the consensus of the meeting that the mandate of the Group of 24 still held and that it could proceed with its work.

The Group of 24 did raise this question, however, in its "Report of the Chairperson of the Group of 24" to the 1976 Manila Third Ministerial Meeting of the Group of 77.[108] In it, the Group of 24 pointed out that after the first stage of reform had been completed with the agreements reached at the January 1976 Kingston meeting of the Interim Committee, the stage of long-term monetary reform had begun; moreover, the Sixth and Seventh Special Sessions of the General Assembly of the United Nations had introduced new considerations into the development discussion. In the light of these factors, the Group of 24 invited the Group of 77

> to re-examine from a political angle the terms of reference initially given to the Group of Twenty-Four in connexion with monetary reform, and to consider the possibility of using the Group as a co-ordinating body with wider terms of reference in the international economic and financial field, including using it as a practical mechanism for strengthening and developing co-operation among the developing countries themselves in those fields.[109]

The Third Ministerial Meeting "took note with appreciation"[110] of this report and recommended that the Group of 24 continue its work in the framework of its expanded mandate and in the light of the guidelines adopted by the Third Ministerial Meeting.

Over the years, the Group of 24 has thus remained a relatively technical group, staffed by highly qualified experts of senior rank. It ensures that the developing countries exercise some influence in the management of the international monetary and financial systems and that the specific interests and economic circumstances of the Third World are at least taken into account. In fact, the Group of 24 observed that,

> in the light of the co-ordinated position of the developing countries, achieved through the Group of Twenty-Four, the variable of the economic development of the Third World was introduced explicitly for the first time in decisions relating to the reform of the international monetary system.[111]

It so far remains the only permanent expert group of the Group of 77. This may be explained by the technicality of its subject matter, its involvement in an on-going process of reform and (through the Group of 9) in the management of the international monetary system, its link with the IMF and the World Bank, its location away from the political centres of the United Nations system, and the fact that the members of the Group are themselves at the ministerial level.

Efforts to institutionalize the group further failed, however: the first set of discussions about the possibility of setting up a technical secretariat for the group was abandoned by the Group of Deputies at their eighth meeting in September 1973 for lack of attendance in a working group created for the consideration of this question; this decision of the deputies was sanctioned by the ministers at their meeting in June 1974. Discussions on this subject were revived again in 1975, when the ministers asked the Bureau to prepare proposals for working arrangements of the Group of 24, and in 1977, when the ministers asked the deputies to examine issues relating to the organization and work of the Group of 24, including the proposal to establish a secretariat. On both occasions, however, there was a consensus in favour of continuing the existing arrangements: the logistic support, especially concerning meeting facilities, translation and secretarial services provided to the Group of 24 (as to the Group of 10) by the IMF; the resources available to the Executive Directors representing developing countries and the co-ordination work carried out by them; the assistance, when necessary, of technical experts recruited to work on specific projects;[112] and the increasing substantive support of the Fund and the Bank.

When the scope of activities of the Group of 24 widened considerably following the nineteenth ministerial meeting of the Group in September 1979, a new effort to establish a secretariat was launched. It was argued that only a secretariat could cope with the detailed preparatory work called for by the Group's programme of action and meet the increasing need to monitor and co-ordinate activities in other international fora in which monetary and financial matters were discussed. In addition, it was argued that the planned expansion of economic co-operation among developing countries called for the establishment of an organizational infrastructure. The arguments, however, failed to convince the April 1980 meeting of the Group of 24 and no progress in the matter of setting up any formal machinery was made. It remains to be seen whether the requirements of the 1980s will lead to some strengthening of the Group's organizational infrastructure.[113]

## 3. *Relations with the Group of 77*

In spite of the origin of the Group of 24 in a decision of the Group of 77, the relationship between the two bodies has not been either simple or stable. When the question of the proper relationship between the two bodies was debated during the first session of the Group, a number of countries argued for strong relations with the Group of 77, i.e., they suggested that the Group of 24 should report to its parent body which, in turn, should provide it with the necessary guidance. Other delegations, led by the largest Latin American countries, urged on the other hand that the Group of 24 should be an independent body of monetary experts which, while reporting its results to the individual members of the Group of 77, would have no direct institutional linkage with the Group of 77 or UNCTAD. This latter view prevailed and, in the years that followed, the Group of 24 remained relatively detached from the Group of 77[114] and maintained a high degree of independence.[115] This was, however, by no means a unilateral preference: many in the Group of 77 considered the Group of 24 to have been co-opted by the Bank and the Fund and, as a result, become a body of managers rather than reformers of the international monetary and financial systems.

Nevertheless, the relationship between the two bodies began to change when the Group of 24, in its report to the 1976 Manila Third Ministerial Meeting, requested (as was mentioned above) a re-examination of its terms of reference and suggested that this be done "from a political angle". As the report of the Group pointed out, the nature of the international development discussion had changed with the politicization of the development issue and the determination of the Third World to work towards the NIEO. Conversely, since the Group of 77 conceived of the NIEO programme as an integrated approach encompassing all major dimensions of North-South interactions, it began to pay greater attention to the IMF and the World

Bank and, eventually, "re-discovered" the Group of 24.[116]

A change also took place within the Group of 24. At the beginning, the developing-country Executive Directors exercised great influence in the Group. They had the technical expertise and the deep familiarity with every aspect of the subject matter that comes from being associated with the management of the daily affairs of the Fund and the Bank. Against this natural advantage of the Executive Directors, the delegations from the capitals were often in an unfavourable position, particularly when they were not briefed as thoroughly as would have been necessary to enable them to participate in the discussions on a basis of equality with the Executive Directors. In this situation, the immediate operational monetary considerations of the Executive Directors—who, after all, were involved in the actual lending activities of their organizations—dominated the deliberations of the Group of 24. And as part of these considerations, the Executive Directors did not favour close ties with the Group of 77, since they considered its competence in monetary matters doubtful and its motives primarily political in nature. For the same reasons, the Group of 24 also kept itself at some distance from UNCTAD, to the extent that it even avoided meeting in Geneva. Over time, however, the delegations from the capitals asserted themselves—partly because they began to command greater expertise, partly because broader considerations began to play a more important role—and the relative influence of the Executive Directors (and their concerns) decreased. The ministers and their deputies, in turn, were much more in tune with the over-all development discussion and, in consequence, saw monetary questions in a broader context and introduced a political-economy perspective into the deliberations of the Group of 24. The inclusion of development finance in the Group's mandate aided this process of detechnicalizing in that it drew the Group deeper into one of the main topics of North-South negotiations and further increased its receptivity to broader development considerations.[117]

By the time the 1979 Fourth Ministerial Meeting of the Group of 77 took place in Arusha, these changes combined to allow for a narrowing of the gap between the Group of 77 and the Group of 24. The final document adopted in Arusha called on the Group of 24 "to intensify its work in accordance with its mandate and to do preparatory work on the fundamental reform of the international monetary system"; it also invited the chairperson of the deputies "to convey reports of all its meetings to the Chairmen of the Group of 77 in Geneva and New York", and requested the three groups "to collaborate with each other on these matters and make arrangements for continuing co-operation".[118] In other words, the Group of 77 began to re-assert its parentage of the Group of 24 and to establish the kind of institutional linkage that the latter had originally sought to avoid. In fact, the Group of 77 went one step further when it suggested that "member Governments of the Group of 77 should avail themselves of the occasion of the Bank/ Fund meeting in Belgrade in 1979 to convene a meeting of the Group of 77 at the level of Ministers of Finance or Economy".[119]

Such a meeting did indeed take place in Belgrade on 29 September 1979—the first gathering of the plenary of the Group of 77 at the level of ministers of finance or economy. The preparatory work was, of course, undertaken by the deputies of the Group of 24. They had completed, during two meetings in Belgrade in July and September 1979, the final draft of an "Outline for a Programme of Action on International Monetary Reform" which set out the principles, objectives and actions for an effective reform of the international monetary system. The Group of 24 approved the "Outline" at its nineteenth meeting on 28 September 1979 and the plenary of the Group of 77 formally and unanimously endorsed it the next day. In a joint press conference of the chairpersons of the Groups of 77 and 24 on the same day, it was released to the public and, later, presented (by the Group of 24) to the Development Committee, the Interim Committee, and the Annual Meetings of the Boards of Governors of the Bank and the Fund.

Although the Group of 77 had neither drafted a text of its own for the Belgrade meeting nor amended the document prepared by the Group of 24—which would certainly have been within its power[120]—it had nevertheless re-asserted its authority over the Group of 24 and, in the process, given additional weight to the work of that Group by supporting it without reservations. At the same time, the Group of 24—which had not regarded without reservation the growing intrusion of the Group of 77 into what it considered its area of competence—had maintained a measure of independence. In addition, its broader mandate had been explicitly confirmed by the "Outline" and, in fact, had been extended beyond matters concerning the Fund and the Bank:

> The Group of 24 should continuously develop and strengthen its work in order to be of maximum assistance to developing countries, coordinating their positions on international monetary and financial matters in all relevant forums.[121]

On the other hand, the Group of 24 recognized that its activities—as those of any organ of the Group of 77—must be carried out in the over-all context of the establishment of the NIEO. It further acknowledged that the proposals decided upon by the Arusha Ministerial Meeting "give a sense of direction to our efforts to achieve a New International Economic Order" and it reaffirmed "the importance of monetary and financial cooperation among developing countries as an integral part of the process of changes in the world monetary and financial order".[122]

Whether or not this balance can be maintained in the future remains to be seen. The impending global negotiations in the General Assembly, in particular, may well tend to strengthen centripetal forces and confer more leadership and authority upon the Group of 77 as a whole. Signs for a further re-integration of the Group of 24 into the mainstream of activities of the Group of 77 can certainly be detected. Thus, members of the Group of 24, including the chairperson of the Deputies of the Group of 24, participated in a "Meeting of Experts of Developing Countries on the Reform of the International Monetary System" which was held in Abu Dhabi from the 25th to the 28th of June 1980[123] to prepare the position of the Group of 77 for the first meeting of UNCTAD's "*Ad Hoc* Intergovernmental High-Level Group of Experts on the Evolution of the International Monetary System" (established by a resolution of UNCTAD V). When the Group of Experts subsequently met in Geneva between the 28th of July and the 5th of August 1980, the chairperson of the Deputies of the Group of 24 was chosen—and agreed—to chair the meeting. Another sign was the participation of the chairperson of the Deputies of the Group of 24 in the second meeting of the co-ordinators of the various centres of the Group of 77 in Geneva on 24 July 1980.[124]

This series of events, which would hardly have been conceivable only a few years ago, represents a clear break with the past: the Group of 24 not only participates actively in an UNCTAD expert group meeting in Geneva on international monetary matters, it even assumes a leading role in it. This is a development that may well signal that the Group of 24 is indeed becoming the monetary and financial arm of the Group of 77 as a whole (instead of being simply a technical body dealing with matters relating to the IMF and the World Bank) and is beginning to feel responsible for maintaining and pursuing a coherent set of policies in all relevant fora. If this is, in fact, the case, a new symbiosis between the Group of 24 and the Group of 77 would seem to have been established.

In the light of the intensified discussions surrounding the IMF and the World Bank, this new relationship acquires particular importance. After the successful 1979 Belgrade gathering, the April 1980 meeting of the Interim Committee would seem to have been a demonstration of the impact that the Group of 24 can have when it is backed by the Group of 77. At that meeting, the Group succeeded in convincing the Interim Committee to request the Managing Director and the Executive Board of the IMF to examine in depth some of the recommendations of the Group of 24, "with a view towards a substantive discussion of these matters at the next session of the Interim Committee."[125] This may well represent the first step towards a greater influence of the Third World on the agenda of the IMF and the World Bank.

## D. The Group of 19

In October 1974, responding to the oil developments in 1973-1974, the President of France called for an international meeting to deal with the energy question. After it had been agreed to broaden the scope of the conference to include all major development issues, the preparatory work for the Conference on International Economic Co-operation began in April 1975, at a meeting attended by seven developing and three developed countries.[126] The meeting laid down the ground rules for the conference:[127] it would be restricted to 19 developing and 8 developed countries (see Table 32); it would open at the ministerial level in Paris in December 1975 and would be presided over by two co-chairpersons, chosen one each by the two participating groups;[128] four commissions (each co-chaired in the same manner) would be set up to deal, respectively, with energy, raw materials, development, and finance; the commissions would function independently of one another but the results of their work would be linked; decisions would be made by consensus; and an international secretariat with an exclusively administrative and technical function would be set up.

The opening ministerial meeting of the Conference took place in Paris from the 16th to the 19th of December 1975. After an organizing session of the co-chairpersons in January 1976—during which the developing countries submitted a list of subjects on which discussions should take place—the commissions (see Table 33) began their work in February of the same year. Meetings also took place at the senior-officials level; and the co-chairpersons continued to play an important mediating role, particularly in September 1976, when the work of the commissions seemed to have reached an impasse. The concluding ministerial meeting took place in Paris, from the 30th of May to the 2nd of June 1977, without, however, reaching the comprehensive agreement that had been sought.[129]

Although the Paris conference was a major North-South encounter, it was to date the only one in which participation was restricted to a selected number of countries. The developing countries agreed to it reluctantly and essentially only to show good faith in responding to a major initiative of France[130] in a critical movement of North-South relations and to explore the possibilities of negotiation in a different framework. Furthermore, since (according to the original timetable) the Conference was scheduled to last only one year, it was from the beginning meant to be a time-limited undertaking.

But the restricted participation in the Conference raised a serious problem of representation. As already indicated, only ten countries were invited to do the preparatory work. They, in turn, assumed the responsibility for designating, from among their respective groups and according to their own procedures, an additional five developed and twelve developing coutries. For the developing countries, this raised the difficult question of which additional four countries from each region should be included. Because the Conference had its origin in the oil developments of 1974, and energy was for the developed countries the most important item on its agenda, the problem of selection was further confounded by the need to ensure a strong OPEC representation. After informal consultations among the members of the Group of 77 in New York,[131] the problem was resolved in favour of the OPEC and the bigger non-oil-exporting developing countries, a solution that did not particularly please the smaller and especially the least-developed members of the Group of 77. Thus, 7 of the 19 developing countries belonged to OPEC, as did three of the four commission chairpersons representing developing countries. In terms of regional distribution, Africa and Latin America were each represented by six countries and Asia by seven countries - a distribution that was neither equal nor equitable and hence was in conflict with one of the main operating principles of the Group of 77.[132]

The nineteen developing countries formed the "Group of 19" whose co-ordinator, Manuel Pérez-Guerrero, was also one of the co-chairpersons of the Paris Conference.[133] At the level of each commission of the Paris Conference, the Group of 19 constituted a committee, each chaired by the developing country co-chairperson of the respective commission. Since all members of the Group of 19 could participate in all committees, they were kept fully informed about the progress of negotiations. The Group of 19 as a whole, as well as each committee, harmonized its views on all issues before the Paris Conference through decisions taken by consensus. The spokespersons of the developing countries acted then on the basis of the mandate given to them. As an offspring of the Group of 77, the function of the Group of 19 was to represent the entire Third World at the Paris Conference. It was clear from the beginning that once its task had been completed, the Group of 19 would be disbanded.

The Group of 19 established, for the duration of the Paris Conference, a "Supporting Team" which reported to the Group's co-ordinator. It consisted of one director and four professional staff-members (assisted, at times, by two junior professionals) each of whom was responsible for one of the substantive areas covered by the four commissions. Apart from assisting the Group of 19 and its committees in all administrative matters, the Supporting Team also made substantive inputs by collecting the necessary background documents, updating analyses, and drafting position papers for the Conference. For such substantive support, the Group of 19 could also rely on the inputs of individual countries and on materials supplied by UNCTAD as well as other United Nations agencies. In fact, since the drafting of these materials forced the developing countries to formulate detailed positions on a wide range of issues in constant interaction with the developed countries, it made a valuable contribution to the further elaboration of the Third World's over-all economic programme.

The problem of selecting the members of the Group of 19 apart, co-ordination also presented some difficulties—if only because the deliberations of the Group of 19 did not take place at a major centre of activity of the Group of 77 as a whole. Fortunately, the 1976 Third Ministerial Meeting of the Group of 77 took place at the beginning of the substantive negotiations in Paris and hence could address itself to this question. The issue of co-ordination had already been raised in the preparatory meeting of the Asian Group of the Group of 77. This Group adopted a resolution that called, *inter alia*, on the co-ordinator countries of the Group of 77 in Geneva and New York jointly to ensure "close co-operation and co-ordination with its Group of 19" and invited the co-chairperson of the Paris Conference representing the Group of 19 "to report on a regular basis to the Group of 77 in Geneva and in New York on the progress and developments" at the conference.[134] The call for close co-ordination was taken up by Houari Boumediènne, who, as President-in-Office of the non-aligned movement and President of an important OPEC country, Algeria, had played a key role in the North-South discussions since 1973. In a message to the 1976 Manila Ministerial Meeting he insisted that "the Group of 19 . . . must receive from the Group of 77 and, in particular, from its Third Ministerial Meeting, guidance, instructions and support. . . ."[135] The Ministerial Meeting had, in fact, before it for its information the "List of Subjects Prepared by the Group of 19 of the Conference on International Economic Co-operation", which the Group of 19 had prepared for the January 1976 discussions between the co-chairpersons of the Paris Conference.

At the Ministerial Meeting, then, the members of the Group of 77 agreed that the Manila Declaration and related documents "should serve as the guidelines of the Group of 19" and that the Third World's co-chairperson at the Paris Conference should "report to the regional group leaders in Geneva and New York who, in turn, are to report to all members of the Group of 77".[136] The Ministerial Meeting itself adopted a decision on the co-ordination between the Groups of 19 and 77, providing, among other things, that arrangements for a constant exchange and flow of information between the Group of 19 and the Group of 77 in Geneva and New York be made and that a liaison group be established in Geneva to supply the Group of 19 with inputs for its negotiations.[137] In a subsequent declaration on 28 April 1976, the Group of 19 confirmed that it considered itself an integral part of the Group of 77 and was guided by the Manila Declaration and Programme of Action.

In practice, co-ordination was carried out in a pragmatic and informal manner. For instance, briefings took place whenever key persons of the various centres of the Group of 77 were in Paris. Co-ordination was also facilitated by the fact that virtually all delegations of the Group of 19 were composed of negotiators from the respective capitals, New York and Geneva, with representatives from Geneva playing a key role in the final round of negotiations. The institutional decisions of Manila thus served more to ensure that there was contact and consultation between the Group of 77 and the Group of 19 than to impose a rigid schedule of implementation. The aim of co-ordination was fully achieved since the Group of 19 always considered itself to be acting on behalf of the Group of 77 and in reference to its wider constituency and since it negotiated on the basis of documents adopted by the Group of 77 as a whole; it seemed inconceivable that the Group of 19 would reach agreements that could not be approved by the Group of 77 as a whole.

While these arrangements seemed to solve the problem of co-ordination, they could not be sufficient to ensure the constant contact between the Group of 19 and the Group of 77 that was required by the ensuing intensive Paris negotiations. Non-participants had only limited opportunities to influence these negotiations—a striking contrast to the procedure in the General Assembly and in UNCTAD where the plenary of the Group of 77 caucuses constantly in all major negotiations to ensure that all points of view are taken into account. Conversely, the possibility could not be ruled out that the Group of 19 would become isolated. The lack of direct participation of all parties interested in the negotiations (not to mention the absence of the Eastern European Group and China), combined with fears that the restricted participation in the Conference would lead to divisions in the Group of 77, made the Paris Conference suspect in the eyes of many developing countries.[138] Ultimately, the failure of the Conference to reach a comprehensive agreement seemed to demonstrate that, their divisive potential apart, negotiations with restricted participation were not necessarily more efficient and effective in reaching successful results. The Group of 19 remained, therefore, an episode in the history of the Group of 77, an experiment that only seemed to confirm the wisdom of the Group's ground-rules. The Paris Conference remained without a follow-up; in fact, it underlined the need to remain in the plenary organs of the United Nations system.

Indeed, efforts to bring the North-South negotiations back into the United Nations system and to keep them there had already started before the Paris Conference formally opened and they continued while it was still in progress. On 15 December 1975, one day before the opening ministerial meeting of the Conference, the Thirtieth Regular Session of the General Assembly adopted resolution 3515 (XXX) in which the Paris Conference was invited to report its conclusions to the General Assembly. It was a precautionary step to ensure that the negotiations in Paris were, indeed, of a limited duration and remained linked to the United Nations system. The ministers took note of this resolution in the final communiqué of their opening meeting and agreed to make the reports of the Conference available to the General Assembly. In resolution 31/14, adopted at its next session in November 1976, the General Assembly reaffirmed its intention to consider during its current session the results of the concluding ministerial meeting, which was at that time scheduled to take place from the 15th to the 17th of December 1976. When the Paris Conference failed to complete its work by that date, a plenary meeting of the Group of 77 in New York on 16 December 1976 reviewed this development, approved the extension of the Conference, and prompted the General Assembly to agree, six days later, that its Thirty-First Regular Session should be resumed at an appropriate time to review the results of the Paris Conference. The Paris Conference ended in June 1977 and its results were, in fact, communicated to the resumed Thirty-First Regular Session of the General Assembly, which was held from the 13th to the 19th of September 1977. Reflecting the lack of agreement in Paris, the resumed session failed to reach agreement even on a final resolution.

The Group of 77 promptly drew the obvious conclusion from this experience and, in a declaration issued at the end of the first meeting of Ministers for Foreign Affairs of the Group of 77, held in New York in September 1977, resolved that "all negotiations of a global nature relating to the establishment of the New International Economic Order [should] take place within the framework of the United Nations

73

system, which is the only appropriate and fully representative forum for these negotiations".[139] As is described below, this set into motion a process that led in December 1977 to the creation of the "Committee Established under General Assembly Resolution 32/174" (the "Committee of the Whole") and, ultimately, to the global negotiations. North-South negotiations were thus firmly brought back into the United Nations system.[140]

## E. The Group of 77 in the United Nations in New York

The 1974 Sixth Special Session of the United Nations General Assembly was the great divide for the activities of the Group of 77 in the United Nations in New York. Before that year, the Group's profile was very low. Only with the Sixth Specil Session did the Group of 77 begin to become a well-organized negotiating agent.

### 1. Before the Sixth Special Session

When the Group met before 1974, it was primarily for discussing matters connected with UNCTAD. The only major exception was the preparation for the Second United Nations Development Decade during 1969-1970. The failure of UNCTAD II to make substantial headway in North-South negotiations precipitated intense efforts to formulate the International Development Strategy for the Second United Nations Development Decade. UNCTAD made an important input on trade and aid matters, but most of the work was undertaken by the developing countries in New York. The negotiations were not, however, conducted along group lines because the Group of 77 (while holding a number of co-ordination meetings[141] and having a position of its own) was still only loosely co-ordinated in New York. Consequently, the developing countries did not prepare substantive input papers. A large part of the negotiations was carried out informally and the Group of 77 did not present a draft of its own. After the International Development Strategy was adopted on 24 October 1970, the Group's activities subsided again and it seldom even introduced resolutions.[142]

As remarked earlier, the main reason for this low profile has to be sought in the prevailing view of the 1960s that economic questions were "low politics". In the United Nations in New York, where the principal issues had been the maintenance of international peace and security, political de-colonization, and disarmament, this view was particularly prevalent. Moreover, the establishment of UNCTAD had provided the development issue with a special forum—elsewhere. Furthermore, as discussed above, the group system's primary *raison d'être* in New York had remained the allocation of posts, which was handled separately by each regional group. There were two other factors. For one thing, the development question was only *one* of the issues before the United Nations, which made a coalescing of the regional groups especially difficult; and, for another, the Group of 77 did not enjoy the same kind of logistical assistance in New York as it did in Geneva.[143]

## 2. *The Ascendancy of the Group of 77 and the Establishment of the Group of 27*

With the politicization of the development question in the early 1970s, the meetings of the Group of 77 became more frequent. And, characteristically, it was an economic event—or, more precisely, a political-economy one—that galvanized the regions and led to the emergence of an active Group of 77 in the United Nations in New York: the 1974 Sixth Special Session of the General Assembly. The session itself did not owe its origin to the activities of the Group of 77, but rather to those of the Non-Aligned Countries. But once the Non-Aligned Countries had ensured that the session would take place, it became the responsibility of the Group of 77 to prepare for it substantively. The time available for this task was very short,[144] but the Fourth Conference of Heads of State or Government of Non-Aligned Countries—which had taken place a few months earlier (September 1973) and had produced the first comprehensive economic programme of the movement (a programme carried by a solid consensus)— provided the Group of 77 with an excellent basis for its work.[145]

To prepare the Sixth Special Session, the plenary of the Group of 77 decided, on 8 February 1974, to establish an open-ended Group of 30 (10 countries from each region). Since most countries attended the meetings of the Group of 30, this body quickly became too cumbersome for drafting work. Hence an open-ended Group of 6 was created on 9 March 1974.[146] It was this Group that drafted the "Declaration on the Establishment of the New International Economic Order" and the "Programme of Action on the Establishment of the New International Economic Order" which in turn became the basis for the final resolutions of the Special Session, adopted by consensus—even though with strong reservations on the part of the developed market economies—on 1 May 1974. The negotiations concerning the final documents, however, were undertaken by a Negotiating Group that had been formed on the 26th of April, i.e., less than one week before the end of the Sixth Special Session.[147]

In the same year, the Group of 77 in New York had to pass another major test in steering the Charter of Economic Rights and Duties of States to adoption.[148] During UNCTAD's 1972 session, the

President of Mexico, Luis Echeverría, had proposed the elaboration of such a charter. An UNCTAD Working Group on the Charter of Economic Rights and Duties of States was established[149] which held four sessions between February 1973 and June 1974.[150] Since the Working Group could not reach agreement on a complete text, its final report identified various alternatives for those paragraphs of the draft Charter on which agreement had not been secured. Although informal consultations began soon after the fourth session of the UNCTAD Working Group, the main efforts were undertaken just befored the Charter was taken up by the Second Committee of the Twenty-Ninth Regular Session of the General Assembly in November 1974. The Group of 77 in New York (under strong leadership of Mexico, which was then the co-ordinator of the Group) conducted a series of informal negotiations, especially with the Western European and Other States Group, to prepare an agreed text for the Committee. When these negotiations failed to lead to the desired result, the Group of 77 drew up a draft Charter on the basis of all agreed paragraphs of the final report of the Working Group and, in cases where consensus had been missing, on the basis of the alternatives proposed by the Group of 77. (The Group tried to incorporate, wherever possible, the points of view expressed by the developed countries.) This text as a whole, which had been amended further in the course of negotiations, was introduced in the Second Committee on 27 November 1974 and was adopted on 6 December 1977 by a roll-call vote of 115 to 6, with 10 abstentions. The General Assembly adopted the Charter as a whole on 12 December 1974 by a vote of 120 to 6, with 10 abstentions.[151]

The Charter of Economic Rights and Duties had hardly been adopted when the preparations for the Seventh Special Session of the General Assembly began. On the basis of its experience during the Sixth Special Session, the Group of 77 decided, prior to the first session of the Preparatory Committee for the Special Session[152] in March 1975, to set up a working group consisting of 27 countries (9 from each region) to undertake the necessary preparatory work (see Table 34). This "Group of 27", as it became known, drafted first a position paper of the developing countries and then a detailed informal working paper for negotiating purposes. The latter paper was the basis for the actual negotiations during the Special Session. In its re-negotiated form it became the resolution on "Development and International Economic Co-operation" which was adopted by consensus (and without major reservations) by the Seventh Special Session on 16 September 1975.

After the Seventh Special Session, the activities of the Group of 77 in New York expanded rapidly.[153] Most of them required preparations, and the need for a smaller body to undertake the preparatory work became quickly apparent. Since the smooth negotiations during the Seventh Special Session had demonstrated the usefulness and effectivenessd of the Group of 27, it was only natural that it should be entrusted with this work. The Group of 27 thus became a continuing working group of the Group of 77.

From the outset, participation in the Group of 27 was open to any member of the Group of 77. The original membership thus lost its importance, although the formal membership of the Group never changed. Rather, both which and how many countries attended a particular meeting came to depend on the subject matter under consideration. Since the Group of 27, which normally meets at the senior officials level, acts only on the instructions of the pleanary,[154] each country is informed about the work of the Group and hence can participate in it. The materials (mostly draft resolutions) prepared by the Group are submitted to the plenary for approval or, if no consensus can be achieved, for further discussion and ultimate arbitration. (The plenary ordinarily meets at the ambassadorial level.) Naturally, the opinions of the Group of 27 can be overruled by the plenary and materials referred back to it for revisions or further work. This is particularly likely to happen if some interested parties have not participated in the initial work. As a rule, however, the proposals of the Group of 27 are accepted by the Group as a whole. All meetings of the Group of 27, like those of the plenary, are chaired by the co-ordinator country, even if that country is not a member of the original 27. Naturally, all decisions are taken by consensus.

Thus, in the absence of a bureau[155] and of strong regional groups, the Group of 27 has come in the space of a few years to assume the functions of a permanent steering and drafting committee of the Group of 77. In carrying out the mandate given to it by the plenary, it prepares and clears a growing number of proposals and, in fact, does most of the. substantive work of the Group of 77, including the preparatory work for ministerial-level meetings in New York. It even creates, as the need arises, smaller *ad hoc* working groups.[156] During sessions of the General Assembly, and particularly at their beginning, the Group of 27 meets almost daily; the plenary may, during certain periods, meet almost as often. In 1979, for instance, there were 241 meetings of the Group of 77 and of its sub-groups (i.e., mostly of the Group of 27)—compared to an average of 33 meetings during the years 1970-1972 (see Table 12). Between sessions, the two Groups meet whenever the need arises, normally in order to prepare for an impending even in the United Nations. Their activities still centre on the economic questions discussed in the Second Committee of the

General Assembly.[157] But the Group of 77 is also beginning to direct its attention to administrative and budgetary questions (Fifth Committee), because of the financial implications of many resolutions; social, humanitarian and cultural matters (Third Committee), especially because of the social dimension of development; some legal issues (Sixth Committee), particularly those touching the legal dimension of the NIEO; and some political issues (Special Political Committee), most notably those relating to information politics[158] and the establishment of the New International Information Order.[159]

The Group of 27 shares its management function with the co-ordinator of the Group of 77 in New York who, until the institutionalization of the Group of 27, was solely responsible for this function. The role of the co-ordinator in New York is the same as that of the co-ordinator in Geneva, except that there are no regional co-ordinators with whom responsibilities could be shared. On the other hand, the Group of 77 is nowhere better represented than in New York: in 1980, 116 of its 122 members had diplomatic missions accredited to the United Nations (see Table 23). However, thirty per cent of the missions had a professional staff of five or fewer persons, and only 4 per cent of them had a staff of 21 or more persons. This compares with, respectively, 11 and 22 per cent for the Western European and Other States Group and 10 and 20 per cent for the Eastern European States Group. (See Table 24.) In addition, the stability of tenure of the chief negotiators, the permanent representatives, was not very high: in 1980, almost half of them had been accredited to the United Nations for one year or less. Only one quarter of the permanent representatives of the Western European and Other States Group on the other hand, had been accredited for so short a time. (See Table 26.)

The institution of the co-ordinator dates back to the 1960s; but it is only since 1974, with the increasing volume of work before the Group of 77, that it has acquired real weight. The office of the co-ordinator rotates annually among the three regions (see Table 35). The co-ordinator country is chosen after informal consultations on the basis of a country's indentification with the work of the Group of 77 and its capacity to fulfill the function for an entire year. It has now become customary for the formal designation of the co-ordinator to be done by the meeting of the ministers for foreign affairs of the Group of 77, which has been held since 1977 at the end of September (i.e., at the commencement of the General Assembly). The co-ordinator assumes office on the day after the meeting.

As a result of the increased activities and better organization of the Group in New York, an increasing number of resolutions have been sponsored by the Group of 77. A conscious effort is made, however, to limit the topics to be dealt with by the Group to the main issues relating to North-South relations and the establishment of the NIEO, i.e., to those topics that are of concern to the Group as a whole and on which unity can be achieved and maintained.[160] Other issues are left to individual countries or groups of countries. The Group of 27 is therefore convened at the beginning of a session of the Genral Assembly to identify the areas that should constitute, at that session, the Group's major foci of attention.

But this effort to confine the work of the Group of 77 to key issues, and hence to avoid an overcrowding of its agenda, does not always succeed to the extent desired. For one thing, since the various aspects of the development task are increasingly seen in relation to one another and many are, in fact, highly interrelated, it is difficult to determine what should be of concern to the Group as a whole and what not. For another, each country or group of countries tends to seek the support of the entire Group for its projects because such support provides it with greater bargaining power in the subsequent search for consensus, or at least assures it a majority in the competent organs of the United Nations. (A country's ability to convince the rest of the Group of the importance of its project is, therefore, an important variable in the determination of the agenda.[161]) As a result, the question of what precisely constitutes a matter for the agenda of the Group of 77 and what does not has no definite answer and the set of matters on the Group's agenda tends to expand continuously. The effect of this expansion is that the Group of 77, qua group, is now participating in all major economic discussions as well as in a growing number of related questions in the United Nations in New York. This represents a profound change in the conduct of business in the General Assembly and it may, as observed earlier, lead to a transformation of all regional groups into co-ordinating bodies for substantive questions, along the lines already described in the context of UNCTAD.

3. *Towards Global Negotiations*

Since the second half of 1977, co-ordination at the ministerial level has been added to the existing organizational structure of the Group of 77 and this has made the Group's activities more political in nature. The beginning was made by the Ministers for Foreign Affairs of the Group of 77 in Fall 1977, with the first in a series of meetings now convened regularly at the commencement of the General Assembly.

The first of these meetings was the result of several developments. Most important among them were the efforts of the co-ordinator country, Pakistan, to obtain a greater institutionalization of the movement and the outcome of the Paris Conference on International Economic Co-operation. Pakistan, not a member of the non-aligned movement and hence interested in a strong Group of 77, was the co-ordinator country of the Group bf 77 in New York during the period 1976-1977 and it vigorously pursued the policy of strengthening the institutional infrastructure of the Group of 77. During the September 1976 Mexico City Conference on Economic Co-operation among Developing Countries, Pakistan, in line with this objective, had pressed strongly for a summit of Third World leaders. When this initiative failed, Pakistan pursued the same objective at lower levels. Thus, when the Paris Conference failed to hold its concluding ministerial meeting (as originally scheduled) in the middle of December 1976, a meeting of the plenary of the Group of 77 in New York was called. It discussed this development and issued a communiqué embodying its conclusions. Among them, it expressed the desire "to consider convening a meeting of the developing countries at an appropriately high political level to assess the situation and to co-ordinate their strategy".[162] The occasion for this meeting, at the level of ministers for foreign affairs, came in September of the next year, when both the Paris Conference and the resumed Thirty-First Regular Session of the General Assembly failed to reach any agreement.[163] As in the case of the Extraordinary Conferences of Ministers of Foreign Affairs of Non-Aligned Countries, the presence of many high-level representatives from the national capitals at the beginning of the General Assembly facilitates greatly the convening of meetings of the Ministers for Foreign Affairs of the Group of 77.

Since 1977, the meetings of the ministers for foreign affairs of the Group of 77 have become a regular institution of the Group. They are held at the end of the co-ordinator's term and at the beginning of the General Assembly. Accordingly, the ministers begin by designating a new co-ordinator country. Then they review the preceding year's developments which are of primary concern to developing countries and provide political impetus and over-all direction to the Group's future work, especially with respect to the principal economic issues on the agenda of the General Assembly.

Thus, at their first meeting on 29 September 1977, the foreign ministers took note of the unsatisfactory negotiations at the Paris Conference and the resumed Thirty-First Regular Session of the General Assembly and resolved (as quoted in full above) that all negotiations of a global nature on the NIEO should take place in the fully representative fora of the United Nations.[164] Accordingly, the ministers suggested that the "General Assembly should provide at its current and future sessions guidelines for the conduct of negotiations in the appropriate bodies within the United Nations system, with a view to reaching concrete and positive results within specific time-frames" and asked that "a special session of the General Assembly" be convened in 1980 (the later Eleventh Special Session of the General Assembly, held between the 25th of August and the 15th of September 1980 in New York) in order

> to assess the progress made in the various forums of the United Nations system in the establishment of the New International Economic Order and, in the light of that assessment, to take appropriate action for further promotion of the development of developing countries  and interntional economic co-operation, including the adoption of the new international development strategy.[165]

These considerations and recommendations led, on 19 December 1977, to the adoption of General Assembly resolution 32/174, creating the "Committee Established under General Assembly Resolution 32/174". The committee became known as the "Committee of the Whole" because its deliberations were open to all states. Between February 1978 and August 1980, it met between the regular sessions of the General Assembly to assist the Assembly by:

> (a) Overseeing and monitoring the implementation of decisions and arrangements reached in the negotiations on the establishment of the new international economic order in the appropriate bodies of the United Nations system;
>
> (b) Providing impetus for resolving difficulties in negotiations and for encouraging the continuing work in these bodies;
>
> (c) Serving, where appropriate, as a forum for facilitating and expediting agreement on the resolution of outstanding issues; [and]
>
> (d) Exploring and exchanging views on global economic problems and priorities.[166]

In establishing the Committee of the Whole, the General Assembly explicitly reaffirmed that "all negotiations of a global nature relating to the establishment of the new international economic order should take place within the framework of the United Nations system" and further underlined its concern that, in these negotiations, "the international community should, with a sense of urgency, make new and resolute efforts to secure positive and concrete results within agreed and specific time-frames".[167] At the same time, and as a final reference point for the work of the Committee of the Whole, the General Assembly decided to convene a special session on development in August 1980

> to assess the progress made in the various forums of the United Nations system in the establishment of the new international economic order and, on the basis of that assessment, to take appropriate action for the

promotion of the development of developing countries and international economic co-operation, including the adoption of a new international development strategy for the 1980s.[168]

With the establishment of the Committee of the Whole, the Group of 77 had re-instated economic negotiations as one of the central tasks of the General Assembly. At the same time, the Group had succeeded in creating a forum for considering the whole range of North-South issues in an integrated and politically aware fashion; and it had made a first step towards creating a permanent forum at the highest level for negotiating with, and putting pressure on, the developed countries in the matter of the establishment of the NIEO.

To ensure that high-level negotiations continue after the Eleventh Special Session and after the adoption of the International Development Strategy for the Third United Nations Development Decade, the 1979 Sixth Conference of Heads of State or Government of Non-Aligned Countries in Havana (acting upon the recommendation of its Co-ordinating Bureau at the Ministerial Level)[169] endorsed a proposal to launch, at the Eleventh Special Session,

> a round of global and sustained negotiations on international economic co-operation for development, such negotiations being action-oriented, allowing for an integrated approach to the main issues involved, proceeding simultaneously on different planes and being open to universal participation;

and it suggested that such negotiations

- take place within the United Nations system with the full participation of all States and within a specified timeframe;
- include major issues in the field of raw materials, energy, trade, development, money and finance; [and]
- make a significant contribution to the implementation of the International Development Strategy for the Third United Nations Development Decade.[170]

The Group of 77 seized upon this proposal without delay and introduced it at the next session of the Committee of the Whole in virtually identical language.[171] Two weeks later, the Ministers for Foreign Affairs lent their strong support to the proposal.[172] The General Assembly subsequently adopted a resolution on the subject, instructing the Committee of the Whole to perform the functions of a preparatory committee and to submit to the Eleventh Special Session its final report containing recommendations on the establishment of the global negotiations.[173] In March 1980, ministers of the Group of 77 met in New York to adopt a draft agenda for the global round of negotiations and to specify their recommendations on procedures and a suitable time-frame. Although neither the Committee of the Whole nor the Preparatory Committee for the New International Development Strategy succeeded in finishing its work, the Eleventh Special Session of the General Assembly—which was preceded by another preparatory ministerial-level meeting of the Group of 77 in New York in August 1980[174]—was held as planned. Negotiations at that Session proved, however, very protracted and, after two extensions of the Session, only one of its twin purposes could be achieved: consensus on the text of the New International Development Strategy for the Third United Nations Development Decade. But agreement was reached neither on the modalities nor the agenda of the global negotiations. Hence the documents relevant to this set of issues were transmitted to the General Assembly at its Thirty-Fifth Regular Session for further deliberations.[175]

These events form an unprecedented series of almost continuous high-level North-South negotiations on the establishment of the New International Economic Order. They reflect the urgency with which the developing countries regard the need to put the NIEO programme into effect, they ensure that the programme receives the proper attention at the proper level, and they are designed to generate the necessary pressure to expedite its implementation. As a result, the development task has become a major concern of the General Assembly, whose "central role . . . as the supreme organ of the United Nations system in the economic and social fields"[176] was explicitly emphasized by the Ministers for Foreign Affairs of the Group of 77 at their 1979 meeting. It is an organ which is attractive to the developing countries not only because they are in the majority in it but also because its almost universal membership makes it a "fully representative forum" that allows "equal participation of all countries in the decision-making process".[177]

The meetings of the ministers for foreign affairs are a natural development; in a sense, they resemble the preparatory ministerial-level meetings of the Group of 77 in the context of UNCTAD and UNIDO, even though they are nowhere near as elaborate.[178] They also indicate that the development task has become thoroughly politicized: the ministers for foreign affairs—not those for economics, finance or commerce—provide the guidance, and this is done in reference to the United Nations General Assembly, an organ at the highest political level.

These rapidly unfolding events may lead to a fundamental change in the multi-central character of the Group of 77. Ministerial-level meetings, it will be recalled, are the supreme organs of the Group of 77. Such meetings are convened only once every three years to prepare for UNCTAD sessions and will be convened once every two years to prepare for UNIDO General Conferences. The General Assembly, on the other hand, is convened every year, as are now the meetings of the foreign ministers of the Group of 77. These latter are further supplemented by meetings of other ministers in connexion with the global negotiations.[179] It is logical, therefore, that most lower-level bodies that meet between ministerial conferences report to the Group of 77 in New York—and this is precisely what has occurred in the case of the Committee of 21[180] and the Preparatory Meeting of Governmental Experts of Developing Countries on Economic Co-operation among Developing Countries (which had met to prepare a meeting of an UNCTAD committee). Besides, the global conferences convened by the General Assembly are often prepared for by the Group of 77 in New York, a responsibility that gives it additional influence on a wide range of topics.[181]

Moreover, if the Group of 77 should, after all, establish a secretariat (an action that may in any event be unavoidable in the long run),[182] it is now very likely to be located in New York and not in Geneva—a step that would further strengthen the position of the New York Group and would, in itself, be an indication of the changing importance of the various centres of the Group of 77. In any event, the annual rotation of the office of the co-ordinator provides the Group of 77 in New York with greater stability of leadership and the stronger presence of the Group in terms of the number and strength of its diplomatic missions in New York gives it better representation and better staff resources than in Geneva. Finally, if the global negotiations are conducted, as the developing countries desire, in a centralized fashion in the framework of a United Nations conference in New York,[183] the Group of 77 in New York would automatically assume a supreme co-ordinating function. (Such co-ordination is, in any case, necessary because it has to be ensured that the Group of 77 moves in the same direction in all fora.) And if the agenda of these negotiations range as broadly as the developing countries propose, the Group in New York would effectively take a leading role in articulating and aggregating the Third World's collective economic interest on all major North-South issues and in representing it in the negotiations with the developed countries.

As UNCTAD loses its supremacy in development questions[184] and is increasingly becoming a technical negotiating forum whose products are legal or quasi-legal instruments,[185] the locus for the formulation of policies in this area and possibly even the focus of all the activities of the Group of 77 may be shifting to New York, from where the Group may well receive its over-all direction in the future.[186] Even if this shift should be accompanied by some tensions between

New York and the other centres of the Group of 77 (and especially Geneva), it may well be a desirable evolution because progress may only be achievable if the development task remains in the centre of political awareness and is continuously pressed at the highest political level and if its pursuit is closely co-ordinated with the non-aligned movement whose political support continues to be a necessity.

Thus, the North-South negotiations have experienced an extraordinary evolution. They began in 1964 in the specialized forum of UNCTAD and, from there, spread to the equally specialized fora of the IMF and the World Bank as well as UNIDO. In 1974, they were elevated to the political level of the General Assembly, albeit only for the limited periods of the Regular Sessions and the Sixth and Seventh Special Sessions of the General Assembly. With the Paris Conference of 1975-1977 followed an experiment in negotiating on the main development issues in a forum of restricted membership outside the United Nations system. When this failed to have the desired results, the negotiations moved back into the United Nations system and, with the Committee of the Whole of the General Assembly, became institutionalized in periodic meetings held in inter-session periods. Finally, although the Eleventh Special Session did not achieve all its objectives, it is only a question of time before sustained global negotiations are launched which will deal in a continuous and centralized fashion with the whole range of development issues at the level of the General Assembly. Work in specialized fora will, of course, continue and care has to be taken that progress being made there is not jeopardized. Together, these events represent a new stage in the long and arduous process of accelerating development through the establishment of the New International Economic Order.

The driving force behind this evolution is the well-organized Group of 77. With the political backing of the Non-Aligned Countries it has changed the status of the development task in a singularly rapid succession of conferences: from being considered only in specialized fora, it has come to be the dominant political-economy item on the agenda of the supreme organ of the United Nations system, the General Assembly.

The only higher level of mobilization, politicization, and pressure that the development task can reach is that of the level of heads of state or government. If the present arrangements do not lead relatively soon to substantial progress—the past few years have shown that events have to move at an accelerated pace—such a final upgrading may well become inevitable. And if the events of the immediate past are a guide, a world congress of heads of state or government on development would have to be open to all heads of state or government; would have to deal with the entire range of development issues in an integrated manner; would have to agree on firm time-frames; would have to be action-oriented towards structural changes; would have to involve binding commitments; and would have to be convened regularly.

Given the dimensions and urgency of the development task, there may be no viable alternative to global negotiations at the highest level. And if negotiations do move to this level, there will be no peaceful alternative to substantial progress in them.

## FOOTNOTES OF PART II

[1] First Ministerial Meeting of the Group of 77, "Charter of Algiers", in Sauvant, document II.D.7.

[2] Apart from UNCTAD, the Group of 77 in Geneva covers also the International Labour Organisation (ILO), the World Health Organization, the World Intellectual Property Organization, and the International Telecommunications Union, all of which are also headquartered in Geneva. The activities of the Group in respect to these organizations have so far been limited mainly to major conferences. In the ILO, whose tripartite structure creates special circumstances, the Group of 77 has made a number of statements that are reflected in the summary records. The "Group of Developing Countries in GATT" is not chaired by the co-ordinator of the Group of 77 in Geneva because, according to the GATT definition, Greece (until 31 December 1980), Israel, Spain, and Turkey are also considered developing countries; in addition, only the contracting parties to GATT participate in its work and few developing countries are contracting parties.

[3] Although this work may well span several years and be of great importance to the conference. This is particularly the case for the Law of the Sea Conference.

[4] In *ibid.*, document I.C.1.a.

[5] First Ministerial Meeting of the Group of 77, Materials before the Conference, "Report of the Chairperson of the Co-ordinating Committee, Ambassador A.F. Azeredo da Silveira", in *ibid.*, document II.D.3.a.

[6] *Ibid.*

[7] See, The Group of 31, "Preparations for the Second Session of the Conference: Meeting of the Group of 77", in *ibid*, document II.A.1. The annex of that document describes briefly the preparations of the regional groups at that stage. The "Co-ordinating Committee" was called "Preparatory Committee" at later Ministerial Meetings and, beginning with the 1976 Third Ministerial Meeting, it was established by the Group of 77 as a whole.

[8] Participation in the Group of 31 was, however, open to all members of the Group of 77.

[9] In *ibid.*, document II.D.7.

[10] See, The Group of 31, "Meeting of the Group of 77 at the Ministerial Level", in *ibid.*, document III.A.1.

[11] Membership in the Co-ordinating Committee that prepared the First Ministerial Meeting was limited to 22 countries.

[12] Thus, for instance, no distinction was made, for Africa and Asia, between core and other members of the Preparatory Committee for the Fourth Ministerial Meeting of the Group of 77.

[13] Since two of the three chairpersons of the previous Preparatory Committees had come from Latin America and one from Africa, it was decided, on the basis of the principle of rotation, that the chairperson of this Preparatory Committee be from Asia.

[14] The rules of procedure provide that in all matters not covered by them, those of the United Nations General Assembly should apply *mutatis mutandis*.

¹⁵Since the functions of the existing working groups are different from those of the sub-committees of the Preparatory Committee and since, furthermore, their membership is larger, the working groups are not used as sub-committees.

¹⁶The regional members of a given Working Group frequently caucus separately to prepare themselves for the sessions of their Working Group. The regional groups may also meet for the purpose of considering questions before a Working Group in order to give the necessary guidance to their representatives in it.

¹⁷This may even happen within the framework of existing Working Groups. Thus, when the negotiations about the Common Fund became intense, the Working Group of 33 on the Integrated Programme for Commodities and the Common Fund first established a sub-group of 12 and then a sub-group of 6 (each based on equal geographical distribution) for consultations on specific matters with other regional groups.

¹⁸The "Interim Progress Report and Annexes" of the Preparatory Committee for the 1979 Fourth Ministerial Meeting, for instance, was over 140 pages long.

¹⁹The Inter-American Economic Council, an organ of the Organization of American States, first established CECLA on a temporary basis, but, in December 1964, CECLA became a permanent organ.

²⁰See, Latin American Co-ordination Meeting for the IVth Ministerial Meeting of the Group of 77 in Arusha with a View to UNCTAD V, "Report and Guidelines of the Position of the SELA Member States for the Fourth Ministerial Meeting of the Group of 77 with a View to UNCTAD V", in *ibid.*, document V.B.3.a.

²¹In fact, a part of the preparations for the Ministerial Meeting is the compilation of a comparative document that re-arranges the regional texts under common headings in order to facilitate the harmonization task to be undertaken by the Ministerial Meeting. At the 1976 Third Ministerial Meeting, the report of the Preparatory Committee was included in this exercise as well.

²²In *ibid.*, document II.D.7.

²³It has become customary for the inaugural meeting of the Ministerial Meeting to be called to order by the president of the preceding Ministerial Meeting.

²⁴The Rapporteur-General has supreme responsibility for the final form of the draft documentation of the meeting, especially the consolidation of the programme of action and its reconciliation with the declaration. A special drafting group, working under the direction of the Rapporteur-General, may be created for this purpose.

²⁵In deference to Tanzania's 1967 "Arusha Declaration" on self-reliance, the final document of the 1979 Arusha Ministerial Meeting was called "Arusha Programme... ."

²⁶Co-ordinating Committee, "Chairperson of the Co-ordinating Committee - A.F. Azeredo da Silveira: Tentative Guidelines for the Work of the Algiers Meeting", in *ibid.*, document II.B.2.

²⁷See, e.g., item 8 on the provisional agenda for UNCTAD V (reproduced in Table 15 as the work area of the Sub-Group of the Preparatory Committee for the Fourth Ministerial Meeting).

²⁸Since facilities were provided for only three simultaneous meetings at the 1979 Arusha Ministerial Meeting and since the Preparatory Committee had established only three sub-committees on substantive questions, only three Working Groups were set up at the Arusha Ministerial Meeting. A limitation to three Working Groups also facilitated the allocation of posts among the regions.

²⁹For instance, the part of the "Arusha Programme for Collective Self-Reliance and Framework for Negotiations" that deals with the items on UNCTAD's agenda is 75 pages long.

³⁰The close relationship between the Preparatory Committee and the Senior Officials Meeting was reflected in the fact that both had the same chairperson.

³¹See, Senior Officials Meeting, "Report on the Work of the Drafting Group of the Plenary", in *ibid.*, document IV.C.3. The close relationship between the Drafting Group and the Co-ordination Committee is reflected in the fact that they were both chaired by the same person and that the 15 countries elected to be members of the Drafting Group were also among the 30 countries elected for the Co-ordination Committee.

³²See, Senior Officials Meeting, "Report and Annexes", annexes I-IV, in *ibid.*, document IV.C.4.

³³If the Ministerial Meeting proper establishes committees or working groups, their officers also become members of the Bureau, according to the rules of procedure

adopted in 1976 in Manila; at the Third Ministerial Meeting, the chairpersons of the four main committees, in addition to the chairperson of the Co-ordination Committee, were, in fact, members of the Bureau.

[34]It should be noted that the bodies are closely co-ordinated. In Arusha, for instance, the same person was Rapporteur-General of the Ministerial Meeting proper and the Senior Officials Meeting and several of the Vice-Presidents of the two bodies were the same.

[35]"Charter of Algiers", in *ibid.*, document II.D.7.

[36]Since the items on UNCTAD's agenda concern, almost by definition, unresolved issues, negotiations are in any case a continuing process. In a sense, therefore, the decisions of a specific meeting of the Group of 77 are only inputs into this process.

[37]For the Fall 1980 session of the Trade and Development Board, a special preparatory committee of 24 was created and the following items were identified for special preparation by Working Groups or *ad hoc* task forces: 1. protectionism and structural adjustment; 2. money and finance, including debt questions; 3. trade relations among countries having different economic and social systems; 4. evaluation and interdependence, shipping and least-developed countries; 5. economic co-operation among developing countries; and 6. rationalization of the permanent machinery of UNCTAD. Each task force has a core membership, but it is open-ended.

[38]In other fora, however, the support of the secretariats of the various organizations - e.g., the United Nations in New York, UNIDO, UNESCO, FAO, UNEP, ILO, the regional commissions - is normally limited to the provision of administrative services.

[39]In particular, OAU, SELA, the ACP Group, and the League of Arab States. Relevant at times are also the secretariats of various development banks (e.g., the Inter-American Development Bank, the African Development Bank), a number of sub-regional banks (such as the Caribbean Development Bank), producers' associations and the secretariats of integration groupings (e.g., Andean Pact, CARICOM, ASEAN, ECOWAS).

[40]See the co-ordinator countries mentioned above, the expert groups that originated in the Dakar Conference of Developing Countries on Raw Materials and the Research and Information System of the Non-Aligned Countries.

[41]In the African Group (every three months) and the Latin American Group (every two months), the chair rotates (in principle) in alphabetical order. In the Asian Group, no rotation takes place since its members have accepted that the Ambassador of the Philippines, Hortencio J. Brillantes, who has been accredited to the United Nations in Geneva since August 1966, continues in the chair.

[42]Before 1968, the rotation took place on a monthly basis, i.e., it followed the pattern of rotation in the regional groups at the United Nations in New York.

[43]This provision reflects the principle of decision-making by consensus. So far, only one incident has occurred in which a country whose turn it was to represent the Group of 77 did not obtain the necessary consensus of its regional group: Chile in the fourth quarter of 1977. Since Mexico and Venezuela, in particular, objected, the preceding co-ordinator country, Yugoslavia, continued in its function until the end of the year.

[44]Many of the diplomatic missions of the African countries in Geneva are very small and have limited facilities. Hence most of these countries pass up the opportunity to assume the office of the co-ordinator.

[45]If other United Nations organs meet at a given centre of the Group of 77, the problem arises of which co-ordinator should chair meetings. This is particularly relevant for meetings of ECOSOC in Geneva, because the issues before ECOSOC overlap a good deal with those before UNCTAD. Normally, prior informal consultations resolve this question on an *ad hoc* basis. But in the event of disagreements, the co-ordinator of the centre at which the meeting takes place seems to have the right to the chair. (A compromise formula is that the co-ordinator from Geneva opens a meeting and then turns it over to the co-ordinator from New York.) This territorial principle is consistent with the general practice that a representative of the country hosting a meeting is elected to chair the meeting. Considerations of this kind can also determine the choice of location for a particular gathering. Thus if a country has a particular interest in a given subject matter, it may volunteer to host a forthcoming meeting. If, on the other hand, a neutral chairperson is being sought, the meeting may be moved to a country without any special interest in its agenda.

[46]A number of countries have also had political motives to press for the establishment of a permanent machinery. Thus, countries like Pakistan and the Philippines - which until recently were excluded from the non-aligned movement - desired an institutional strengthening of the Group of 77 because they would have liked to see this Group (in which they were prominent members) become the most important Third World organization. This also explains why the Asian Group of the Group of 77 took a lead in this matter on several occasions. Important is, however, also that the Asian Group has no regional institution of its own. As already discussed, the African and Latin American Groups, on the other hand, have their own regional institutions.

[47]Co-ordinating Committee, "Reference Document of the Co-ordinating Committee on Items 11 and 14 of the Provisional Agenda of the Ministerial Meeting of the Group of 77", in *ibid.*, document II.B.1. It should be noted, however, that the part of the "Reference Document" which dealt with the future activities of the Group of 77 had not been approved by the Committee as a whole but rather was an individual contribution by its chairperson.

[48]See, First Ministerial Meeting of the Group of 77 "Charter of Algiers", in *ibid.*. document II.D.7.

[49]Actually, a "Working Party of Nine on Future Activities of the Group of 77 at Geneva" was established after UNCTAD II on 13 May 1968 to examine, *inter alia*, the need for a machinery to promote joint action by the Group of 77, including the question of the continuation of the Co-ordinating Committee. The Working Party proposed to create a standing committee and, in fact, even thought of setting up two consultative committees (which would report to the Group of 77 and the Group of 31): one to prepare the joint positions of the Group of 77 on all substantive matters and the other to examine whether and when a Ministerial Meeting should be held and to consider questions relating to other international conferences held in Geneva. The Latin American Group, on the other hand, wanted to establish only one consultative committee, which would report to the Group of 77 and would constitute a steering committee. These questions were never resolved and no final report of the Working Party was adopted.

[50]Second Ministerial Meeting of the Group of 77, "The Declaration and Prinici- of the Action Programme of Lima", in *ibid.*, document III.E.6.

[51]The Asian Group of the Group of 77 had already made arrangements for itself to assure some continuity between its Ministerial Meetings: the Bureau of these gatherings holds office until the next meeting. At the Fourth Ministerial Meeting of the Asian Group of the Group of 77, the Bureau was further requested to hold consultations with the members of the Group and to co-ordinate their activities whenever the need arose (see "Colombo Declaration and Programme of Action", in *ibid.*, document V.B.2.a.

[52]Third Ministerial Meeting of the Asian Group of the Group of 77, "Jakarta Declaration Programme of Action, Joint Communiqué, and Report of the Third Ministerial Meeting of the Asian Group of the Group of 77", in *ibid.*, document IV.B.2.a.

[53]The representative of the host country would thus have acquired a position similar to that of the President-in-Office of the non-aligned movement.

[54]Third Ministerial Meeting of the Group of 77, "Resolutions and Decisions", in *ibid.*, document IV.D.7.

[55]See, Working Group of the Group of 77 - Manila Decision No. 2, "Report on the Proposed Establishment of a Secretariat of the Group of 77", in *ibid*, document IV.F.2.a.

[56]A fact that was later reflected in the hesitation of the Group of 77 in Geneva to bring into operation the committee that was entrusted to deal with this question.

[57]Fourth Ministerial Meeting of the Group of 77, "Resolutions and Decisions", in *ibid.*, document V.D.5. The Committee was established in April 1979 by decision of the Group of 77 in Geneva.

[58]Committee of 21 of the Group of 77 at Geneva, "Report on a Special Technical Support Machinery for the Group of 77", in *ibid.*, document V.F.1.a.

[59]A working group eventually produced a paper that was submitted to the Group of 27 which ciruculated it to governments for comments.

[60]See, Ministers for Foreign Affairs, Fourth Meeting, "Decisions", in *ibid.*, document X.B.4.b.

[61]The section of the "Report" of the Committee of 21 arguing against the establishment of a secretariat identified this option as one of the ways in which the present arrangements could be reinforced.

[62]Some developed market economies are not averse to the establishment of a Group of 77 secretariat because they expect that such a technical body would tend to de-politicize negotiations and because it would encourage the UNCTAD Secretariat to adopt a more neutral stance.

[63]For this reason, the Group of 77 encouraged its members from the very beginning to establish permanent missions in Geneva or, at least, to instruct one of their embassies close to Geneva (e.g., Berne, Bonn, Brussels, Paris) to perform the functions of such a mission.

[64]The turn-over rate is the same for countries members of Groups B and D, but they can rely, as was pointed out earlier, on strong national and regional support systems as well as being able to draw on a greater pool of expertise and experience.

[65]One observer (Kenneth D. Hall, "Technical and Organizational Support for Developing Countries on International Economic Negotiations: A Report", in *The Group of 77: Strengthening Its Negotiating Capacity* (Nyon: Third World Forum, 1979), p.18 remarked:

> The organisational structure of the Group of 77 has resulted in a pattern where effectiveness in negotiations is largely a question of personal attributes related to such variables as familiarity with the issues, technical competence, experience in international negotiations and tenure at the particular post. The personal input assumes even greater importance in a context where the heads of missions are the only ones from the resident missions directly involved in various international aspects of the negotiations. Transfer of that officer might result in the total absence of information and expertise with the new incumbent having to undertake the not inconsiderable task of self-briefing. Decision making under such circumstances could be further adversely affected by new appointees who are unable to participate effectively in on-going discussions or in the uninformed, irrelevant or contradictory interventions which could threaten delicately agreed positions thereby delaying consideration of new issues while colleagues spend valuable time explaining the situation.

[66]If financing were to be shared on the basis of the key that determines the contributions to the budget of the United Nations, the Latin American countries would have to make relatively high payments - a perspective which probably explains the reluctance of some of them to consent to establishing a secretariat.

[67]The summer sessions of ECOSOC, held in Geneva, offer such opportunities on a regular basis.

[68]See below, the section on the Group of 77 in the United Nations in New York.

[69]Frequently, the missions of those countries that are co-ordinators elsewhere serve as conduits for information. For instance, if the co-ordinator in Vienna is Tunisian, contact with the other centres of the Group of 77 is maintained through the Tunisian missions in Geneva, New York, etc.

[70]It is thought that the venue of the January meeting would rotate while the July meeting would be held in Geneva, during the summer session of ECOSOC.

[71]General Assembly resolution 2089 (XX) of 20 December 1965.

[72]The developing countries present at the symposium did, of course, table a set of recommendations which, together with those prepared by the industrialized countries, were adopted as the final action of the conference (see UNIDO, "Report of the International Symposium on Industrial Development", ID/B/21 of 2 February 1968, pp. 43-52).

The Athens meeting was prepared by four regional symposia that had been sponsored by the regional commissions of the United Nations: Manila, 6-20 December 1965; Cairo, 27 January - 10 February 1966, Kuwait, 1-10 March 1966, and Santiago, 14-25 March 1966. Developed countries members of the regional commissions also participated in these symposia. Developed countries are members of the Economic Commission for Africa (South Africa - but the country does not participate in the work of the Commission), the Economic and Social Commission for Asia and the Pacific (Australia, France, Japan, the Netherlands, New Zealand, the USSR, the United Kingdom, and the United States), and the Economic Commission for Latin

America (Canada, France, the Netherlands, Spain, the United Kingdom, and the United States). In addition, China and Mongolia are members of the Economic and Social Commission for Asia and the Pacific.

[73]In May 1970, the Industrial Development Board of UNIDO (the equivalent of UNCTAD's Trade and Development Board) recommended that the General Assembly convene a Special International Conference of UNIDO. The General Assembly concurred in November of the same year and scheduled the conference for the 1st to the 8th of June 1971 in Vienna.

[74]The Conference was, however, discussed in regular meetings of various geographical groups, and in other intergovernmental and regional meetings that took place at the beginning of 1971: the Common Afro-Malagasy-Mauritius Organization (Fort Lamy, 27-30 January 1971); the ECAFE Committee for Industry and Natural Resources (Bangkok, 29 January - 6 February 1971); the tenth session of the Economic Commission for Africa (Tunis, 1-13 February 1971); the Special Committe on Latin American Co-ordination (Brasilia, 2-11 February 1971); and the Industrial Development Centre for Arab States (Cairo, 13-15 February 1971). A number of these meetings made pronouncements pertaining to UNIDO.

[75]Following the Geneva example, it was decided that the office of the co-ordinator should rotate among the regions every three months. The Permanent Representative of Zaire, H. Waku, who had played a key role in the establishment of the Group of 77 in Vienna, was designated as the first co-ordinator. His mandate was later extended until the Special Conference.

Before the first meeting of the first session of the Industrial Development Board on 10 April 1967, the 25 developing countries that were members of the Board had formed a group known as the Group of 25, which also elected a chairperson. (See, *Summary Records of the First Meeting of the First Session of the Industrial Development Board*, ID/B/SR.1 of 18 July 1967, p. 8.)

[76]The membership of the Standing Committee was enlarged in March 1971 to 15 to include 3 members each from Geneva and Bonn - an action that reflected the under-representation of the developing countries in Vienna. In fact, only 16 developing countries had, in December 1970, permanent missions accredited to UNIDO that were located in Vienna; an additional eight countries had embassies in the city but these were not accredited to UNIDO. This presented a serious problem of representation for the Group of 77 in Vienna - for instance, only four African countries had missions or embassies located in Vienna. The problem was solved by involving, as far as possible, developing-country representatives from missions or embassies in Geneva and Bonn. Since the Group of 77 in Vienna was in its formative stage, it was, in any event, important to benefit from the experience gained by the Group in Geneva. Since the latter Group accepted the over-all responsibility of the Group of 77 in Vienna for the formulation and adoption of a common position for the Conference, co-operation between the two centres proceeded harmoniously.

[77]For instance, the Group of Nordic countries acted separately and the Latin American Group was not unanimous in its statement on the final document.

[78]That the organization of the Group of 77 in Vienna underwent a slow evolution is indicated by the fact that it was still unclear to several delegations during the First Ministerial Meeting whether or not that meeting was supposed to be at the ministerial level (see, First Ministerial Meeting of the Group of 77 in Preparation for UNIDO II, "Report", in Sauvant, document VII.B.3 ). One of the reasons for this uncertainty may have been that the developing countries participated in the over-all preparations for UNIDO II which were carried out by the Industrial Development Board and its Permanent Committee (which functioned as the Preparatory Committee of the Conference) and in the framework of which the Group of 77 met as well to elaborate a common approach. The First Ministerial Meeting was, in fact, held in conjunction with the work of the Preparatory Committee, i.e., it was less formal than a normal Ministerial Meeting; there were, for example, no formal opening speeches.

[79]This document was passed on to Groups B and D and an unofficial exchange of views on it took place before UNIDO II was convened.

[80]The United States voted against its adoption by UNIDO II. The Group of 77 (together with Romania) had prepared for UNIDO II draft resolutions on strengthening the role of UNIDO (ID/CONF.3/L.5), on international co-operation in the transfer of technology (ID/CONF.3/L.7/Rev.1), on permanent sovereignty over natural resources and industrialization of the developing countries (ID/CONF.3/L.8

/Rev.1), and on the establishment of an insurance system for guaranteeing contracts concluded by the developing countries with enterprises from the developed countries (ID/CONF.3/L.9). (See "Report of the Chairperson of the Group of 77 on the Mandate Given Him by the Second Ministerial Meeting of the Group of 77 Held at Algiers", in Sauvant, document VII.E.1.) UNIDO II decided to pass on these draft resolutions to the Industrial Development Board for consideration.

[81] Until then, a working group of the Group of 77 had handled the input of the Group into the discussions of the constitution.

[82] See, UNIDO, *Constitution of the United Nations Industrial Development Organization* (Vienna: UNIDO, 1979).

[83] Morocco, Senegal and Zaire entered reservations concerning paragraph 29 of the declaration.

[84] On the insistence of Cuba, Chapter VIII of the Plan of Action, dealing with special measures for the least developed, land-locked, island, and most seriously affected developing countries, as well as for the Palestinian and Namibian peoples and for Zaire, was strengthened considerably.

[85] As already indicated, the 1967 Athens Symposium was prepared exclusively through regional symposia organized in the framework of the United Nations regional commissions and hence with the participation of developed countries. For UNIDO I, no separate regional meetings were organized. The regional declarations for UNIDO II were all prepared by gatherings in which (exceptionally) only developing countries participated. In the case of UNIDO III, finally, the documents of the African and Arab regions were drafted by meetings of the developing countries alone, those of the Asian and Latin American regions by meetings in the framework of regional commissions in which developed countries also participated.

[86] The declarations adopted by the Arab states nonetheless constitute a recognized contribution to the deliberations of the relevant ministerial meetings of the Group of 77 in Vienna as well as to those of UNIDO's General Conferences.

[87] Possibly because of the effectiveness of the Task Force, the question of a secretariat has not yet arisen in Vienna. Eventually, the Task Force may be expanded to include the regional co-ordinators.

[88] General Assembly resolution 2152 (XXI) of 17 November 1966, which spelled out UNIDO's terms of reference, also stipulated that the election of the members of the Board and of the Bureau should give due regard to the principle of equitable geographical representation. The "Rules of Procedure of the Industrial Development Board" (E.78.II.B.2) determined the cycle of rotation of the Board's offices.

[89] The Group of 77 in Vienna has no formal rules of procedure; as at other centres, it acts on the basis of precedent. When choosing a co-ordinator of the Group of 77 as a whole, the regional groups designate, after informal consultations, a country that has played a leading role in the Group, has the necessary resources for the task, and shows interest in it. Each regional group also has its own co-ordinator who is generally chosen on an alphabetical basis and who is elected to serve for one year.

[90] Such groups are especially established during sessions of the Industrial Development Board to deal with specific questions, e.g., the system of consultations.

[91] As elsewhere, the co-ordinator can designate someone else to chair meetings or to speak on behalf of the Group of 77. This is, for example, necessary when the co-ordinator country is not a member of the Industrial Development Board or the Board of Governors of the International Atomic Energy Agency.

[92] The co-ordinator is also responsible for representing the interests of the developing countries in the International Atomic Energy Agency, which is also headquartered in Vienna. It was only during the General Conference of the Agency in 1978 that the Group of 77 in Vienna constituted itself formally in the Agency (informal consultations among the developing countries had, however, taken place before, even though only on an *ad hoc* basis). Since then, the Group of 77 (and especially those developing countries that are members of the Agency's Board of Governors) has begun to meet relatively regularly and now also receives some services from the Agency when need arises. An *ad hoc* working group (whose core members include those of the Task Force) has been formed to follow the deliberations of the Agency's Committee on Assurance of Supply. As for UNIDO, the Task Force is responsible for the substantive preparatory work of the Group of 77 in relation to the Agency, while the regional groups concentrate on the allocation of posts. (Until the beginning of 1981, the Latin American Group even had a separate co-ordinator for the Agency.)

[93]Belgium, Canada, France, the Federal Republic of Germany, Italy, Japan, the Netherlands, Sweden, the United Kingdom, and the United States. Switzerland (not a member of the IMF) later joined the group as an associate member.

[94]Second Ministerial Meeting of the Group of 77, "The Declaration and Principles of the Action Programme of Lima", in Sauvant, document III.E.6.

[95]*Ibid.* The proposal to establish such a group had originated in the Latin American Group of the Group of 77. It is contained in resolution 27/XII of "The Consensus of Lima", adopted by the Twelfth Meeting of the Special Committee on Latin American Co-ordination (CECLA) during its session in Lima from the 20th to the 27th of October 1971 in preparation for the Second Ministerial Meeting of the Group of 77; the resolution also contains the draft of the terms of reference of the intergovernmental group. In *ibid.*, document III.C.3.a.

[96]Originally, the group was meant to have 15 members. But since it was difficult to agree which 5 from each region should be selected, membership was enlarged to 8 from each region, thus accommodating all those that were interested.

[97]As in other bodies of the Group of 77, the representation of the African countries - because of lack of specialized personnel - continues to be weak.

[98]Under the Articles of Agreement of the International Monetary Fund, all powers of the Fund are vested in the Board of Governors, which consists of one Governor and one Alternate appointed by each member. Under the authority of the Board of Governors, the Board of Executive Directors is responsible for the conduct of the general operations of the Fund, including the appointment of a Managing Director. (The arrangements in the World Bank are the same.) In 1979, 6 Executive Directors were appointed by individual countries (United States, United Kingdom, Federal Republic of Germany, France, Japan, and, since 1979, Saudi Arabia) and 15 others were elected by the Governors representing the remaining members. (The appointed Directors cast all the votes of the countries that appointed them, and the elected Directors cast as a unit all the votes of the countries that elected them.) Only 8 of these 15 are elected exclusively by developing countries (the remaining developing countries are represented by Directors from developed countries). The "Group of 9" had started to meet informally as early as 1966 and continued to do so quite frequently after the Group of 24 was established. (The nine developing-country Executive Directors on the Board of the World Bank meet separately as well, but not as frequently or in as organized a fashion as those of the IMF.) Since the Executive Directors of the developing countries have access to the resources of the Fund, they make an important input into the meetings of the Group of 24 and provide a part of the background material required for its deliberations.

[99]The Managing Director of the IMF had attended meetings of the Group of 24 from the very beginning; the President of the World Bank began attending in September 1974, when the Development Committee was created.

[100]Originally, it was thought that the meetings of the Group (as those of the Ministerial Meetings of the Group of 77) would rotate among the regions and that the chair would be occupied by the representative of the country in which the Group met; hence the first chairperson of the Group (who presided over its first five meetings) was from Venezuela. Since it soon became established practice that the Group of 24 would be convened immediately before the meetings of the Committee of 20 and, later, before those of the Interim Committee (whose venue the developing countries could not determine), this procedure was not workable for practical reasons. In an arrangement that was designed to combine equity with continuity, it was therefore decided by the fifth meeting of the Group of 24 in September 1973 that the chair should rotate on an annual basis among the regions. One of the vice-chairpersons (who are determined by the regions using their own procedures) should become chairperson and be replaced by a vice-chairperson from the same geographical region as the former chairperson. The vice-chairperson from Africa became the chairperson at the next meeting of the Group of 24 in January 1974. Since then, the chair has changed at the first meeting each year.

[101]By October 1980, the Group of 24 had met 21 times at the ministerial level and 31 times at the level of deputies.

[102]With one exception, each session of the Group of 24 at the ministerial meeting ended with the adoption of a communiqué based on the report of the Deputies. At first, the Deputies issued communiqués as well (although at irregular intervals), but this practice was discontinued.

[103]Intergovernmental Group of 24 on International Monetary Affairs, First Ministerial Meeting, "Communiqué", in *ibid.*, document IX.C.1.a.

[104]See footnote[98].

[105]See, IMF, *International Monetary Reform: Documents of the Committee of Twenty* (Washington: IMF, 1974).

[106]Committee of 20, Sixth Meeting, "Communiqué", in Sauvant, document IX.E.6.a.

[107]Apart from this link through the Development Committee and the participation of the Executive Directors of the World Bank in the work of the Group of Deputies, the Group of 24 has no formal relationship with the World Bank.

[108]See, Third Ministerial Meeting of the Group of 77, Materials before the Conference, "Report of the Chairperson of the Group of 24", in *ibid.*, document IX.A.1.a.

[109]*Ibid.* The Group of 24 also invited the Group of 77 to consider the possibility that the number of its official members be increased on an *ad hoc* basis (and without prejudice to the geographical distribution originally agreed upon) when co-ordination needs required the presence of other members. Since the Ministerial Meeting did not pronounce itself on this matter, no such changes were made in the membership.

[110]Third Ministerial Meeting of the Group of 77, "Organizational and Other Matters", in *ibid.*, document IV.D.5.

[111]Third Ministerial Meeting of the Group of 77, Materials before the Conference, "Report of the Chairperson of the Group of 24", in *ibid.*, document IX.A.1.a.

[112]Thus, for instance, several technical studies, financed by UNCTAD and UNDP, were prepared for the Group of 24 before its September 1979 Belgrade meeting.

[113]As in other centres of the Group of 77, the proponents of greater institutionalization point to the organizational infrastructure of the developed market economies. Thus, the Group of 10 has had, from the beginning, an *ad hoc* secretariat of three persons and its members meet monthly in Basle to review developments of interest to them.

[114]The Group of 24 does, however, keep the individual member-states of the Group of 77 informed about its activities.

[115]The factors that explain why the Group of 24 has been the only permanent expert group of the Group of 77 play a role in this context as well.

[116]Since the developing countries have greater influence in UNCTAD than in the Fund or the Bank, that body has always been their preferred forum for the consideration of international monetary and financial questions. Links between the Group of 24 and UNCTAD did, however, exist; mention has already been made of the technical support provided by UNCTAD. In addition, the Secretary-General of UNCTAD was always invited to attend the meetings of the Group of 24.

[117]It is not inconceivable, especially in the light of the broader mandate of the Group of 24, that the Group may experience another change: the emergence of regional groups. In the Fund and the Bank, regional caucuses are common. The Latin American and the Commonwealth countries, in particular, have a long history in this respect. The African countries have begun to hold regional meetings only recently, while the Asian group, possibly because it lacks a regional framework like the OAU or SELA or because some of its most important members participate in the Commonwealth Group, is the least organized. The Latin American Group is the most cohesive Group in the Fund and the Bank. It regularly prepares a common position before the Annual Meetings of the Boards of the Bank and the Fund and expresses it through a single spokesperson. Since matters are also discussed at these meetings that are on the agenda of the Group of 24, the Latin American Group has a co-ordinated stand in the Group of 24 as well - which, of course, places it at a certain advantage vis-à-vis countries from other regions.

[118]Fourth Ministerial Meeting of the Group of 77, "Arusha Programme for Collective Self-Reliance and Framework for Negotiations", in *ibid.*, document V.D.4.

[119]*Ibid.* The Government of Yugoslavia (the host country) was requested to make the necessary arrangements in consultation with the chairperson of the Group of 24.

[120]There had been considerable discussion at the meeting of the Group of 24 whether or not the Group of 77 could change the text of the "Outline", with the consensus being that this should be avoided. The Group of 77 respected this wish - which, after all, was supported by the ministers of finance or economy or the governors of central banks of 24 of its members who had lobbied to ensure that the text remain intact - and no changes were made. However, at the Ministerial Meeting of the

94

Group of 77, the issue of observer status for the PLO in the Fund and the Bank was raised, an issue that introduced strong political overtones into the subsequent Annual Meetings of the Boards of the Bank and the Fund.

[121] In *ibid.*, document IX.C.19.b.

[122] *Ibid.*

[123] The expert group had its origin in a resolution of UNCTAD V.

[124] The date of this event had been scheduled to take advantage of the presence of the chairperson of the Deputies on account of the meeting of the *Ad Hoc* Group of Experts. The Group of 24 had also been invited to the first meeting of the co-ordinators on 14 February 1980, but it did not send a representative.

[125] See, Interim Committee, Fourteenth Meeting, "Communiqué", in Sauvant, document IX.F.14.a. Only once before, in the context of the discussions about the use of the Fund's gold, had the Group of 24 succeeded in a similar manner.

[126] The developing countries were Algeria, Brazil, India, Iran, Saudi Arabia, Venezuela, and Zaire (i.e., the most important OPEC countries and one non-oil-exporting country from each region); the developed countries were the European Community, Japan, and the United States. They had been chosen on the basis of informal consultations between France and Saudi Arabia.

[127] See, First and Second Preparatory Meetings, "Final Declaration and Related Documents", in *ibid.*, document XII.B.1.

[128] The co-chairpersons were Manuel Pérez-Guerrero (Venezuela) and Allan J. MacEachen (Canada).

[129] The Paris Conference did, however, give impetus to some North-South negotiations, e.g., on the Common Fund and debt relief.

[130] France continued to play a separate role within the OECD on the question of energy. Some developing countries looked favourably upon this role and hence supported the separate French initiative. In addition, developed market economies had frequently argued that the nearly universal framework of the General Assembly does not allow fruitful and efficient negotiations. Besides, a more restrictive framework tended to exclude countries with extreme critical positions — something favoured by the developed countries.

[131] Since a number of important members of the Group of 77 could not be included, efforts were made at a later stage to add three additional countries: Colombia, Ivory Coast and Malaysia. (In the rare instance of a vote taken in the Asian Group in New York on the question of who should represent that Group at the Conference, Malaysia had been the runner-up.) The developed market economies, however, objected because all their major sub-groups were already adequately represented: since the European Community participated as an entity, its nine member countries were associated with the proceedings; the Scandinavian group was represented by Sweden; and the Southern European group by Spain.

[132] Asia was over-represented because the most important oil-exporting countries of that region had to participate in the Conference.

[133] Given the innovative nature of the Group of 19, it adopted its own rules of procedure; in *ibid.*, document XII.A.1.a.aa. They also specify the terms of reference of the Supporting Team described in the next paragraph.

[134] See, Third Ministerial Meeting of the Asian Group of the Group of 77, "Jakarta Declaration, Programme of Action, Joint Communiqué, and Report of the Third Ministerial Meeting of the Asian Group of the Group of 77", in *ibid.*, document IV.B.2.a.

[135] Third Ministerial Meeting of the Group of 77, Statements, "Message from President Houari Boumedienne, President of the Revolutionary Council and Head of Government of the People's Democratic Republic of Algeria and President-in-Office of the Conference of Heads of State or Government of Non-Aligned-Countries", in *ibid.*, document IV.D.4.d.

[136] Third Ministerial Meeting of the Group of 77, Materials before the Conference, "Statement by the Hon. Manuel Collantes - Secretary-General of the Third Ministerial Meeting - on Matters Related to the Conference on International Economic Co-operation", in *ibid.*, document IV.D.3.g.

[137] Third Ministerial Meeting of the Group of 77, "Resolutions and Decisions", in *ibid.*, document IV.D.7.

[138] The origin of the Conference, and especially the initial intention to restrict it to developed market economies and OPEC countries only, certainly further compromised the idea of restricted meetings.

[139] Ministers for Foreign Affairs of the Group of 77, First Meeting, "Declaration", in *ibid.*, document X.B.1.a.

[140] Actually, this was already foreshadowed in the "Report" of the Concluding Ministerial Meeting of the Paris Conference. There, the members of the Conference agreed "to recommend that intensive consideration of outstanding problems should be continued within the United Nations system and other existing, appropriate bodies" (in *ibid.*, document XII.C.5.a).

[141] The meetings were not even always identified as those of the Group of 77, but at times as those of the "Afro-Asian-Latin American Groups".

[142] An exception is draft resolution A/C.2/L.1199/Rev. of 30 November 1971 on the international monetary situation which was sponsored by the members of the Group of 77, even though it was not identified as a resolution of the Group of 77. In the subsequent debate in the Second Committee, however, it was made clear that the Group of 77 as a whole stood behind the draft; and a spokesperson of the developing countries pointed out that "the action of the sponsors of draft resolution A/C.2/L.1199/Rev.1 was without precedent in that the text proposed had been worked out by the Group of 77". See *Official Records of the General Assembly, Twenty-Sixth Session, Second Committee*, p. 505. At that time, virtually all resolutions in the Second Committee of the General Assembly (the committee dealing with economic questions) were introduced "on behalf of the sponsors", which did not necessarily mean all developing countries. Similarly, the countries introducing resolutions normally spoke "in the name of the sponsors" and not "in the name of the Group of 77".

[143] The Group of 77 does, however, make use of the meeting facilities of the United Nations in New York, just as it does of those in Geneva.

[144] The formal request to convene the Sixth Special Session was made to the Secretary-General of the United Nations on 30 January 1974 by President Houari Boumediènne, in his capacity as President-in-Office of the non-aligned movement. Since this request was immediately supported by more than the minimum number of countries necessary, the Special Session was called for the 9th of April 1974.

[145] See, the "Economic Declaration" and the "Action Programme for Economic Co-operation", in Jankowitsch and Sauvant. On the relationship between the economic programme of the Non-Aligned Countries and that of the Sixth Special Session, see Jankowitsch and Sauvant, "The Initiating Role of the Non-Aligned Countries", in Sauvant, *Changing Priorities on the International Agenda*.

[146] The members were Algeria and Senegal for Africa, India and the Philippines for Asia and Argentina and Mexico for Latin America. The co-ordinator of the Group of 77 (Iran) chaired the meetings of the Group and Yugloslavia was later added as rapporteur. The average attendance at the Group's meetings was 25-30 countries.

[147] The members of this Group were: Algeria, Egypt, Ivory Coast, Madagascar, Nigeria, and Zaire for Africa; Afghanistan, India, Iraq, Pakistan, the Philippines, and Yugoslavia for Asia; and Argentina, Cuba, Guyana, Mexico, and Venezuela for Latin America. The Group was again chaired by the co-ordinator of the Group of 77.

[148] In the intervening period, however, the Group of 77 constituted itself in the Third Conference of the United Nations on the Law of the Sea, whose first substantive session opened only six weeks after the Sixth Special Session in Caracas. The Group of 77 has played a major role in that Conference.

[149] UNCTAD resolution 45 (III), contained in Sauvant. For a discussion of the Charter, see Robert F. Meagher, *An International Redistribution of Wealth and Power: A Study of the Charter of Economic Rights and Duties of States* (New York: Pergamon, 1979). The drafting process is described in detail in Romeo Flores Caballero, "La elaboración de la Carta: Antecedentes de un nuevo orden internacional", in Kurt Waldheim *et al., Justicia económica internacional* (Mexico City: Fondo de Cultura Económico, 1976), pp. 25-80.

[150] The reports of the Working Group on its four sessions are contained in documents TD/B/AC.12/1 of 6 March 1973, TD/B/AC.12/2 and Add.1 of 8 and 9 August 1973, TD/B/AC.12/3 of 8 March 1974, and TD/B/AC.12/4 and Corr.1 of 1 and 21 August 1974.

[151] Belgium, Denmark, the Federal Republic of Germany, Luxembourg, the United Kingdom, and the United States voted against the Charter.

[152] The Preparatory Committee had been established by the Economic and Social Council on 2 August 1974.

153After the Special Session, the Group of 77 had immediately to prepare itself for the General Assembly, where it increasingly introduced resolutions under its name.

154Sometimes the Group of 27 does deal directly with draft resolutions when these (because of on-going negotiations) require immediate attention; in these cases, the Group of 27 merely reports to the Group of 77.

155Neither the Group of 77 nor the Group of 27 in New York has a bureau or, for that matter, formal rules of procedure. (Presumably, the rules of procedure of the Ministerial Meetings in preparation of UNCTAD Sessions apply.)

156Such sub-groups, whose chairpersons are normally designated by the chairperson of the Group of 77 or 27 and whose membership may often number less than 10 countries, are mostly established during sessions of the General Assembly, when the workload is highest. But they may also be created at other times; thus, for instance, such a group undertook a substantial part of the preparatory work for the Development Strategy for the Third United Nations Development Decade.

157The activities of the Group of 77 focus on committees of the whole or other plenary gatherings. In the Economic and Social Council (ECOSOC), whose membership is limited, resolutions are therefore normally introduced by individual developing countries, although usually with the support of the other developing countries that are participating. (The same practice generally applies to other nonplenary organs.) The developing countries members of ECOSOC do, however, meet to co-ordinate their policies and these meetings are open to all other members of the Group of 77.

158The focal point of discussion for this question is UNESCO, where the Non-Aligned Countries have assumed a leading role.

159As in other centres in which the Group of 77 is active, the Group of 77 in New York covers all agencies of the United Nations system headquartered there. Since all of them, in the final analysis, report to the General Assembly, the Group of 77 has not constituted itself formally in these agencies. On occasion, however, issues discussed in some of them - e.g., the United Nations Development Programme - command the attention of the Group of 77 and attract concrete inputs from it.

160For instance, during the Thirty-Fourth Regular Session of the General Assembly, the Group of 27 decided, at the beginning of October 1979, to attach special importance to the following topics from the agenda of the Second Committee: the establishment, by UNIDO, of a network for the exchange of technological information and an industrial and technological information bank; co-operation in the field of the environment concerning natural resources shared by two or more states; desertification; food problems; habitat; technical co-operation among developing countries; the acceleration of the transfer of real resources to developing countries; the United Nations Conference on New and Renewable Sources of Energy; UNCTAD; the United Nations Conference on Science and Technology for Development; the Report of the Committee of the Whole and the global negotiations; the New International Development Strategy; the preparations for the Eleventh Special Session; multilateral development assistance for the exploration of natural resources; economic co-operation among developing countries; the transport and communications decade in Africa; the restructuring of the economic and social sectors of the United Nations system; United Nations Development Programme; transnational corporations; and the question of special categories of countries. For a number of these items, drafting groups were established to prepare draft resolutions for the consideration of the Group of 27 and the final approval of the Group of 77.

161On the other hand, since such projects surface often in the midst of negotiations, time may not allow it to clear a project with the Group of 77.

162The Group of 77 in the United Nations, New York, "Communiqué", in Sauvant, document XII.A.2.a.aa. This was the first formal public statement by the plenary of the Group of 77 in New York.

163Thus, the First Meeting of Ministers for Foreign Affairs of the Group of 77, which only lasted one day, was a compromise gesture towards Pakistan. Pakistan remained the co-ordinator of the Group of 77 in New York until the end of September in order to be able to chair this meeting.

164During the next year's gathering, the same view was underlined again by the ministers and the reasons for it were made even more explicit: "In this regard, and reaffirming the need for equal participation of all countries in the decision-making process, they emphasize the central role of the General Assembly". See, Ministers for

Foreign Affairs of the Group of 77, Second Meeting, "Declaration", in *ibid.*, document X.B.2.a.

[165]Ministers for Foreign Affairs of the Group of 77, First Meeting, "Declaration", in *ibid.*, document X.B.1.a.

[166]General Assembly resolution 32/174 of 19 December 1977.

[167]*Ibid.*

[168]*Ibid.* A preparatory committee was established to draft the New International Development Strategy. For the report on the meetings of the Committee of the Whole (which also contains various statements made on behalf of the Group of 77 as well as materials presented by it) to the Thirty-Third Regular Session of the General Assembly, see *Official Records of the General Assembly, Thirty-Third Session, Supplement No. 34, A/33/34, Report of the Committee Established Under General Assembly Resolution 32/174*, vols. I and II; for its reports to the Thirty-Fourth Regular Session of the General Assembly and to the Eleventh Special Session of the General Assembly, see respectively, documents A/34/34 and .A/S-11/1. For the reports of the Preparatory Committee for the New International Development Strategy to the Thirty-Fourth Regular Session of the General Assembly, see *Official Records of the General Assembly, Thirty-Fourth Session, Supplement No. 44, A/34/44, Report of the Preparatory Committee for the New International Development Strategy*, vols. I-III; for its report to the Eleventh Special Session of the General Assembly, see document A/S-11/2.

[169]See Jankowitsch and Sauvant, vol. V.

[170]*Ibid.*, Economic Resolution No. 9.

[171]See, draft resolution A/AC.191/L.4 of 13 September 1979. The summit of the Non-Aligned Countries had ended on 9 September 1979, the next meeting of the Committee of the Whole began on 10 September 1979.

[172]Ministers for Foreign Affairs of the Group of 77, Third Meeting, "Declaration", in Sauvant, document X.B.3.a.

[173]General Assembly resolutions 34/138 and 34/139 of 14 December 1979.

[174]The need for this meeting, as part of the preparations for the Eleventh Special Session, had already been agreed upon during the September 1977 meeting of the Ministers for Foreign Affairs that called for the Eleventh Special Session.

[175]By decision S-11/24 of 15 September 1980 of the Eleventh Special Session of the General Assembly. Because of the failure to launch the global negotiations, the New International Development Strategy was not formally adopted by that Session.

[176]Ministers for Foreign Affairs of the Group of 77, Third Meeting, "Declaration", in Sauvant, document X.B.3.a.

[177]See the citation above.

[178]It would not be surprising, however, if they were to become as elaborate and if the institution of a preparatory committee were to emerge at some point in the future, although the Group of 27 already performs this function to a certain extent.

[179]As has already been indicated, the first such meeting took place in New York between the 11th and the 14th of March 1980; a second such meeting took place on the 21st and 22nd of August 1980, preceded by a meeting of senior officials. In *ibid.*, documents X.C.1.a and X.C.3.a.

[180]As was pointed out earlier, the decision of the February 1979 Fourth Ministerial Meeting of the Group of 77 to have the Committee of 21 report to the September 1979 Meeting of Ministers for Foreign Affairs of the Group of 77 in the United Nations in New York marks the first time that such a decision was not followed up within the UNCTAD framework.

[181]The developing countries' draft programme of action on science and technology for development for the United Nations Conference on Science and Technology for Development (held in Vienna from the 20th to the 31st of August 1979), for instance, was prepared by the Group of 77 in New York.

[182]See the discussion above, in the section on the Group of 77 in UNCTAD. In this context, it should be noted that the debates about the desirability of the establishment of a technical support machinery have moved from Geneva to New York.

[183]The framework of a United Nations conference permits the participation of countries that are not members of the United Nations (e.g., the Democratic People's Republic of Korea, the Republic of Korea, Switzerland) and, therefore, ensures universality.

[184]This is underscored by the failure of UNCTAD, at its fifth session in Manila in May-June 1979, to be recognized as *the* principal instrument of the General Assembly for international economic negotiations relating to the establishment of the NIEO and by its failure to formulate an agreed input into the discussions for the International Development Strategy for the Third United Nations Development Decade.

[185]See, for instance, the instruments pertaining to multimodula transport, restrictive business practices, the Common Fund, rubber, and the transfer of technology.

[186]Some of the practical work may be moved to New York as well, especially when it has a political dimension. Thus, the New York Group of 77 was entrusted with making the necessary arrangements (which include detailed technical work at the national level) for the preparations for the conference on economic co-operation among developing countries, planned for 1981. This development was not seen without some displeasure by the Geneva centre of the Group of 77 which considers this area as its domain.

**ANNEX I**
**TABLES**

## TABLE 1
### The members of the Group of 77, Fall 1980*

| | | |
|---|---|---|
| 1. Afghanistan | 41. Grenada | 81. Papua New Guinea |
| 2. Algeria | 42. Guatemala | 82. Paraguay |
| 3. Angola | 43. Guinea | 83. Peru |
| 4. Argentina | 44. Guinea-Bissau | 84. Philippines |
| 5. Bahamas | 45. Guyana | 85. Qatar |
| | | |
| 6. Bahrain | 46. Haiti | 86. Republic of Korea |
| 7. Bangladesh | 47. Honduras | 87. Romania |
| 8. Barbados | 48. India | 88. Rwanda |
| 9. Benin | 49. Indonesia | 89. Saint Lucia |
| 10. Bhutan | 50. Iran | 90. Samoa |
| | | |
| 11. Bolivia | 51. Iraq | 91. Sao Tomé and Principe |
| 12. Botswana | 52. Ivory Coast | 92. Saudi Arabia |
| 13. Brazil | 53. Jamaica | 93. Senegal |
| 14. Burma | 54. Jordan | 94. Seychelles |
| 15. Burundi | 55. Kenya | 95. Sierra Leone |
| | | |
| 16. Cape Verde | 56. Kuwait | 96. Singapore |
| 17. Central African Republic | 57. Lao People's Democratic Republic | 97. Solomon Islands |
| | | 98. Somalia |
| 18. Chad | 58. Lebanon | 99. Sri Lanka |
| 19. Chile | 59. Lesotho | 100. St. Vincent and the Grenadines |
| 20. Colombia | 60. Liberia | |
| | | 101. Sudan |
| 21. Comoros | 61. Libyan Arab Jamahiriya | 102. Suriname |
| 22. Congo | | 103. Swaziland |
| 23. Costa Rica | 62. Madagascar | 104. Syrian Arab Republic |
| 24. Cuba | 63. Malawi | 105. Thailand |
| 25. Cyprus | 64. Malaysia | |
| | 65. Maldives | 106. Togo |
| 26. Democratic Kampuchea | | 107. Tonga |
| 27. Democratic People's Republic of Korea | 66. Mali | 108. Trinidad and Tobago |
| | 67. Malta | 109. Tunisia |
| 28. Democratic Yemen | 68. Mauritania | 110. Uganda |
| 29. Djibouti | 69. Mauritius | |
| 30. Dominica | 70. Mexico | 111. United Arab Emirates |
| | | 112. United Republic of Cameroon |
| 31. Dominican Republic | 71. Morocco | 113. United Republic of Tanzania |
| 32. Ecuador | 72. Mozambique | 114. Upper Volta |
| 33. Egypt | 73. Nepal | 115. Uruguay |
| 34. El Salvador | 74. Nicaragua | |
| 35. Equatorial Guinea | 75. Niger | 116. Venezuela |
| | | 117. Viet Nam ** |
| 36. Ethiopia | 76. Nigeria | 118. Yemen |
| 37. Fiji | 77. Oman | 119. Yugoslavia |
| 38. Gabon | 78. Pakistan | 120. Zaire |
| 39. Gambia | 79. Palestine Liberation Organization | |
| 40. Ghana | 80. Panama | 121. Zambia |
| | | 122. Zimbabwe |

  * The 77 signatories of the 1964 Joint Declaration of the Seventy-Seven are underlined.
  ** Before: Republic of Viet-Nam.

| | |
|---|---|
| 1. Algeria | 26. Malawi |
| 2. Angola | 27. Mali |
| 3. Benin | 28. Mauritania |
| 4. Botswana | 29. Mauritius |
| 5. Burundi | 30. Morocco |
| | |
| 6. Cape Verde | 31. Mozambique |
| 7. Central African Republic | 32. Niger |
| 8. Chad | 33. Nigeria |
| 9. Comoros | 34. Rwanda |
| 10. Congo | 35. Sao Tome and Principe |
| | |
| 11. Djibouti | 36. Senegal |
| 12. Egypt | 37. Seychelles |
| 13. Equatorial Guinea | 38. Sierra Leone |
| 14. Ethiopia | 39. Somalia |
| 15. Gabon | 40. Sudan |
| | |
| 16. Gambia | 41. Swaziland |
| 17. Ghana | 42. Togo |
| 18. Guinea | 43. Tunisia |
| 19. Guinea-Bissau | 44. Uganda |
| 20. Ivory Coast | 45. United Republic of Cameroon |
| | |
| 21. Kenya | 46. United Republic of Tanzania |
| 22. Lesotho | 47. Upper Volta |
| 23. Liberia | 48. Zaire |
| 24. Libyan Arab Jamahiriya | 49. Zambia |
| 25. Madagascar | 50. Zimbabwe |

* The country in the chair rotates on a monthly basis, following alphabetical order. The African National Congress (ANC), the Pan-Africanist Congress (PAC), and the South-West Africa People's Organization (SWAPO) participate at the discretion of the Secretariat of the Organization of African Unity. South Africa belongs geographically to the African region, but it has not been accepted by the African Group as a member; South Africa does not participate in any regional group.

## TABLE 3
## Regional groups in the United Nations, New York, Fall 1980: The Asian Group*

| | | | |
|---|---|---|---|
| 1. | Afghanistan | 21. | Maldives |
| 2. | Bahrain | 22. | Mongolia |
| 3. | Bangladesh | 23. | Nepal |
| 4. | Bhutan | 24. | Oman |
| 5. | Burma | 25. | Pakistan |
| 6. | China | 26. | Papua New Guinea |
| 7. | Cyprus | 27. | Philippines |
| 8. | Democratic Kampuchea | 28. | Qatar |
| 9. | Democratic Yemen | 29. | Samoa |
| 10. | Fiji | 30. | Saudi Arabia |
| 11. | India | 31. | Singapore |
| 12. | Indonesia | 32. | Solomon Islands |
| 13. | Iran | 33. | Sri Lanka |
| 14. | Iraq | 34. | Syrian Arab Republic |
| 15. | Japan | 35. | Thailand |
| 16. | Jordan | 36. | Turkey |
| 17. | Kuwait | 37. | United Arab Emirates |
| 18. | Lao People's Democratic Republic | 38. | Viet Nam |
| 19. | Lebanon | 39. | Yemen |
| 20. | Malaysia | | |

\* The country in the chair rotates on a monthly basis, following alphabetical order. Japan belongs to this group merely for election purposes; it participates in the Western European and Other States Group for the purpose of the discussion of some policy issues. For election purposes, Turkey is nominated by the Western European and Other States Group. Israel belongs geographically to the Asian region, but it has not been accepted by the Asian Group as a member; Israel does not participate in any regional group.


## TABLE 4
## Regional groups in the United Naitons, New York, Fall 1980:
## The Eastern European Group*

| | | | |
|---|---|---|---|
| 1. | Albania | 7. | Poland |
| 2. | Bulgaria | 8. | Romania |
| 3. | Byelorussian SSR | 9. | Ukrainian SSR |
| 4. | Czechoslovakia | 10. | USSR |
| 5. | German Democratic Republic | 11. | Yugoslavia |
| 6. | Hungary | | |

\* The country in the chair rotates on a monthly basis, following alphabetical order. Until 1975, i.e., until the country had been accepted as a member of the Latin American Group (and hence received an opportunity to obtain offices on that Group's quota), Cuba had joined this Group for some election purposes (before some elections, the Eastern European Group announced that Cuba, for the purpose of a specific election, would be considered as a member of that Group and hence qualify for one of the posts allocated to the Eastern European Group). Albania does not participate in the work of this Group. Yugoslavia participates only for election purposes.

## TABLE 5
## Regional groups in the United Nations, New York, Fall 1980:
## The Latin American Group *

| | | | |
|---|---|---|---|
| 1. | Argentina | 16. | Guyana |
| 2. | Bahamas | 17. | Haiti |
| 3. | Barbados | 18. | Honduras |
| 4. | Bolivia | 19. | Jamaica |
| 5. | Brazil | 20. | Mexico |
| | | | |
| 6. | Chile | 21. | Nicaragua |
| 7. | Colombia | 22. | Panama |
| 8. | Costa Rica | 23. | Paraguay |
| 9. | Cuba | 24. | Peru |
| 10. | Dominica | 25. | Saint Lucia |
| | | | |
| 11. | Dominican Republic | 26. | Suriname |
| 12. | Ecuador | 27. | Trinidad and Tobago |
| 13. | El Salvador | 28. | Uruguay |
| 14. | Grenada | 29. | Venezuela |
| 15. | Guatemala | | |

* The country in the chair rotates on a monthly basis, following alphabetical order. Until 1975, Cuba was not accepted by this Group and it participated in the Eastern European Group.

## TABLE 6
## Regional groups in the United Nations, New York, Fall 1980:
## The Western European and Other States Group*

| | | | |
|---|---|---|---|
| 1. | Allemagne, République Fédérale d' | 16. | Norvège |
| 2. | Australie | 17. | Nouvelle-Zélande |
| 3. | Autriche | 18. | Pays-Bas |
| 4. | Belgique | 19. | Portugal |
| 5. | Canada | 20. | Royaume-Uni |
| | | | |
| 6. | Danemark | 21. | Suède |
| 7. | Espagne | 22. | Turquie |
| 8. | Finlande | | |
| 9. | France | | |
| 10. | Grèce | | |
| | | | |
| 11. | Irlande | | |
| 12. | Islande | | |
| 13. | Italie | | |
| 14. | Luxembourg | | |
| 15. | Malta | | |

Observers:

1. Monaco
2. Suisse
3. Saint-Siège

* The country in the chair rotates on a monthly basis, following counterclockwise alphabetical order in French. The participation of the United States is decided on a case-by-case basis. Japan participates for the purpose of the discussion of some policy issues.

TABLE 7
**The permanent members of the Security Council**

| | |
|---|---|
| 1. China | 4. Union of Soviet Socialist Republics |
| 2. France | 5. United States of America |
| 3. United Kingdom of Great Britain and Northern Ireland | |

**TABLE 8**
**The Arab countries in the United Nations, New York, Fall 1980\***

| | |
|---|---|
| 1. Algeria | 16. Somalia |
| 2. Bahrain | 17. Sudan |
| 3. Democratic Yemen | 18. Syrian Arab Republic |
| 4. Djibouti | 19. Tunisia |
| 5. Iraq | 20. United Arab Emirates |
| 6. Jordan | 21. Yemen |
| 7. Kuwait | |
| 8. Lebanon | |
| 9. Libyan Arab Jamahiriya | |
| 10. Mauritania | |
| 11. Morocco | |
| 12. Oman | |
| 13. Palestine Liberation Organisation | |
| 14. Qatar | |
| 15. Saudi Arabia | |

\* The country in the chair rotates on a monthly basis, following alphabetical order in Arabic. The League of Arab States may also participate in this Group.

## TABLE 9
### The regional groups in the United Nations, New York, and UNCTAD, Geneva: Frequency of meetings, 1965-1979*
#### (Number)

| Year | African States Group and sub-groups New York | Geneva | Asian States Group and sub-groups New York | Geneva | Afro-Asian States Group and sub-groups, New York | Latin American States Group and sub-groups New York | Geneva | Eastern European States Group and sub-groups** New York | Geneva | Western-European and Other States Group and sub-groups** New York | Geneva | Arab States, New York |
|---|---|---|---|---|---|---|---|---|---|---|---|---|
| 1965 | 48 | 17 | 6 | 6 | 47 | 61 | 49 | - | 35 | 25 | 114 | - |
| 1966 | 66 | 11 | 6 | 8 | 56 | 56 | 34 | 1 | 9 | 26 | 87 | - |
| 1967 | 37 | 15 | 17 | 9 | 67 | 94 | 59 | - | 28 | 29 | 82 | - |
| 1968 | 54 | 100 | 12 | 61 | 95 | 97 | 122 | 1 | 38 | 68 | 255 | - |
| 1969 | 48 | 105 | 15 | 75 | 87 | 47 | 144 | - | 50 | 37 | 217 | - |
| 1970 | 50 | 121 | 19 | 79 | 41 | 54 | 188 | - | 63 | 49 | 212 | - |
| 1971 | 61 | 62 | 24 | 55 | 33 | 57 | 108 | 1 | 75 | 44 | 181 | - |
| 1972 | 62 | 98 | 24 | 95 | 33 | 42 | 168 | 1 | 39 | 54 | 320 | - |
| 1973 | 84 | 115 | 32 | 93 | 30 | 42 | 147 | 1 | 92 | 53 | 233 | - |
| 1974 | 84 | 80 | 31 | 67 | 17 | 33 | 114 | - | 101 | 42 | 221 | 5 |
| 1975 | 50 | 49 | 23 | 44 | 12 | 37 | 99 | 4 | 82 | 40 | 279 | 17 |
| 1976 | 69 | 83 | 30 | 48 | - | 33 | 120 | 1 | 172 | 39 | 481 | 13 |
| 1977 | 93 | 145 | 38 | 104 | - | 45 | 167 | - | 187 | 41 | 520 | 14 |
| 1978 | 94 | 112 | 27 | 81 | - | 45 | 108 | - | 159 | 46 | 585 | 17 |
| 1979 | 90 | 199 | 15 | 111 | | 57 | 163 | 1 | 253 | 35 | 862 | 29 |

Source: Various documents of the Committee on Conferences and own research on the basis of the Journal of the United Nations.

*Excluding meetings in relation to specialized conferences, e.g., the United Nations Conference on the Laws of the Sea and Habitat: United Nations Conference on Human Settlements. For Geneva, the data refer to meetings held in relation to sessions of UNCTAD bodies, as well as meetings held outside sessions of UNCTAD bodies (except for 1965, for which data could only be obtained for the first category).

**In Geneva: Group D and Group B. These Groups and their sub-groups (e.g., the Vinci Group in New York) frequently meet in Permanent Missions; these meetings are not reflected in these statistics.

**TABLE 10**
## The group system in UNCTAD: Membership 1964-1979

1. UNCTAD I, 1964

### Group A

| | | |
|---|---|---|
| 1. Afghanistan | 22. Jordan | 42. Samoa |
| 2. Algeria | 23. Kenya | 43. Saudi Arabia |
| 3. Benin | 24. Kuwait | 44. Senegal |
| 4. Burma | 25. Lao People's Democratic | 45. Sierra Leone |
| 5. Burundi | Republic | 46. Somalia |
| 6. Central African Republic | 26. Lebanon | 47. South Africa |
| 7. Chad | 27. Liberia | 48. Sri Lanka |
| 8. China | 28. Libyan Arab Jamahiriya | 49. Sudan |
| 9. Congo | 29. Madagascar | 50. Syrian Arab Republic |
| 10. Democratic Kampuchea | 30. Malaysia | 51. Thailand |
| 11. Egypt | 31. Mali | 52. Togo |
| 12. Ethiopia | 32. Mauritania | 53. Tunisia |
| 13. Gabon | 33. Mongolia | 54. Uganda |
| 14. Ghana | 34. Morocco | 55. United Republic of Cameroon |
| 15. Guinea | 35. Nepal | 56. United Republic of Tanzania |
| 16. India | 36. Niger | 57. Upper Volta |
| 17. Indonesia | 37. Nigeria | 58. Viet Nam |
| 18. Iran | 38. Pakistan | 59. Yemen |
| 19. Iraq | 39. Philippines | 60. Yugoslavia |
| 20. Israel | 40. Republic of Korea | 61. Zaire |
| 21. Ivory Coast | 41. Rwanda | |

### Group B

| | | |
|---|---|---|
| 1. Australia | 11. Holy See | 22. Portugal |
| 2. Austria | 12. Iceland | 23. San Marino |
| 3. Belgium | 13. Ireland | 24. Spain |
| 4. Canada | 14. Italy | 25. Sweden |
| 5. Cyprus | 15. Japan | 26. Switzerland |
| 6. Denmark | 16. Liechtenstein | 27. Turkey |
| 7. Finland | 17. Luxembourg | 28. United Kingdom of Great |
| 8. France | 18. Monaco | Britain and Northern |
| 9. Germany, Federal | 19. Netherlands | Ireland |
| Republic of | 20. New Zealand | 29. United States of America |
| 10. Greece | 21 Norway | |

### Group C

| | | |
|---|---|---|
| 1. Argentina | 9. Ecuador | 16. Nicaragua |
| 2. Bolivia | 10. El Salvador | 17. Panama |
| 3. Brazil | 11. Guatemala | 18. Paraguay |
| 4. Chile | 12. Haiti | 19. Peru |
| 5. Colombia | 13. Honduras | 20. Trinidad and Tobago |
| 6. Costa Rica | 14. Jamaica | 21. Uruguay |
| 7. Cuba | 15. Mexico | 22. Venezuela |
| 8. Dominican Republic | | |

### Group D

| | | |
|---|---|---|
| 1. Albania | 4. Czechoslovakia | 7. Romania |
| 2. Bulgaria | 5. Hungary | 8. Ukrainian SSR |
| 3. Byelorussian SSR | 6. Poland | 9. Union of Soviet Socialist Reps. |

2. Additions at UNCTAD II, 1968

### Group A

| | | |
|---|---|---|
| 1. Botswana | 4. Lesotho | 7. Mauritius |
| 2. Democratic Yemen | 5. Malawi | 8. Singapore |
| 3. Gambia | 6. Maldives | 9. Zambia |

/...

(Table 10 cont'd)

### Group B

1. Malta

### Group C

1. Barbados      2. Guyana

3. Additions at UNCTAD III, 1972

### Group A

1. Bahrain      4. Equatorial Guinea      7. Swaziland
2. Bangladesh      5. Fiji      8. United Arab Emirates
3. Bhutan      6. Qatar

4. Additions at UNCTAD IV, 1976

### Group A

1. Angola
2. Cape Verde      5. Guinea-Bissau      8. Papua New Guinea
3. Comoros      6. Mozambique      9. Sao Tome and Principe
4. Democratic People's      7. Oman
   Republic of Korea

### Group C

1. Bahamas      2. Grenada      3. Suriname

### Group D

1. German Democratic Republic

5. Additions at UNCTAD V, 1979 *

### Group A

1. Djibouti      2. Tonga

---

\* At the first part of its nineteenth session, the Trade and Development Board decided that, pending action by the Conference in pursuance of paragraph 6 of General Assembly resolution 1995 (XIX), Saint Lucia should, for the purposes of elections, be treated as if it were one of the group of countries listed in part C of the annex to the said resolution. A similar decision was taken later regarding St. Vincent and the Grenadines.

## TABLE 11
## UNCTAD: Rotation of groups in the election of the president and rapporteur of the Trade and Development Board, 1980-1982*

| 1980 | | 1981 | | 1982 | |
|---|---|---|---|---|---|
| First regular session | Second regular session | First regular session | Second regular session | First regular session | Second regular session |

### President

| | | | | | |
|---|---|---|---|---|---|
| Group D | African states in Group A | Group B | Asian states plus Yugoslavia in Group A | Group C | Group B |

### Rapporteur

| | | | | | |
|---|---|---|---|---|---|
| African states in Group A | Group D | Group C | Asian states plus Yugoslavia in Group A | Group B | |

Source: UNCTAD, Rules of Procedure of the Trade and Development Board (Geneva: UNCTAD, 1973), as per amendment of January 1980 (TD/B/16/Rev.2/Amend.3).

\* This cycle is repeated, for the president, after every six sessions as from the first regular session in 1983 onwards and, for the rapporteur, after every five sessions as from the second regular session in 1982 onwards. The rules of procedure specify: "At no regular session shall representatives of States from any one of the five categories mentioned above be elected for the offices of both President and Rapporteur. At the regular sessions at which, in accordance with the established system of rotation, both the President and the Rapporteur would belong to the same Group, that Group shall postpone presentation of a candidate for the office of Rapporteur, and the Group next in line shall hold the post of Rapporteur."

## TABLE 12
## The Group of 77 and the Non-Aligned Countries in the United Nations, New York, and UNCTAD, Geneva: Frequency of meetings, 1965-1979*
### (Number)

| Year | Group of 77 and sub-groups ** | | Non-Aligned Countries and sub-groups, New York |
|------|-----------|--------|---------------------|
|      | New York  | Geneva |                     |
| 1965 | N.A. | 105 | 6 |
| 1966 | 11   | 121 | 4 |
| 1967 | 22   | 164 | 14 |
| 1968 | 2    | 243 | – |
| 1969 | 35   | 211 | 10 |
| 1970 | 36   | 148 | 28 |
| 1971 | 29   | 188 | 24 |
| 1972 | 35   | 253 | 27 |
| 1973 | 62   | 155 | 38 |
| 1974 | 91   | 189 | 23 |
| 1975 | 100  | 376 | 26 |
| 1976 | 140  | 405 | 54 |
| 1977 | 173  | 579 | 49 |
| 1978 | 197  | 762 | 42 |
| 1979 | 241  | 625 | 60 |

Source: Various documents of the Committee on Conferences and own research on the basis of the Journal of the United Nations.

* Excluding meetings in relation to specialized conferences, e.g., the United Nations Conference on the Law of the Sea and Habitat: United Nations Conference on Human Settlements. For Geneva, the data refer to meetings held in relation to sessions of UNCTAD bodies as well as meetings held outside sessions of UNCTAD bodies (except for 1965, for which data could only be obtained for the first category).

** For the earlier years, it is not always clear whether or not meetings of sub-groups have been included in the figures for New York. For the years 1966, 1967, 1972, and 1973, the data pertaining to meetings of the Afro-Asian-Latin American Group in New York have been included in those of the Group of 77. Sub-groups include, for instance, working groups.

## TABLE 13
### Co-ordinating Committee for the 1967 First Ministerial Meeting:
### Membership and members of the Sub-Committees

| Committee and Sub-Committee | Members | | |
|-----------------------------|---------|------|---------------|
|                             | Africa  | Asia | Latin America * |
| Co-ordinating Committee | Algeria ** | India | Argentina |
|                         | Egypt | Iraq | Brazil |
|                         | Ethiopia | Pakistan | Chile |
|                         | Ghana | Philippines | El Salvador |
|                         | Madagascar | Republic of | Mexico |
|                         | Nigeria | Viet Nam | Peru |
|                         | Tunisia | Sri Lanka | Venezuela |
|                         | Zaire | Yugoslavia | |

Sub-Committee I (on substantive documents for the Ministerial Meeting) and
Sub-Committee II (on administration and organization of the Ministerial Meeting) were Sub-Committees of the whole and, hence, had the same membership as the Co-ordinating Committee

* Jamaica and Uruguay were substitute members.

** The host country of the Ministerial Meeting.

**TABLE 14**
**Preparatory Committee for the 1979 Fourth Ministerial Meeting: Membership***

| Africa | Asia | Latin America | |
|---|---|---|---|
| Algeria | Bangladesh | Argentina[+] | Romania |
| Egypt | India | Bolivia [+] | |
| Ethiopia | Indonesia | Brazil | |
| Gabon | Iran | Chile [+] | |
| Ghana | Iraq | Colombia [+] | |
| | | | |
| Ivory Coast | Jordan | Cuba[+] | |
| Libyan Arab Jamahiriya | Malaysia | Ecuador [+] | |
| Nigeria | Pakistan | El Salvador[+] | |
| Somalia | Philippines | Jamaica | |
| Sudan | Qatar | Mexico[+] | |
| | | | |
| Tunisia | Sri Lanka | Nicaragua | |
| United Republic of | Thailand | Peru[+] | |
| Tanzania | Yugoslavia | Trinidad and Tobago [+] | |
| Zaire | | Uruguay | |
| | | Venezuela | |

\* Bangladesh named the chairperson, Jamaica the vice-chairperson, and
Egypt the vice-chairperson-cum-rapporteur. The ten core members of the Latin
American Group are indicated by daggers (+); those of the other groups
could not be ascertained.

## TABLE 15

**Preparatory Committee for the 1979 Fourth Ministerial Meeting: Membership and allocation of work to the Sub-Committees and the Sub-Group**

| Sub-Committee | Membership * Africa | Asia | Latin America | Work areas |
|---|---|---|---|---|
| Sub-Committee I | Ivory Coast Nigeria Sudan Tunisia Zaire <br><br> Madagascar | Bangladesh Indonesia Malaysia Sri Lanka <br><br> Saudi Arabia | Argentina Chile Cuba Mexico Peru | Integrated Programme for Commodities Economic co-operation among developing countries Trade relations among countries having different economic and social systems Institutional questions Least developed among developing countries, island developing countries and land-locked developing countries |
| Sub-Committee II | Egypt Ethiopia Ghana Ivory Coast | India Iraq Thailand Yugoslavia | Brazil Colombia Ecuador Mexico Trinidad and Tobago | Manufactures and semi-manufactures Multilateral trade negotiations Restrictive business practices Transport: shipping and multimodal Transfer of technology and strengthening of the technological capacity of developing countries Protectionism |
| Sub-Committee III | Algeria Gabon Ghana Sudan United Republic of Tanzania | Iran Pakistan Qatar Syrian Arab Republic | Cuba El Salvador Jamaica Venezuela | Monetary and financial questions Transfer of real resources for development Interdependence of problems of the international financial, monetary and trade systems Invisibles |

(Table 15 cont'd)

| Sub-Committee | Membership * | | | | Work areas |
|---|---|---|---|---|---|
| | Africa | Asia | Latin America | | |
| Sub-Committee on Organizational Matters | Algeria Ethiopia Gabon United Republic of Tanzania ** | Jordan Philippines Sri Lanka | Argentina Cuba Peru | | Organizational matters |
| Sub-Group on Item 8 of the Provisional Agenda *** | Nigeria | Pakistan | Jamaica Trinidad and Tobago | | Evaluation of the world trade and economic situation and consideration of issues, policies and appropriate measures to facilitate structural changes in the international economy, taking into account the interrelationships of problems in the areas of trade, development, money and finance with a view to attaining the establishment of a new international economic order and bearing in mind the further evolution that may be needed in the rules and principles governing international economic relations and UNCTAD's necessary contribution to a New International Development Strategy for the Third United Nations Development Decade |

*' The country in the chair is underlined, the country designating the vice-chairperson-cum-rapporteur is underlined in broken lines.

** As the host country, this sub-committee did not have a vice-chairperson-cum-rapporteur.

*** One member from each of the three regional groups was added.

115

## TABLE 16
### Co-ordinating Committee for the 1967 First Ministerial Meeting: Work areas and membership of the Working Parties

| Working Party and work area | Member * | | |
| --- | --- | --- | --- |
| | Africa | Asia | Latin America |
| Working Party on Commodities | Ethiopia<br>Ghana | Philippines<br>Sri Lanka | Uruguay<br>Venezuela |
| Working Party on Manufactures and Semi-Manufactures | Nigeria<br>Zaire | India<br>Pakistan | Chile<br>Mexico |
| Working Party on Invisibles and Financing, Including Shipping | Tunisia<br>Egypt | Iraq<br>Yugoslavia | Brazil<br>Peru |
| Working Party on Other Matters, Including General Trade Policy (Trade Expansion and General Integration) | Algeria<br>Madagascar | India<br>Republic of Viet Nam | Argentina<br>El Salvador |
| Working Party on Other Matters, Including General Trade Policy (the Least Developed among the Developing Countries) | Algeria<br>Madagascar | India<br>Republic of Viet Nam | Argentina<br>El Salvador |

\* The country in the chair is underlined.

116

## TABLE 17
### Working Groups of the Group of 77 in UNCTAD: Membership, September 1980

| Group | Member * | | |
|---|---|---|---|
| | Africa | Asia | Latin America |
| Working Group of 33 on the Integrated Programme for Commodities and the Common Fund | Algeria<br>Egypt<br>Gabon<br>Ghana<br>Ivory Coast<br>Libyan Arab Jamahiriya<br>Nigeria<br>Sudan<br>Tunisia<br>Zaire | Bangladesh<br>India<br>Indonesia<br>Iran<br>Kuwait<br>Malaysia<br>Pakistan<br>Philippines<br>Sri Lanka<br>Syrian Arab Republic<br>Yugoslavia | Argentina<br>Bolivia<br>Brazil<br>Chile<br>Colombia<br>Ecuador<br>Jamaica<br>Mexico<br>Peru<br>Trinidad and Tobago<br>Venezuela |
| Working Group of 15 on Institutional Questions | Algeria<br>Egypt<br>Ethiopia<br>Ghana<br>Libyan Arab Jamahiriya | Bangladesh<br>India<br>Iraq<br>Malaysia<br>Yugoslavia | Argentina<br>Brazil<br>Colombia<br>Trinidad and Tobago<br>Venezuela |
| Working Group of 30 on Economic Co-operation among Developing Countries | Algeria<br>Egypt<br>Gabon<br>Ivory Coast<br>Libyan Arab Jamahiriya<br>Nigeria<br>Somalia<br>Sudan<br>Zaire | Bangladesh<br>India<br>Indonesia<br>Iran<br>Iraq<br>Pakistan<br>Philippines<br>Sri Lanka<br>Thailand<br>Yugoslavia | Argentina<br>Brazil<br>Colombia<br>Cuba<br>Ecuador<br>Guatemala<br>Jamaica<br>Mexico<br>Peru<br>Venezuela |

(Table 17 cont'd)

| Group | Africa | Member *<br>Asia | Latin America |
|---|---|---|---|
| Working Group of 15 on Monetary and Financial Issues | Egypt<br>Ghana<br>Nigeria<br>Sudan<br>Zaire | Bangladesh<br>India<br>Iran<br>Pakistan<br>Yugoslavia | Bolivia<br>Chile<br>Honduras<br>Jamaica<br>Venezuela |
| Co-ordinating Committee on Multi-lateral Trade Negotiations ** | Algeria<br>Egypt<br>Ethiopia<br>Gabon<br>Ghana<br>Ivory Coast<br>Nigeria<br>Senegal<br>Tunisia<br>Zaire | India<br>Indonesia<br>Iraq<br>Iran<br>Malaysia<br>Pakistan<br>Philippines<br>Singapore<br>Sri Lanka<br>Thailand<br>Yugoslavia | Argentina<br>Brazil<br>Bolivia<br>Colombia<br>Cuba<br>Chile<br>Dominican Republic<br>Ecuador<br>El Salvador<br>Jamaica<br>Mexico<br>Nicaragua<br>Peru<br>Trinidad and Tobago<br>Uruguay<br>Venezuela |
| Working Group of 15 on Transfer of Technology | Algeria<br>Egypt<br>Ivory Coast<br>Kenya<br>Nigeria<br>Senegal<br>Zaire | India<br>Indonesia<br>Iraq<br>Pakistan<br>Philippines<br>Sri Lanka<br>Yugoslavia | Argentina<br>Brazil<br>Chile<br>Colombia<br>Jamaica<br>Mexico<br>Venezuela |

118

## (Table 17 cont'd)

| Group | Member * | | |
|---|---|---|---|
| | Africa | Asia | Latin America |
| Working Group of 15 on Restrictive Business Practices | Burundi Egypt Ghana Tunisia Uganda | India Malaysia Pakistan Qatar Sri Lanka | Argentina Brazil Chile Colombia Trinidad and Tobago |
| Working Group of 15 on the International Development Strategy | Burundi Ghana Libyan Arab Jamahiriya Nigeria Sudan | India Indonesia Iraq Pakistan Thailand | Argentina Brazil Colombia Mexico Venezuela |
| | OAU *** SIECA *** | Yugoslavia *** | El Salvador *** Jamaica *** |
| Working Group of 15 on Manufactures | Algeria Ghana Morocco Nigeria Zaire | Bangladesh India Iraq Malaysia Philippines | Brazil Chile Cuba El Salvador Mexico |

\* The country in the chair is underlined.

\*\* No fixed membership.

\*\*\* Other participants.

119

## TABLE 18
### Presidents and Rapporteurs-General of the Ministerial Meetings in Preparation for UNCTAD

| Ministerial Meeting | President | Rapporteur-General |
|---|---|---|
| Algiers 1967 | Mr. Bouteflika (Algeria) | Mr. Stanovnik (Yugoslavia) |
| Lima 1971 | Mr. Mercado-Jarrin (Peru) | Mr. Naik (Pakistan) |
| Manila 1976 | Mr. Romulu (Philippines) | Mr. Kiano (Kenya) |
| Arusha 1979 | Mr. Jamal (United Republic of Tanzania) | Mr. Jaramillo (Colombia) |

## TABLE 19
### Composition and membership of the Bureau of the Ministerial Meeting proper, 1967-1979

| Officer | Ministerial Meeting | | | |
|---|---|---|---|---|
| | 1967 Algiers | 1971 Lima | 1976 Manila | 1979 Arusha |
| President | Algeria | Peru | Philippines | Tanzania |
| Vice Presidents: | | | | |
| Africa | Nigeria Sudan United Republic of Tanzania United Republic of Cameroon | Central African Republic Ethiopia Nigeria Senegal Tunisia | Central African Republic Ivory Coast Tunisia Zambia | Burundi Mozambique Senegal |
| Asia | Indonesia Iran Sri Lanka | Iran Malaysia Lebanon | Indonesia Qatar Sri Lanka | Iraq Malaysia Sri Lanka Yugoslavia |
| Latin America | Bolivia Guatemala Jamaica | Ecuador Mexico | Ecuador Guyana Mexico | Cuba Mexico Uruguay |
| Rapporteur-General | Yugoslavia | Pakistan | Kenya | Colombia |
| Chairpersons, and vice-chairpersons-cum-Rapporteurs of the four main committees | | | Bangladesh Botswana Ghana Iran, Iraq Jamaica Mexico Venezuela | |
| Chairperson of the Co-ordination Committee | | | Argentina | |
| Regional co-ordinators | | | | Ethiopia Sri Lanka Venezuela |
| Chairperson of the Senior Officials Meeting | | | | United Republic of Tanzania |

**TABLE 20**
**Regional composition of the Group of 31 and the Bureau of the Ministerial Meeting proper, 1967-1979**

| Region | Group of 31 | 1967 Algiers | 1971 Lima | 1976 Manila | 1979 Arusha |
|---|---|---|---|---|---|
| Africa . . . . | 12 | 5 | 5 | 7 | 6 |
| Asia . . . . . | 10 | 4 | 4 | 7 | 5 |
| Latin America. . | 9 | 3 | 3 | 7 | 5 |
| Total . . . | 31 | 12 | 12 | 21 | 16 |

**TABLE 21**
**Regional distribution of the officers of the Senior Officials Meeting, 1971-1979***

| Officials and regions | Ministerial Meeting 1971 Lima | 1976 Manila | 1979 Arusha** |
|---|---|---|---|
| Chairperson | Ivory Coast | Philippines | Tanzania |
| Vice-chairpersons Africa | | | Tunisia Zaire |
| Asia | India | | Kuwait Pakistan |
| Latin America | Peru | Nicaragua | Cuba Uruguay |
| Rapporteur-General | | Kenya | Colombia |
| Chairpersons, vice-chairpersons and rapporteurs of the Working Groups Africa | | | Egypt Ghana Malawi |
| Asia | | | India Iraq Sri Lanka |
| Latin America | | | Guyana Haiti Mexico |
| Chairpersons and vice-chairpersons of the Drafting Group | | | Indonesia Tanzania |
| Co-ordinators of the regional groups | | | Ethiopia Sri Lanka Venezuela |

* No Senior Officials Meeting took place at the 1967 Algiers Ministerial Meeting

** The Bureau of the Senior Officials Meeting, according to the rules of procedure.

## Table 22
## The co-ordinator countries of the Group of 77 in Geneva, 1967-1980

| Year | Country |
|------|---------|
| 1967 | Trinidad and Tobago, Tunisia, Lebanon, Uruguay, United Arab Republic, Pakistan, Argentina, Philippines |
| 1968 | Bolivia, Zaire, Saudi Arabia, Brazil |
| 1969 | Ghana, Syrian Arab Republic, Chile, Egypt |
| 1970 | Yugoslavia, Ecuador, Ethiopia, India |
| 1971 | El Salvador, Ghana, Sri Lanka, Guatemala |
| 1972 | Ivory Coast, Indonesia, Honduras, Egypt |
| 1973 | Iran, Jamaica, Chad, Iraq |
| 1974 | Mexico, Algeria, Pakistan, Panama |
| 1975 | Nigeria, Sri Lanka, Argentina, Ethiopia |
| 1976 | Philippines, Bolivia, Sudan, Bangladesh |
| 1977 | Brazil, Egypt, Yugoslavia  */ |
| 1978 | Zaire, Syrian Arab Republic, Colombia, Algeria |
| 1979 | Thailand, Cuba, Ivory Coast, India |
| 1980 | El Salvador, Burundi, Indonesia, Mexico |

*/ Yugoslavia continued in the fourth quarter because Chile, whose turn it was, did not obtain the necessary consensus in the Latin American Group.

## TABLE 23
## Diplomatic missions located in New York, Geneva and Vienna: Number, by group of countries, 1980*
## (Number of countries)

| Group of countries and region | Number of countries | Number of countries with missions in: New York | Geneva | Vienna |
|---|---|---|---|---|
| Group of 77 | | | | |
| Africa | 50 | 48 | 18 | 7** |
| Asia | 41 | 39 | 30 | 16 |
| Latin America*** | 31 | 29 | 22 | 14 |
| TOTAL | 122 | 116 | 70 | 37 |
| Group B**** | 27 | 27 | 27 | 25 |
| Group D***** | 10 | 10 | 9 | 6 |
| China | 1 | 1 | 1 | 1 |

* Included are only those missions that are located in the respective cities or their immediate vicinity.
** Including Kenya, which has only a liaison office in Vienna.
*** Including Romania.
**** Including Israel and South Africa, but excluding Cyprus and Malta as well as Liechtenstein, Monaco, and San Marino.
***** Including Mongolia, but excluding Romania.

# TABLE 24
## Diplomatic missions in New York, Geneva and Vienna: Size, by group of countries, 1980 *
### (Number of professional staff)

| Group of countries and region | Number of countries with missions (1) | Number of missions with a professional staff of 1-5 (2) | 6-10 (3) | 11-15 (4) | 16-20 (5) | 21+ (6) | (2) As percentage of (1) | (2)+(3) As percentage of (1) | (6) As percentage of (1) |
|---|---|---|---|---|---|---|---|---|---|
| **Group of 77** | | | | | | | | | |
| *Africa* | | | | | | | | | |
| New York | 48 | 22 | 18 | 6 | 1 | 1 | 46 | 83 | 2 |
| Geneva | 18 | 4 | 8 | 4 | 1 | 1 | 22 | 67 | 6 |
| Vienna** | 7 | 3 | 4 | - | - | - | 43 | 100 | 0 |
| *Asia* | | | | | | | | | |
| New York | 39 | 12 | 17 | 5 | 4 | 1 | 31 | 74 | 3 |
| Geneva | 30 | 16 | 7 | 7 | - | - | 53 | 77 | 0 |
| Vienna | 16 | 10 | 5 | 1 | - | - | 63 | 94 | 0 |
| *Latin America\*\*\** | | | | | | | | | |
| New York | 29 | 10 | 8 | 3 | 5 | 3 | 34 | 62 | 10 |
| Geneva | 22 | 9 | 7 | 3 | 2 | 1 | 41 | 73 | 5 |
| Vienna | 14 | 12 | 2 | - | - | - | 86 | 100 | 0 |
| **Group B\*\*\*\*** | | | | | | | | | |
| New York | 27 | 3 | 10 | 8 | - | 6 | 11 | 48 | 22 |
| Geneva | 27 | 5 | 10 | 4 | 4 | 4 | 19 | 54 | 15 |
| Vienna | 25 | 21 | 4 | - | - | - | 84 | 100 | 0 |
| **Group D\*\*\*\*\*** | | | | | | | | | |
| New York | 10 | 1 | 4 | 3 | - | 2 | 10 | 50 | 20 |
| Geneva | 9 | 3 | 2 | 3 | - | 1 | 33 | 56 | 11 |
| Vienna | 6 | 5 | - | 1 | - | - | 83 | 83 | 0 |
| **China** | | | | | | | | | |
| New York | 1 | - | - | - | - | 1 | 0 | 0 | 100 |
| Geneva | 1 | - | - | - | - | 1 | 0 | 0 | 100 |
| Vienna | 1 | 1 | - | - | - | - | 100 | 0 | 0 |

* Included are only those missions that are located in the respective cities or their immediate vicinity.
** Including Kenya, which has only a liaison office in Vienna.
*** Including Romania.
**** Including Israel and South Africa, but excluding Cyprus and Malta as well as Liechtenstein, Monaco, and San Marino.
***** Including Mongolia, but excluding Romania.

123

## TABLE 25
## Official meetings of UNCTAD, 1966-1979
## (Number)

| Year | Number of meetings |
|------|--------------------|
| 1966 | 340 |
| 1967 | 446 |
| 1968 | 887 |
| 1969 | 612 |
| 1970 | 777 |
| | |
| 1971 | 572 |
| 1972 | 861 |
| 1973 | 987 |
| 1974 | 712 |
| 1975 | 691 |
| | |
| 1976 | 657 |
| 1977 | 1071 |
| 1978 | 1272 |
| 1979 | 2083 |

<u>Source</u>: Various documents of the Committee on Conferences.

124

TABLE 26
## Length of tenure of the permanent representatives in New York, Geneva and Vienna, by group of countries, 1980*
### (Years)

| Group of countries and region | Number of countries with missions | 1 year or less** | 2 | 3 | 4 | 5 | 6 | 7 | 8 | 9 or more |
|---|---|---|---|---|---|---|---|---|---|---|
| **Group of 77** | | | | | | | | | | |
| *Africa* | | | | | | | | | | |
| New York . . . . | 48 | 24 | 6 | 1 | 6 | 4 | 1 | 2 | – | 4 |
| Geneva . . . . | 18 | 3 | 6 | 2 | 3 | 3 | 1 | – | – | – |
| Vienna . . . . | 7 | 2 | 1 | 1 | 1 | – | 1 | 1 | – | – |
| *Asia* | | | | | | | | | | |
| New York . . . . | 39 | 16 | 10 | 3 | 2 | 1 | 2 | – | 1 | 4 |
| Geneva . . . . . | 30 | 10 | 9 | 1 | 3 | 2 | 2 | 2 | – | 1 |
| Vienna . . . . . | 16 | 4 | 6 | 2 | 4 | – | – | – | – | – |
| *Latin America**** | | | | | | | | | | |
| New York . . . . | 29 | 13 | 5 | 5 | 1 | 3 | 1 | – | 1 | – |
| Geneva . . . . . | 22 | 10 | 5 | 1 | 3 | 1 | 2 | – | – | – |
| Vienna . . . . . | 14 | 4 | 2 | 4 | 3 | – | 1 | – | – | – |
| TOTAL | | | | | | | | | | |
| New York . . . | 116 | 53 | 21 | 9 | 9 | 8 | 4 | 2 | 2 | 8 |
| Geneva . . . . | 70 | 23 | 20 | 4 | 9 | 6 | 5 | 2 | – | 1 |
| Vienna . . . . | 37 | 10 | 9 | 7 | 8 | – | 2 | 1 | – | – |
| **Group B***** | | | | | | | | | | |
| New York . . . . | 27 | 7 | 6 | 4 | 5 | – | 1 | 3 | – | 1 |
| Geneva . . . . | 27 | 14 | 1 | 3 | 4 | 2 | 2 | 1 | – | – |
| Vienna . . . . . | 25 | 6 | 5 | 7 | 4 | 2 | 1 | – | – | – |
| **Group D****** | | | | | | | | | | |
| New York . . . . | 10 | 5 | 1 | 1 | 2 | –* | – | 1 | – | – |
| Geneva . . . . . | 9 | 2 | 3 | 1 | 1 | 1 | – | – | – | 1 |
| Vienna . . . . . | 6 | 1 | 1 | 2 | 2 | – | – | – | – | – |
| **China** | | | | | | | | | | |
| New York . . . . | 1 | 1 | – | – | – | – | – | – | – | – |
| Geneva . . . . | 1 | 1 | – | – | – | – | – | – | – | – |
| Vienna . . . . | 1 | 1 | – | – | – | – | – | – | – | – |

\* Included are only those missions that are located in the respective cities or their immediate vicinity.

\*\* Including missions currently without a permanent representative.

\*\*\* Including Romania.

\*\*\*\* Including Israel and South Africa, but excluding Cyprus and Malta as well as Lichtenstein, Monaco and San Marino.

\*\*\*\*\* Including Mongolia, but excluding Romania.

## TABLE 27
### The Task Force of the Group of 77 in Vienna

| Africa | Asia | Latin America | |
|---|---|---|---|
| Egypt | India | Brazil | |
| Tunisia | Pakistan | Venezuela | Romania |

## TABLE 28
## UNIDO: Rotation of Groups in the election of officers for the Bureau of the Industrial Development Board, 1978-1982*

| 1978 | 1979 | 1980 | 1981 | 1982 |
|---|---|---|---|---|
| | | President | | |
| Group B | Group C | Group D | African states in Group A | Asian states plus Yugoslavia in Group A |
| | | Vice Presidents | | |
| Group C | Group D | African states in Group A | Asian states plus Yugoslavia in Group A | Group B |
| Group D | African states in Group A | Asian states plus Yugoslavia in Group A | Group B | Group C |
| African states in Group A | Asian states plus Yugoslavia in Group A | Group B | Group C | Group D |
| | | Rapporteur | | |
| Asian states plus Yugoslavia in Group A | Group B | Group C | Group D | African states in Group A |

Source:  UNIDO, Rules of Procedure of the Industrial Development Board (Vienna:  UNIDO, 1978).

  * This cycle is repeated every five years as from 1983 onwards.


## TABLE 29
## The co-ordinator countries of the Group of 77 in Vienna, 1974-1981

| Year | Country |
|---|---|
| 1974 | Zaire * |
| 1975 | India |
| 1976 | Brazil |
| 1977 | Nigeria |
| 1978 | Philippines/Indonesia ** |
| 1979 | Peru |
| 1980 | Tunisia |
| 1981 | Pakistan |

  * Zaire continued into 1975.

  ** The Philippines had been designated as the co-ordinator country for 1978.  In July of that year, however, the ambassador of that country left and Indonesia was designated as the co-ordinator for the balance of the year.

126

## TABLE 30
## Membership in the Intergovernmental Group of 24 on International Monetary Affairs

| Africa | Asia | Latin America |
|--------|------|---------------|
| Algeria | India | Argentina |
| Egypt | Iran | Brazil |
| Ethiopia | Lebanon | Colombia |
| Gabon | Pakistan | Guatemala |
| Ghana | Philippines | Mexico |
| Ivory Coast | Sri Lanka | Peru |
| Nigeria | Syria | Trinidad and Tobago |
| Zaire | Yugoslavia | Venezuela |

## TABLE 31
## The presiding countries of the Group of 24

| Year | Country |
|------|---------|
| 1972 | Venezuela |
| 1973 | Venezuela |
| 1974 | Algeria |
| 1975 | Sri Lanka |
| 1976 | Peru |
| 1977 | Ghana |
| 1978 | Pakistan |
| 1979 | Mexico |
| 1980 | Nigeria |

## TABLE 32
## The participants in the Conference on International Economic Co-operation

| Group | Members |
|-------|---------|
| Developed countries | Australia, Canada, European Community, Japan, Spain, Sweden, Switzerland, United States |
| Developing countries: | |
| Africa | Algeria, Egypt, Nigeria, United Republic of Cameroon, Zaire, Zambia |
| Asia | India, Indonesia, Iran, Iraq, Pakistan, Saudi Arabia, Yugoslavia |
| Latin America | Argentina, Brazil, Jamaica, Mexico, Peru, Venezuela |

## TABLE 33
## Membership in the four commissions of the Conference on International Economic Co-operation

| Commission | Members * | |
| | Developing countries | Developed countries |
| --- | --- | --- |
| Energy | Algeria, Brazil, Egypt, India, Iran, Iraq, Jamaica, Saudi Arabia, Venezuela, Zaire. | Canada, European Community, Japan, Switzerland, United States |
| Raw materials | Argentina, Indonesia, Mexico, Nigeria, Peru, United Republic of Cameroon, Venezuela, Yugoslavia, Zaire, Zambia | Australia, European Community, Japan, Spain, United States. |
| Development | Algeria, Argentina, India, Jamaica, Nigeria, Pakistan, Peru, United Republic of Cameroon, Yugoslavia, Zaire | Canada, European Community, Japan, Sweden, United States |
| Finance | Brazil', Egypt, India, Indonesia, Iran, Iraq, Mexico, Pakistan, Saudi Arabia, Zambia | European Community, Japan, Sweden, Switzerland, United States |

\* The co-chaircountries are underlined.

## TABLE 34
## The Group of 27

| Africa | Asia | Latin America |
| --- | --- | --- |
| Algeria | Bangladesh | Argentina |
| Egypt | India | Brazil |
| Ethiopia | Indonesia | Colombia |
| Kenya | Iran | Guatemala |
| Morocco | Iraq | Haiti |
| Nigeria | Malaysia | Jamaica |
| Tunisia | Nepal | Mexico |
| Zaïre | Pakistan | Peru |
| Zambia | Yugoslavia | Venezuela |

## TABLE 35
## The co-ordinator countries of the Group of 77 in New York, 1970-1981

| Year | Country |
| --- | --- |
| 1970-71 | India |
| 1971-72 | Peru |
| 1972-73 | Egypt |
| 1973-74 | Iran |
| 1974-75 | Mexico |
| 1975-76 | Madagascar |
| 1976-77 | Pakistan |
| 1977-78 | Jamaica |
| 1978-79 | Tunisia |
| 1979-80 | India |
| 1930-81 | Venezuela |

128

# ANNEX II
## SELECTED DOCUMENTS OF THE GROUP OF 77

## A. Address by His Excellency Mwalima Julius K. Nyerere, President of the United Republic of Tanzania, to the Fourth Ministerial Meeting of the Group of 77, Arusha, 12-16 February 1979*

It is my duty and my pleasure to welcome this meeting, and everyone of you, to Tanzania and to Arusha. I suspect that some of you may have found that your accommodation gives you too frequent a reminder that this meeting is being held in an under-developed country. I want to assure you that we tried hard! I hope, however, that you will not find your rooms or the facilities so unsatisfactory that you cannot do your work properly. I also hope that there will be an opportunity for you to see something of Tanzania. We have a lovely country, and we would like you to enjoy your stay here as well as to serve your countries and the whole Third World.

The Agenda of your Conference is very long; it deals with very important matters. Many technical questions are involved, in which details and percentages can mean the difference between the usefulness or otherwise of a proposal or suggested negotiating position. And these details are the reality of working for a New International Economic Order; unless careful attention is given to them (especially by those entrusted with negotiating power) the Third World demands are mere rhetoric.

But there is also a danger in details. When a Third World negotiator has, after exhausting hours of argument, pushed the other side of the table from 30 per cent to 45 per cent he will feel a sense of achievement, and urge acceptance upon his colleagues. We should all sympathize! I am not a military man. But I am told that an Army Commander looks at a platoon's advance in the light of its effect on the total battle front. If that advance can be held without cost, or can be used to harass the opposing forces - fine! But if it exposes his troops pointlessly, or weakens the general strategy, then he congratulates the Platoon Commander and his men, and tells them to withdraw again.

At this Conference you will be looking at the details of past and present negotiations in relation to the aim of securing fundamental changes in the present International Economic Order. I do not propose to comment! The delegates here are much better equipped than I am to assess the negotiations about a Common Fund, changes in the power structure of world financial institutions, tariff and other restrictions on Third World trade, and so on. All that I intend to do is to share with you some thoughts about the future.

The Group of 77 developed out of a felt need for the Third World to speak with one voice at UNCTAD Conferences and other meetings concerned with world economic matters. It was our separate weakness which impelled us towards multilateral consultations, and which has caused forty more nations to join Group of 77 meetings since Algiers in 1967. Whatever the economic philosophy of our nations, we had all found that individual efforts to develop our own national economy kept running into a solid wall of power - the power of the rich nations and the rich transnational corporations.

Newly decolonized nations, and the older countries of Latin America, had all inherited the same idea from the dominant Euro-American culture: work hard and you will become prosperous. Gradually we all discovered that hard work and prosperity were not cause and effect; something external to ourselves always seemed to break the reputed connexion! The so-called neutrality of the world market place turned out to be a neutrality between the exploiter and the exploited, between a bird of prey and its victim. If in our effort to find resources for survival - let alone development - we carried out the textbook procedures for raising capital, we always seemed to end up under the virtual control of the transnational corporations or subject to IMF deflationary policies - or both. We did not achieve progress; we simply moved from the frying pan into the deep-freezer! Even if we tried to do nothing except sell our traditional exports and buy our traditional imports, we found that we could buy less and less with more and more of our hard work.

So we came together in order to negotiate with the industrialized States

*Reprinted from Sauvant, document V.D.3.a.

for changes in the laws and practices of world exchange and finance. The present system has been developed by the industrialized States to serve their purposes. This is a matter of historical fact, not a moral judgement! The result is that the group of industrialized nations - which do act as a group when dealing with outsiders - control the levers of international exchange and finance, and also control the wealth accumulated through centuries of colonialism, gun-boat diplomacy, and an initial advantage in mass production techniques. Once again I am stating facts, not making moral judgements. If morality enters into the matter - as I believe it does - it refers to the future. For we, the Third World, are now demanding that the systems which make the rich richer and the poor poorer must be changed to keep pace with other changes in the world - the ending of colonialism, the advance of technology, and mankind's new consciousness of human equality and human dignity.

We make this demand, as the Third World, in full awareness of certain basic facts, and because of them. Seventy per cent of the world's population - the Third World - commands together no more than 12 per cent of the Gross World Product. Eighty per cent of the world's trade and investment, 93 per cent of its industry, and almost 100 per cent of its research is controlled - in the words of Barbara Ward - by the industrial rich. The income gap is getting wider, even between the industrialized and the so-called "higher-income" Third World countries. The Third World still does most of its trade with the developed nations; its transport links are predominantly with the developed world; the technology it uses is technology developed by and for the developed world - which also controls its use.

In other words, the Third World nations did not shape the world's institutions of production and exchange and have virtually no say in them. But we are dominated by them. It is this domination by forces over which we have no control that each one of us has rejected. And our coming together in the Group of 77 has the purpose of enabling us to deal on terms of greater equality with an existing Centre of Power. Ours is basically a unity of opposition. And it is a unity of nationalisms.

For it was our separate nationalisms which caused us to come together, not the ideals of human brotherhood, or human equality, or love for each other. The immediate reason for each nation joining the Group of 77 depended on the point at which it had experienced the economic frustrations of power external to itself. Whether it wanted to "be developed" or "be industrialized", or "to overcome poverty", or even just to be able to operate as an independent nation, it wanted to do that thing while remaining African, Latin American, or Asian - and within those groups, Tanzanian, Argentinian or Malaysian. It was practical experience of the fact that legal independence did not mean economic freedom which made most of us think in terms of co-operating with others similarly placed.

I stress the fact that it was our nationalism which has forced us together because we have to understand ourselves in order to achieve our purposes. The Group of 77 does not share an ideology. Some of us are avowedly "Scientific" Socialists, some just plain socialist, some capitalist, some theocratic, and some fascist! We are not necessarily friendly with each other - some countries represented here are currently engaged in a war with each other. Our national income per head varies from about $100 a year to $2,000 a year. Some of us have minerals, some do not; some of us are landlocked and others are isolated in huge oceans. The Group of 77 cannot be defined by any of these or any other economic, social, or ideological categories - membership cuts across them all.

The immediate interests and the negotiating priorities, of different Group of 77 members are therefore very different. Consequently, there is a tendency for sub-groups to develop within the Group of 77. We have OPEC, the Most Seriously Affected, the Least Developed, the Newly Industrialized Countries, the Landlocked and so on; sometimes these classifications are made by us and sometimes by others but accepted by us for working purposes. For this kind of subdivision of the Group of 77 can be useful; it enables us to carry on particular detailed negotiations with the industrialized countries, and it also helps us to ensure that all interests within the Group of 77 are covered in the working out of our general strategy.

But this kind of subdivision is also very dangerous. Subgroups inevitably develop their own internal accommodations and their own sense of unity - which can become a unity against the other subgroups rather than with them against the existing world order. When this happens it becomes difficult to use a negotiating advantage in one area to make a break-through in an area where the advantage is with the other side of the table. "Divide and rule" is an old technique of domination; the developed nations are not unaware of its usefulness.

But our diversity exists in the context of one common and overriding experience. What we have in common is that we are all, in relation to the developed world, dependent - not interdependent - nations. Each of our economies has developed as a by-product and a subsidiary of development in the industrialized North, and is externally oriented. We are not the prime movers of our own destiny. We are ashamed to admit it; but economically we are dependencies - semi-colonies at best - not sovereign States.

This is true for every one of us represented here. The members of OPEC united and set the price of oil in 1973. This historic action shook the world, greatly improved the bargaining power of the oil exporting countries and encouraged other primary producers. But since then OPEC has learned, and we have all learned once again, that however powerful it is, a single trade union which only covers one section of a total enterprise cannot change the fundamental relationship between employers and employees.

Then there are the Third World giants - India, Indonesia and Brazil. If these three countries, representing about 900 million people, were to separate themselves from other Third World countries and speak as one, they would still not be able to escape from the reality of domination by the group of developed countries -- at best they could get marginal and temporary concessions. For the reality is that the unity of even the most powerful of the subgroups within the Third World is not sufficient to allow its members to become full actors, rather than reactors, in the world economic system. The unity of the entire Third World is necessary for the achievement of fundamental change in the present world economic arrangements.

Yet the pressures towards disunity are strong. The more advantageously placed among the Group of 77 are being flattered and wooed and offered concessions in this or that matter which is of immediate interest to them. And there are forces within every subgroup - from OPEC to the Least Privileged - which are inclined to take offers of special treatment, or special representation, and then - instead of using these as a base for further Third World advance - to lose interest in the wider struggle. Those forces have not yet won within any country, but it would be stupid to pretend that they do not exist. For they will not just disappear. We are all feeling the cold winds of a European recession, and in our desperation there is a strong temptation to look inwards to ourselves as individual nations rather than inwards to our group as a whole.

I have been saying out loud some of the things which are being said privately. I have done so because a danger can be dealt with only when it is acknowledged. And disunity would be a terrible setback to the prospects of all of us, and would mean discarding a great potential source of power. For the diversity within the Third World could be our strength rather than our weakness if we can hold to our political decision for unity in negotiation and in action.

Sometimes we politicians talk as if change in the present world economic order has to come either through dialogue or through confrontation with the rich nations. I have done this myself when talking in developed countries. For it is a kind of shorthand - a quick way of pointing out that what is true within countries is also true between countries. If there is not planned change in the old order then confrontation is inevitable, nationally and internationally. But we have gone on from there, and talked as if the Third World had to make a strategic choice between negotiating and declaring all-out economic war on the rich States. On that basis we have become very apologetic - to our own people and to others. When participating in dialogue we become apologetic, as if to negotiate is somehow to surrender or to soften about the objective. And if dialogue gets us nowhere we become apologetic about confrontation, as if we were being unreasonable - even irrational - and provoking an all-out economic war which we cannot win.

I do not believe that is the kind of choice we face. We do not have to choose between dialogue and confrontation with the rich: there is no reason why we should be apologetic about negotiating, or about refusing to go on with a particular discussion and resorting to direct action. Ours is a kind of trade union of the poor. Sometimes - perhaps most of the time - we will negotiate about different aspects of the demand for a New International Economic Order and settle for the best compromise we can reach at that time. Sometimes, however, we may be forced to call a strike in order to show that certain things are no longer acceptable!

But a trade union is strong in proportion to its unity. And when deciding upon the acceptability or otherwise of any potential compromise we have to recognize political realities - in our case all 117 of them. For the Third World does not have a strike fund, and hunger strikes are not the weapon of the starving. Asking countries like Zambia and Chile to stop exporting copper to the industrialized nations, for example, is asking them to commit suicide. Their Governments will naturally not agree to do that, and asking them to do so would therefore be equivalent to breaking the unity of the Third World. This weakness of ours can be exaggerated. But our conditions are well known to the developed nations; threatening talk of confrontation as an alternative to dialogue does not frighten them.

But it is also true that the kind of dialogue we have been conducting - at UNCTAD, Paris, Geneva, New York and everywhere else - has brought no fundamental changes in the world economic order. This is not to say that it has been useless. There are now groups of people, and even small nations, in the industrialized world which have realized that the present inequities cannot be allowed to continue, and that planned change is necessary in their own interests as well as ours. That is a helpful movement. But the problem remains: we have not succeeded in changing the structure of power. The world order still works against the interests of the poor.

I believe this unsatisfactory result from our efforts is because we have been making the mistake of acting as if negotiation is exclusively a matter of reason and morality, which has nothing to do with the strength of the participants. The truth is that we need power to negotiate, just as we need power to go on strike. So far we have been negotiating as noisy and importunate supplicants. We need to negotiate from a position of steadily increasing power.

The basic question we should be asking ourselves now, after years of hard talking and little progress, is this. What can we do, among ourselves, to strengthen our position in future negotiations?

My first answer is just what I have been saying until now. We must maintain and strengthen our unity. We must ensure that we continue to speak with one voice and that none of us makes a separate bilateral or multilateral deal which weakens the overall Third World bargaining position. This will not get easier as time goes on.

In all our countries there are groups which identify themselves with the powerful and privileged of the world and who aim only to join them - regardless of the poor in their own nation and elsewhere. In all our countries there are those who have no patience with international negotiations or agreements. In Governments, and as Oppositions, the Third World has reactionaries and radicals of different gradations. If we are to maintain Third World unity we all have to work together when operating within non-Third World organizations for Third World objectives.

I do not believe this means that we must never protest about brutality, tyranny, and racism within the Third World; that would be intolerable - and it would not serve the interests of our peoples. It does mean, however, that we may have to co-operate functionally with governments which we intensely dislike and disapprove of. For the object is to complete the liberation of the Third World countries from external domination. That is the basic meaning of the New International Economic Order. And unity is our instrument - our only instrument - of liberation.

But we have to do more than stand united when negotiating as the Group of 77. We have to work together; our nations have to co-operate economically. This is where the diversity of the Third World can be our strength also.

We have to build up trade among ourselves, and we have to do this quite deliberately. For it will not happen through the workings of laissez faire. We each have to search out the possibilities of purchase from other Third World nations, or sale to other Third World nations.

134

We have to co-operate in establishing Third World Multinational Corporations, owned by us and controlled by us, to serve our purposes and to remain independent of the great transnational corporations which now dominate the world economic scene. We need Third World Shipping Lines to carry our goods, to open new links between us - and to break the stragling monopoly of the conference lines. We need Third World international insurance; it is absurd that our reinsurance premiums should provide capital for the industrialized world. We need to have institutions of research and development directed at serving our needs and developing our resources. We need to plan jointly-owned industries when our separate markets are too small for the economic viability of certain production processes. And it may be that we should be considering the idea of having our own Third World financial clearing institutions instead of paying each other through London, New York, or Paris.

All these things are possible on three conditions. That there is, on balance, equal benefit for all the participating Third World countries in each package of co-operation. That we treat obligations - financial or commercial - to each other as seriously as we treat those to the rich and powerful nations, or even more seriously. And that we should all give preference to Third World institutions when these compete with those of the industrialized world.

Building up Third World self-reliance, nationally and collectively, is not a miraculous answer to our problems. It will take time - a long time. And it will be very difficult. Certainly Tanzania is not the one to underestimate the difficulties of this prescription: East Africa is an example of a tragic failure in Third World co-operation. There have been other failures, and there may be more in the future. Yet every successful effort at co-operation strengthens the whole Third World in its dealings with the developed world. We must all keep trying. And we must all encourage and give what help we can to every attempt which is made, whether it is functional or general, neighbourly, regional, or intercontinental. All that we should ask before giving our backing, is that it is a truly Third World co-operative effort, and that it is designed to strengthen the independence and the economy of Third World countries.

This question is on your Agenda. Economic Co-operation among Developing Countries is Item 18! Yet this position on the Agenda need not matter too much; co-operation among ourselves can be a feature of the discussion on almost any subject if the approach is always "what can we do among ourselves, for ourselves?". And there are corridors in this building!

The final point I wish to mention is not on your Agenda at all. But I am sometimes appalled by the handicap under which Third World negotiators enter into important meetings - either among ourselves or with others. We in Tanzania take these questions fairly seriously, yet our delegations have very little help. They get, from Tanzanian economists who have very heavy domestic responsibilities, a short paper commenting on the major issues; they read articles in international journals; and they have the papers which UNCTAD staffs present to us all. I believe a similar situation exists for most, if not all, Third World delegations to United Nations or North/South meetings. And with this kind of support they go to meet highly experienced people, armed with all the preparatory material done by sophisticated domestic and OECD staffs and their computers!

Many dedicated Third World experts work for UNCTAD, and other staff members see the need for changes in the international system of exchange and finance. But UNCTAD is, by definition, a world organization. One job of its staff is to help meetings to reach agreement. It is the job of the Third World to develop and state its own position.

The same lack of technical preparation may be hindering our efforts to expand economic co-operation among ourselves. It is at present no one's job to search out potential areas of co-operation and present them to our overworked Ministers, and then follow up an interest. Once again, UNCTAD and other United Nations servants are helpful; we owe a lot to them. But some members of the United Nations appear to have their own feelings about United Nations secretariats serving the interests of one side - even the weaker side - in a world negotiation!

There is considerable suspicion about international bureaucracies and new institutions - I am not immune myself! They tend to be very expensive, especially if the staffs are paid at what are called "international standards" - which usually means the highest wages anywhere! But it may be that the Group of 77 should be

135

looking again at this question of whether it needs its own full-time economists and other professional people as a technical aid to the policy-makers and negotiators. I would only add that, if we decide this to be the case, then we must pay for that technical office ourselves. He who pays the piper calls the tune!

As I understand it, our purpose in the Group of 77 is to try to secure changes in the world's economic arrangements because we see these as unfair, detrimental to our interests, and indeed contrary to the interests of world stability and progress. Our goal is economic liberation, and on that goal there can be no compromise. But during the process of liberation it may sometimes be necessary to compromise; we have no desire to contract out of the world in which we live.

I have been arguing that to achieve our purposes we need to maintain and even strengthen our unity in the Group of 77, and to expand functional co-operation among ourselves. Nothing I have said is new. It can only be a reminder of well-known truths as you embark upon your labours.

For these are no miraculous answers to our problems. Changing the world order is a process. It can be speeded; it can be directed; and it can be made less turbulent. But it will remain a process. The next UNCTAD Conference - for which you are preparing yourselves - is an event along the way. Your preparations for it should also be preparations for later stages in the process we are trying to influence.

## B. Arusha Programme for Collective Self-Reliance and Framework for Negotiations, Adopted by the Fourth Ministerial Meeting of the Group of 77, Arusha, 12-16 February 1979*

CONTENTS

I. The setting

II. Programme for Collective Self-Reliance

III. Framework for negotiations

Item 8 of the provisional agenda for UNCTAD V

Evaluation of the world trade and economic situation and consideration of issues, policies and appropriate measures to facilitate structural changes in the international economy, taking into account the interrelationships of problems in the areas of trade, development, money and finance with a view to attaining the establishment of a new international economic order and bearing in mind the further evolution that may be needed in the rules and principles governing international economic relations and UNCTAD's necessary contribution to a New International Development Strategy for the Third United Nations Development Decade

Item 9 of the provisional agenda for UNCTAD V

Developments in international trade

Item 10 of the provisional agenda for UNCTAD V

Commodities

Item 11 of the provisional agenda for UNCTAD V

Manufactures and semi-manufactures

Item 12 of the provisional agenda for UNCTAD V

Monetary and financial issues

Item 13 of the provisional agenda for UNCTAD V

Technology

Item 14 of the provisional agenda for UNCTAD V

Shipping

Item 15 of the provisional agenda for UNCTAD V

Least developed among developing countries

Item 16 of the provisional agenda for UNCTAD V

Land-locked and island developing countries

Item 17 of the provisional agenda for UNCTAD V

Trade relations among countries having different economic and social systems

*Reprinted from Sauvant, document V.D.4.

CONTENTS (continued)

## I. THE SETTING

1.   We, the representatives of the developing countries, members of the Group of 77, having met in our fourth ministerial session at Arusha, United Republic of Tanzania, from 12 to 16 February 1979, to reaffirm our spirit of solidarity and collective self-reliance and to decide on a collective negotiating strategy for the fifth session of the United Nations Conference on Trade and Development to be held in Manila in May 1979, as well as on a programme of action on collective self-reliance and mutually beneficial co-operation among ourselves.

2.   Recognizing that our meeting takes place in the midst of the severest crisis of the world economy after the Second World War,

3.   Conscious of the responsibility placed on the developing countries to find effective solutions to the acute social and economic problems facing them and to work out strategies which will promote self-reliance and effect basic structural changes, permanently remove the conditions of underdevelopment and accelerate the rapid socio-economic and technological transformation of our societies,

4.   Recalling General Assembly resolutions 3201 (S-VI) and 3202 (S-VI) on the Declaration and the Programme of Action on the Establishment of a New International Economic Order and 3201 (XXIX) on the Charter of Economic Rights and Duties of States, as well as 3362 (S-VII) on Development and International Economic Co-operation,

5.   Recalling also the Manila Declaration and Programme of Action adopted by the Third Ministerial Meeting of the Group of 77, which consolidated the negotiating positions of developing countries for the fourth session of the United Nations Conference on Trade and Development in May 1976,

6.   Recalling the initiatives taken at the fourth session of UNCTAD and subsequent decisions of that Conference to commence international negotiations on a wide range of issues in the field of trade and development, as part of the effort of developing countries to restructure economic relations with developed countries and to work towards the establishment of the New International Economic Order,

7.   Convinced that just peace is not only the absence of war but also must provide conditions for political freedom, the sustained and accelerated development of developing countries and for the promotion of world orderly development,

8.   Convinced also that economic and social consequences of the arms race are so detrimental that its continuation is obviously incompatible with the implementation of the New International Economic Order and that resources released as a result of the implementation of disarmament measures should be used in a manner which will help to promote the well-being of all peoples and to improve the economic conditions of the developing countries,

9.   Having reviewed the recent developments in the world economy and evaluated the results so far achieved in the negotiations initiated, especially at the fourth session of UNCTAD,

10.   Express deep disappointment and grave concern that the negotiations undertaken since the fourth session of UNCTAD have not yielded the expected results so far and that no significant progress has been achieved in the implementation of the Programme of Action on the Establishment of a New International Economic Order owing to the lack of political will on the part of most of the developed countries;

138

11.  Record profound dissatisfaction at the failure to make adequate progress and produce concrete results in the negotiations on the Integrated Programme for Commodities, primarily owing to the persistent intransigence on the part of most of the developed countries and their refusal to adopt constructive positions on the basic objectives and goals of the programme;

12.  Express further our profound dissatisfaction that, despite the commitment made at the fourth session of UNCTAD and in many other fora, most developed countries have not yet evinced the political will necessary for the successful conclusion of the negotiations on a Common Fund which will serve as a key instrument to attain the objectives of UNCTAD resolution 93 (IV) and express the hope that a discernible change of attitude will be shown at the resumed negotiating session so that the negotiations will be successfully concluded;

13.  View with deep concern the trends in the Multilateral Trade Negotiations which indicate that, unless corrective measures are introduced the outcome of these negotiations will fall far short of the objectives set forth for the trade of developing countries by the Tokyo Declaration and may result in the continuation of a trading system which would be increasingly unfavourable to developing countries;

14.  Express profound disappointment that the negotiations on the adoption of the International Code of Conduct for the Transfer of Technology have not yet reached a successful conclusion and hope that the forthcoming resumed session will achieve positive results;

15.  Strongly urge that developed countries should adopt a more constructive approach and co-operate to bring the on-going negotiations to a successful conclusion before the fifth session of UNCTAD, to enable the fifth session to meet in a positive atmosphere and chart the course for more constructive and fruitful international co-operation in trade and development in the 1980s;

16.  Express grave apprehension that failure to achieve concrete results in on-going negotiations before the fifth session could lead to a serious loss of confidence in the international negotiating process and seriously jeopardize the prospect for international co-operation;

17.  View with growing concern the persistent crisis in the international economic order, which is manifested in the developed countries, such as in their inability to control the chronic imbalances in their international payments, in the continuing high levels of unemployment and inflation, combined with new structural rigidities in the economies and long-term prospects of low growth, and whose features in the developing countries include mainly the continuing deterioration in the terms of trade, new barriers to exports of their manufactures and consequently new constraints on export earning capacity, the growing burden of external indebtedness, persistent mass poverty and inadequate level of transfer of real resources;

18.  View with deep concern the inequities and injustices in the prevailing order which have cast an avoidable and intolerable proportion of the global burden of readjustment on the developing countries and seriously retarded their development effort;

19.  Express alarm at the serious disruptive impact which the disorder in the international monetary system, global inflation and the high degree of instability in exchange rates of major currencies continue to have on the developing countries, especially in the heavy loss of revenues on their raw materials and other exports and the consequent effect on the management of the economies;

20.  Strongly deplore the policies adopted by developed countries in the field of trade, specifically the intensification of protectionism and their attempts to formulate arbitrary concepts, such as graduation, selectivity and access to supplies, which constitute serious obstacles to the development of developing countries;

21.  Emphasize that the continuing malaise in the international economic system cannot be regarded as a cyclical phenomenon but needs to be recognized as the manifestation of a deep-seated structural mal-functioning which, therefore, calls for fundamental structural changes in the international economic system;

22.  Stress that the existing international economic order not only fails to

support the development process of the developing countries but is also functioning inefficiently;

23.  Reaffirm the urgent need to greatly enhance the transfer of resources from the developed countries to the developing countries so as to promote rapid economic development and thus enable them to eradicate mass poverty and improve the standard of living of the people of the developing countries;

24.  Underscore the need for developed countries to recognize the structural nature of the current economic crisis and the ineffectiveness of pursuing policies which assume that their economic recovery can be achieved independently of the structural reform of the international economic system;

25.  Recognize that on the part of both developed and developing countries there is the emerging perception of the interdependence of nations and the close interrelationship of issues in the fields of trade, money, finance and development;

26.  Consider, therefore, that it is necessary to promote genuine mutuality of interests in the structural changes that are needed in the international economic system and to recast the world order within a framework of independence, equity and genuine sovereign equality;

27.  Consider it imperative therefore that the international community accelerate the implementation of the Programme of Action on the Establishment of the New International Economic Order;

28.  Consider that the essential economic elements  of such an accelerated implementation of the programme include negotiated shifts in the prevailing patterns of trade and production which eliminate protectionism in manufacturing agricultural and other sectors, promote an equitable global distribution of productive capacity and accelerate the industrialization of developing countries; the restructuring and development of the primary commodity sector in the world economy, with improved terms of trade and greater shares for developing countries in processing, marketing and distribution; an international framework conducive to the rapid growth of technological capacity of developing countries and an effective framework for international financial co-operation which ensures to developing countries vastly increased access to resources;

29.  Reaffirm that the preparation and implementation of the new International Development Strategy for the third United Nations Development Decade should come within the framework of the implementation of the Programme of Action on the Establishment of the New International Economic Order;

30.  Consider further that the basic structural and economic problems facing the least developed countries are so severe that extraordinary additional measures, especially designed in a comprehensive programme as an essential feature of the New International Economic Order, are required;

31.  Consider also that there is a need for specific action to overcome economic problems arising from the geographical handicaps facing the land-locked and island developing countries as well as the economic problems facing the most seriously affected countries;

32.  Reiterate the vital importance of basing the restructured world economic order and international economic relations within it on full respect for the principles of sovereign equality among independent States, non-intervention in internal affairs, respect for different economic and social systems and the right of each State to exercise full and permanent control over its own natural resources and all its economic activities without suffering any kind of economic aggression or discrimination;

33.  Emphasize that the governments and peoples of developing countries shall continue to mobilize their resources in support of their common struggle against colonialism, foreign aggression and occupation, racism, apartheid and all forms of foreign domination and exploitation, so as to put an immediate end to these major obstacles to development.  They reiterate their unswerving support for the heroic struggles of the peoples of Namibia, Zimbabwe, Azania and Palestine to achieve their liberation and to regain effective control over their natural resources and economic activities.  They are determined to exercise full permanent sovereignty over their wealth, natural resources and economic activities and the

right to restitution and full compensation for the exploitation and depletion of and damages to the natural and all other resources of the peoples, countries and territories subjected to those practices.

34. Recognize that developing countries need to enhance their collective bargaining strength and exercise their countervailing power, thereby creating the compulsions which would make the developed countries willing to negotiate the desired changes in the international economic system;

35. Reaffirm that such countervailing power flows from the individual and collective self-reliance of developing countries, and that the basis of collective self-reliance rests on the intensification and strengthening of economic linkages among developing countries;

36. Underline the vital importance of intiatives which member governments of the Group of 77 take to accelerate the development and transformation of their economies through the process of collective self-reliance which include an intensification of their joint and concerted efforts to mobilize their resources and markets for building a structure of genuine economic interdependence and complementarity between their economies and explore areas of communality of interest as well as the strengthening of their solidarity in their negotiations with the developed countries for the establishment of the New International Economic Order;

37. Resolve therefore to give the highest priority to implementing economic co-operation among developing countries based, inter alia, on the Mexico City Programme as well as on the Buenos Aires Plan of Action and resolutions adopted by the United Nations Conference on TCDC, as an essential element in the establishment of the New International Economic Order and to consider the development of an appropriate institutional framework to help in its implementation, as well as strengthen the negotiating capacity of developing countries;

38. Reaffirm our commitment to the solidarity of the developing countries which makes it possible to harmonize diversity of interests, solve unified positions and strengthen the collective bargaining power of developing countries;

39. Emphasize that developed countries need to undertake a restructuring of their economies which enable them to adjust speedily and smoothly to the shifting patterns of comparative advantage in the international division of labour, and at the same time should seek to initiate more basic reorientations in their patterns of consumption growth and development to create the conditions for a more rational and more equitable use of the earth's resources;

40. Reaffirm that developing countries perceive the structural changes in the international economic system as being significant and essential for creating the external environment conducive to carrying through the socio-economic and institutional transformation within their societies which will rapidly modernize and expand their production system, increase their technological capability, promote their self-reliance, eliminate mass poverty, and establish an equitable social order;

41. Consider it imperative, as a key element of the reform of the institutional framework of international economic relations, that developing countries should have an equitable share in global decision-making and management of the world economy, and for this purpose, they need to participate more effectively in the management of the international economy to ensure not only that policies in the field of trade, money and finance are mutually consistent and are supportive of development, but also that they promote the movement towards long-term restructuring;

42. Consider, at the same time, that with the breakdown of the monetary and trading system established after the Second World War and the emergence of major new elements in the international system, there is urgent need to recast the existing rules of principles governing international trade and economic relations and to align them with the requirements of a restructured world economic order;

43. Urge that, in order to ensure that the international negotiating process functions effectively and facilitates the implementation of the structural reform of the international economic order, the machinery for negotiations within the United Nations system should be adequately strengthened;

44. Recognize the evolving role of UNCTAD as a major forum for the evaluation

and review of world economic developments in the context of its mandate, for initiating discussions on new concepts and policies and even more for negotiations on a wide range of issues relevant to international economic relations and, in this context, the need to enhance its capacity to perform its evolving functions effectively;

45.    Recognize further UNCTAD as the principal instrument of the General Assembly for international economic negotiations on international trade and development particularly in the context of negotiations on the establishment of the New International Economic Order; and reaffirm this role;

46.    Therefore unanimously adopt, inter alia, the following Programme for Collective Self-reliance and Framework for Negotiations.

## II.  PROGRAMME FOR COLLECTIVE
## SELF-RELIANCE

Strongly aware that the attainment of collective self-reliance among developing countries calls for meaningful implementation measures over a sustained period of time,

The Fourth Ministerial Meeting of the Group of 77

Recalling General Assembly resolutions 1995 (XIX) of 30 December 1964, as amended, 3177 (XXVIII) of 17 December 1973, 3241 (XXIX) of 29 November 1974, 3442 (XXX) of 9 December 1975, 31/119 of 16 December 1976, 32/180 of 19 December 1977 and 33/195 of 29 January 1979 on Economic Co-operation among Developing Countries,

Reaffirming the principles established in the Declaration and the Programme of Action on the Establishment of a New International Economic Order, contained in General Assembly resolutions 3201 (S-VI) and 3202 (S-VI) of 1 May 1974;  the Charter of Economic Rights and Duties of States, adopted in General Assembly resolution 3281 (XXIX) of 12 December 1974;  and the provisions of General Assembly resolution 3362 (S-VII) of 16 September 1975 on development and international economic co-operation,

Reaffirming further the principles contained in Concerted Declaration 23 (II) adopted by the United Nations Conference on Trade and Development on 26 March 1968; Conference resolution 48 (III) of 18 May 1972 on trade expansion, economic co-operation and regional integration among developing countries, as well as Conference resolutions 90 (IV) and 92 (IV) of 31 May 1976 and Trade and Development Board decisions 142 (XVI) of 23 October 1976 on the establishment of the Committee on Economic Co-operation among Developing Countries and 161 (XVII) of 2 September 1977 on the terms of reference of the Committee on Economic Co-operation among Developing Countries,

Recalling also the Action Programme on Economic Co-operation and the pertinent resolutions approved by the Fifth Conference of Heads of State or Government of Non-Aligned Countries held in Colombo from 16 to 19 August 1976, relative to co-operation among developing countries, as well as the recommendations on this item made by the Conference of Ministers of Foreign Affairs of the Non-Aligned Countries, held at Belgrade from 24 to 29 July 1978,

Recalling its programme on economic co-operation among developing countries contained in resolution adopted at the Third Ministerial Meeting of the Group of 77 held at Manila from 26 January to 7 February 1976, which provided a basic framework for the development of further action to turn into reality the objectives of economic self-reliance of the developing countries,

Recalling further the Buenos Aires Plan of Action and resolutions adopted at the United Nations Conference on Technical Co-operation among Developing Countries, held from 30 August to 12 September 1978,

Mindful that a strategy of collective self-reliance should be viewed as an integral part of a global economic system, specifically as an essential element of an over-all strategy for development encompassing the restructuring of international economic relations, and that Economic Co-operation among Developing

Countries is a key element in a collective self-reliant strategy and thus becomes both an essential part of and an instrument for the necessary structural changes required for a balanced and equitable process of world economic development, ushering in a new set of relationships based on mutual interests and accommodations,

Aware that a strategy of collective self-reliance embodies the potential for joint action by developing countries that will strengthen their capacity to negotiate with developed countries and reduce their dependency on them and that intensifying trade and economic linkages among developing countries is part of the structural change needed for a more rational international division of labour, leading to a more efficient use of world resources,

Convinced that more intensive economic co-operation among developing countries is beneficial to the entire international economy,

1. Welcomes with great satisfaction the decisions adopted at the Conference on Economic Co-operation among Developing Countries, held at Mexico City from 13 to 22 September 1976, which developed further the programme for economic co-operation among developing countries in accordance with paragraph 14 of resolution No. 1 adopted at the Third Ministerial Meeting of the Group of 77;

2. Takes note of the recommendations made by the Working Party on Trade Expansion and Regional Economic Integration among Developing Countries, pursuant to decision A.I.1 of the Mexico City Conference on Economic Co-operation among Developing Countries;

3. Takes note of the measures of support and co-ordination of activities undertaken within the United Nations system in the field of economic co-operation among developing countries, as reported by the Secretary-General of the United Nations to the thirty-third session of the General Assembly; 1/

4. Welcomes the establishment of the UNCTAD Committee on Economic Co-operation among Developing Countries;

5. Welcomes further the substantive work carried out by UNCTAD in pursuance of the work programme adopted by the Committee on Economic Co-operation among Developing Countries;

6. Considers that, in accordance with the Manila Declaration and Programme of Action and the Mexico City Conference, the time has now come for concrete action;

7. Considers furthermore that during the last three years considerable progress has been made in elaborating further the details of the programme on economic co-operation among developing countries and that the technical information already available justifies the adoption of detailed operational guidelines and objectives for implementation of the economic co-operation among developing countries over the next few years; and therefore,

8. Decides on the implementation of the following First Short Medium-Term Action Plan for Global Priorities on Economic Co-operation among Developing Countries, which should be reviewed regularly at future Ministerial Meetings of the Group of 77 and at least once at Senior Officials level in the period between the Ministerial Meetings, acting on the principle that economic co-operation among developing countries constitutes a long-term process where progress should be sought on all fronts as opportunities for co-operation are detected on the basis of sound and technically justified proposals.

First Short Medium-Term Action Plan for Global Priorities on Economic Co-operation among Developing Countries

1. A first Short Medium-Term Action Plan for Global Priorities on Economic Co-operation among Developing Countries is adopted, to be reviewed at the Fifth Ministerial Meeting of the Group of 77, calling for specific action in the following priority areas of economic co-operation among developing countries and in accordance with the following principles and objectives.

2. Economic co-operation among developing countries is a basic component of their efforts towards the establishment of the New International Economic Order (NIEO).

1/ "Economic Co-operation among Developing Countries." Report of the Secretary-General A/33/367.

143

3.   Owing to the fact that economic co-operation among developing countries is a matter that chiefly concerns the developing countries, it should be formulated and implemented by them, at the subregional, regional, interregional and global levels.

4.   In this context, the developed countries and the organizations of the United Nations system should give a strong support to this process in fulfilment of the different General Assembly and UNCTAD resolutions.

A.   A global system of trade preferences among developing countries (GSTP)

5.   The Ministers recommend that:

    (i)   a long-term objective on a global system of trade preferences must be established among developing countries;

    (ii)   as a first step, priority should be given to the strengthening and linking up of the existing subregional, regional and interregional preferential schemes, as well as expanding the scope of bilateral arrangements;

    (iii)   the following principles, pending the completion of the meetings proposed in paragraph (iv) below, should provide guidelines for work in this field:

        (a)   the recognition that a GSTP would constitute a major instrument for the promotion of trade, production and employment among developing countries;

        (b)   the recognition of the complexities and difficulties involved in the creation of a GSTP, which calls for a realistic step-by-step approach on the part of all interested governments;

        (c)   that a GSTP should not rely only on traditional tariff concessions, but in addition to covering non-tariff barriers it ought to be progressively interrelated with other measures in the field of production, marketing, payments, finance and transport;

        (d)   the strengthening of existing and the establishment of new subregional and regional trade preferences among developing countries;

        (e)   the GSTP would need to be based on the principle of mutuality of advantages, so as to yield benefits to all participants; taking into account the respective levels of economic and industrial development, trade patterns and trade regimes of individual developing countries;

        (f)   in addition to non-reciprocal trade preferences, effective special treatment would be required in favour of products of export interest to least developed countries, land-locked and island developing countries on a non-reciprocal basis;

        (g)   subregional, regional and interregional groupings of developing countries could participate as such, whenever they consider it desirable, in the negotiations for a GSTP;

        (h)   the GSTP should be open to the participation of all interested developing countries;

        (i)   the gradual establishment of a GSTP should be accomplished by a parallel strengthening of subregional, regional and interregional integration groupings, which have a highly important role to play in this respect;

        (j)   the global preferential trading arrangement should consist of a coherent set of closely related components, including such elements as the adoption of indicative targets for increasing mutual trade, special techniques and modalities on preferential negotiations and for concessions on quantitative restrictions, agreements on direct trade measures and the use of long-term contracts, recourse to sectoral negotiations when appropriate, provisions on rules of origin and safeguards, and other essential provisions of preferential trade arrangements. The GSTP should furthermore incorporate appropriate mechanisms and regular medium-term reviews for evaluating progress;

(k) product coverage should include not only manufactures but also commodities and agricultural products in their raw and processed forms;

(l) in addition to the GSTP, all other appropriate means of expanding trade should be considered by developing countries, including the use of bilateral arrangements; and

(m) a trade information system in support of the GSTP should be established.

(iv) (a) The studies on the Global System of Trade Preferences, prepared by UNCTAD, should be duly analysed as a first step by each government.

(b) Subsequent to these analyses, during the fourth quarter of 1979, there shall be a regional evaluation by means of meetings of government experts with the support of the relevant regional economic organizations as appropriate.

(c) After the above stages, an interregional meeting of government experts of the Group of 77 should be held within the framework of UNCTAD before the end of 1979 to prepare recommendations on the studies set forth in (iv) (a) above.

B. Co-operation among State-trading organizations (STOs)

6. The Ministers recommend that:

(i) Specific open-ended meetings of STOs should be convened by the Group of 77 with the assistance of UNCTAD, regional economic commissions and subregional groupings of developing countries to discuss the essential features of co-operation arrangements among themselves. UNCTAD and the regional economic commissions should co-operate with international centres for public enterprises in developing countries such as that established in Ljubljana.

(ii) The above meetings should also consider studies already undertaken by the UNCTAD Secretariat and APEC-TTI in this area.

(iii) The following measures should be adopted by the international community:

(a) the compilation of a comprehensive and regularly updated handbook of STOs of developing countries, which could serve as a tool for the promotion of their mutual business contacts, should be undertaken by UNCTAD on a priority basis. This handbook should become a significant means of providing information on STOs;

(b) in view of the universally-stressed need for organizing intensive training facilities for STOs, it is recommended that the STOs needs at the national, subregional and regional levels should be evaluated with a view to the organization of seminars and longer-term training programmes for senior and middle-level managerial personnel respectively, tailored to include the specific needs for the co-operation process; and

(c) advisory and consultancy services to individual STOs should be provided on request by international agencies with a capacity in the field of international marketing and procurement. Special regional units for training and consultancy services to STOs should be created and located at a central point in each region, initially for one year, to extend the above services. Among the services to be extended by such units are in-depth studies of those strategic commodities which must lend themselves to joint action.

(iv) (a) The studies on the State Trading organizations, prepared by UNCTAD, regional economic commissions and APEC-TTI, should be duly analysed as a first step by each government.

(b) Subsequent to these analyses, during the fourth quarter of 1979, there shall be a regional evaluation by means of meetings of government experts with the support of the relevant regional organizations as appropriate.

(c) After the above stages, an interregional meeting of government experts of the Group of 77 may be held within the framework of UNCTAD before the end of 1979, to prepare recommendations on the subjects set forth in (iv) (a) above.

C. Establishment of multinational marketing enterprises (MMEs)

7. The Ministers recommend that the following action programme for the promotion of MMEs should be implemented:

(i) support to initiatives generated by public and private promotional schemes (e.g. proposals emerging from State Trading organizations, producers' associations, the Council of Producers' Associations, subregional and regional integration and co-operation schemes, regional and subregional Chambers of Commerce and Industry, and other private and public, national and multinational promoters). Such support would consist of the provision of technical and financial assistance, when requested, to projects for multinational marketing arrangements emerging from such organizations.

(ii) Undertaking direct promotional action through sectoral studies and promotion of open-ended sectoral and multi-sectoral meetings of producers and exporters to detect opportunities and promote new initiatives for multinational marketing action at the subregional, regional and interregional levels, as the case may be, for the commodities identified by the UNCTAD secretariat on the basis of consultations with governments and public and private enterprises.

(iii) The UNCTAD secretariat should expand its research programme to include the analysis of opportunities for the establishment of marketing ventures concerned with import procurement and with the provision of services, with a view to identifying opportunities for expanding the action programme to include such type of activities.

(iv) (a) The studies on multinational marketing enterprises, prepared by UNCTAD, should be duly analysed as a first step by each government.

(b) Subsequent to these analyses, during the fourth quarter of 1979, there shall be a regional evaluation by means of meetings of government experts with the support of the relevant regional economic organizations as appropriate.

(c) After the above stages, interregional meetings of government experts of the Group of 77 may be held within the framework of UNCTAD before the end of 1979, to prepare recommendations on the subjects set forth in (iv) (a) above.

D. Strengthening of subregional, regional and interregional economic integration and co-operation

8. The member governments of the subregional and regional economic groupings of the developing countries should analyse the Report of the Meeting of the Working Group on the Expansion of Trade and Regional Economic Integration among Developing Countries, composed of representatives of the secretariats of the subregional and regional economic groupings of the developing countries, to evaluate its conclusions and within the regional organizations and groupings to which they belong, to give guidelines for possible work in the future by the Intersecretariat Consultative Group proposed in the said report, including a statement about its possible institutionalization. The results of the meeting of these economic groupings would subsequently be compiled in a sufficiently high level meeting of the Group of 77 so that final recommendations may be adopted.

9.  The Ministers recommend that a meeting of the secretariats of economic
co-operation groupings of developing countries on subregional, regiona and
interregional economic co-operation and integration among developing countries
be sponsored in due course by UNCTAD.

E.  Co-operation in the transfer and development of technology

10. The Ministers recommend that:

(i)   UNCTAD should provide support and assistance not only for the strengthening
      or establishment of sectoral, national, subregional and regional centres
      for the transfer and development of technology, but also in the
      establishment of links among such centres in order to elaborate joint
      policies, plans, institutional structures and skill exchange required
      for accelerating the technological capacity of developing countries in
      accordance with their needs, in terms of employment, production and
      income, and with their specific requirements in sectors of critical
      importance to them.

(ii)  In the light of activities being undertaken in the pharmaceutical sector,
      UNCTAD could assist developing countries in identifying and undertaking
      specific action at the subregional and regional levels with respect to
      other sectors of great importance to developing countries.

(iii) Account should be taken of UNCTAD's studies concerning the following
      sectors:  petrochemicals, fertilizers, capital goods in the iron and
      steel sector, electronics, consultancy design and engineering services
      and food processing.

(iv)  Co-operation among developing countries for the exchange of skills should
      be expanded and in this respect UNCTAD in co-operation with other
      United Nations agencies could assist _inter alia_ in the creation of skilled
      manpower pools;  co-ordination among developing countries in education
      and manpower training on a medium-term and long-term basis, creation of
      institutions of developing countries in education and training;
      initiation of technological co-operation programmes funded and managed
      directly by the developing countries, establishment of joint consultancy
      agencies, and establishing a link between skill flows and capital transfer.

(v)   Adequate resources should be made available in order to enable UNCTAD to
      assist actively developing countries in their endeavours.

(vi)  The UNCTAD secretariat should assist developing countries, _inter alia_
      in the elaboration of schemes of preferential treatment among developing
      countries for the exchange of technology.

(vii) The Advisory Service on Technology of UNCTAD should have the means
      commensurate with its task in order to enable it to actively assist
      developing countries in the above endeavours.  In carrying out these
      tasks, the UNCTAD secretariat should co-operate closely with other
      United Nations agencies to ensure co-ordination and avoid duplication.

F.  Least developed countries

11. The Ministers recommend that:

1.  In addition to the major steps to be taken by the developed countries in
support of the efforts of the least developed countries, the developing countries
themselves should provide important support in a number of areas, within the
framework of economic co-operation among developing countries.

2.  A New Programme of Action for the 1980s for the least developed countries
should be launched at UNCTAD V, as recommended by the Intergovernmental Group on
the Least Developed Countries with the following elements:

(a) in addition to non-reciprocal trade preferences, under GSTP, effective special
treatment would be required in favour of products of export interest to least
developed countries, including land-locked and island developing countries on a
non-reciprocal basis;

(b) within regional co-operation schemes among developing countries,

147

arrangements should be made:  (i) for the establishment of multinational ventures
in the least developed countries with a guaranteed regional market;  (ii) for
joint exploitation of common river-basin or other resource potentials, with special
support provisions for participating least developed countries;  (iii) for regional
and subregional training programmes, with special attention to the needs of the
least developed countries in a regional grouping;

(c) developing countries should whenever ready to do so substantially expand
the flow of financial and/or technical assistance support to the least developed
countries;

(d) developed countries and international institutions should assist the
flow of technical and commodity assistance from other developing countries to the
least developed countries by helping to offset the foreign exchange costs of such
flows;

(e) the Secretary-General of UNCTAD, as part of the preparations for the
New Programme of Action for the 1980s for the least developed countries, should
convene a meeting of the developing countries to consider the various measures they
can provide in support of this programme.  Progress and problems in this regard
should be reviewed at subsequent meetings of this type.

## G.    Land-locked and island developing countries

### Land-locked developing countries

12.  In the context of economic co-operation among developing countries and in a
spirit of collective self-reliance, activities among the developing countries
should be intensified, wherever necessary at subregional, and regional and
interregional levels, with a view to solving transit-transport problems keeping
in mind the needs of the least developed countries and the land-locked among them.
In this context, it was recognized that various studies had been conducted by UNCTAD
and at the regional level, and that programmes and activities had been initiated
for least developed countries and land-locked countries among them.

13.  It was also recognized that measures to deal with transit problems of the land-
locked countries require effective co-operation and close collaboration between the
land-locked countries and their transit neighbours.  Where any study is to be
undertaken in any transit country, such study shall be undertaken with the approval
or consent of the transit country concerned.  Where any programme or action is to
be undertaken in or in relation to any transit country, such programme or action
will be undertaken with the approval or consent of that transit country.  Any
proposals in relation to special measures to reduce the transit costs shall be
given due consideration by the transit country.

14.  The Ministers recommend that the adoption of the integrated planning approach
to the transit countries should be based on the following elements:

(a)  full co-operation between land-locked countries and their transit
neighbours;

(b)  clear recognition that major efforts to reduce the cost of access to the
sea and to world markets facing land-locked developing countries may necessitate
improved procedures and new investments both in land-locked and in transit countries
and therefore needed supportive financial assistance by the international community
should be normally extended on especially concessional terms;

(c)  the need to look at and compare all aspects of the problem of transit
transport, including procedures and regulations, pricing policies, management,
training, legal and organizational arrangements, maintenance of existing
infrastructure and new infrastructure requirements.  Past studies have tended to
focus on one or another of these elements, but seldom on their interrelations as
alternative or as complementary ways of reducing real transit costs;

(d)  possibility of alternative routes wherever this is feasible, for each
land-locked developing country, in order to ensure against any difficulties that
may arise on other transit routes;

(e)  the need for providing planners from land-locked and transit countries
with basic information on all the available options.

148

Island developing countries

15. **The Ministers recommend that** co-operative arrangements in favour of island developing countries should be intensified in areas such as the development of shipping, air services, telecommunications, tourism, insurance and re-insurance.

H. **Subregional, regional and interregional insurance and re-insurance schemes among developing countries**

16. **The Ministers recommend that** a medium-term action plan for enhanced support should be aimed at intensifying present efforts in order to:

  (i)   strengthen national insurance markets in developing countries, as particularly called for in UNCTAD resolution 42 (III);

  (ii)  the UNCTAD secretariat should intensify its work programme in the field of insurance and report on progress of work to the Committee on Invisibles and Financing related to Trade;

  (iii) increased reciprocal exchange of re-insurance business aimed at a corresponding decrease of the existing dependence of developing countries on outside developed re-insurance markets; and

  (iv)  promote technical and institutional mechanisms, adequate professional skills and operational methods with a view to generating insurance service fully adapted to the increasing needs and specific requirements of developing countries.

I. **Monetary and financial co-operation**

17. **The Ministers recommend that:**

  (i)  **Multilateral payments and credit arrangements**

    (a.)  The strengthening of the existing arrangements is considered to be a priority task. It is to be expected that, as more experience is gained in the operation of multilateral schemes, the scope of these mechanisms will be widened. Furthermore, the setting up of new payments arrangements needs to be encouraged.

    (b)   The establishment and development of subregional payments arrangements has shown that they constitute an appropriate starting point to foster a gradual approach towards the creation of a global network of multilateral schemes open to all developing countries, the expectation being that at a later stage, an important element of reciprocal credits to support mutual trade flows will be incorporated. Fundamental importance is attached to the need for adopting all necessary steps aimed at promoting a gradual but prompt linking up of multilateral payments arrangements within a global strategy for the expansion of trade.

    (c)   The creation of the Co-ordination Committee on Multilateral Payments Arrangements and Monetary Co-operation as the first forum of monetary co-operation at the interregional level among arrangements of developing countries is a most positive step and its objectives deserve strong support. The Committee, without being a formal institution, is capable of bringing together the technical expertise required and has an open-ended membership which allows for universal coverage of the developing countries in their objectives of improving existing arrangements, establishing new ones and then progressively creating links among them. The Group of 77 should invite the Co-ordination Committee to prepare a balanced strategy for the linkage of payments arrangements and to provide the necessary assistance through its Technical Secretariat to achieve this objective.

    (d)   UNCTAD can play an important role as Technical Secretariat of the Committee in the achievement of its goals in collaboration with economic regional commissions, IMF and other relevant international and regional institutions. The facilitation of the exchange of information and experience between the various multilateral

149

arrangements with the financial support of UNDP and other sources should be continued and strengthened.

(ii) Trade financing

(a) The progress made in recent years in several developing areas in the establishment, strengthening and expansion of regional and subregional financial institutions as well as of national mechanisms that provide direct financing of exports of interested developing countries, deserves to be underlined. Developing countries should continue devising mechanisms to finance trade together with the reinforcement of the system for exchanging commercial information, including the availability and supply of goods, through national and regional export promotion institutions.

(b) Without prejudice to the efforts being made in regard to an Export Credit Guarantee Facility, and as a part of the Programme of Work on economic co-operation among developing countries, the Secretary-General of UNCTAD should be requested to present proposals for the setting up of a Financing Facility exclusively aimed at the expansion of trade among developing countries, with special attention to the situation of the least developed countries.

(iii) A bank of developing countries

Consideration should be given to strengthening the importance of existing subregional and regional development banks to ensure that such institutions fully respond to the needs of developing countries. In addition the UNCTAD secretariat should be requested to submit a report on the practical feasibility of establishing a bank for developing countries on sound banking practices taking into account existing institutions. The report should be submitted by the Secretary-General to a group of governmental representatives of developing countries, for subsequent consideration.

(iv) Mobilization of resources among developing countries

(a) The UNCTAD secretariat should continue its efforts in the preparation of reports on financial flows among developing countries on an annual basis as a part of the work programme of economic co-operation among developing countries, covering all financial flows and contributions in accordance with Part IV, 26, of the Mexico City mandate.

(b) A special study of the capital markets of developing countries should be undertaken by the UNCTAD secretariat for the purpose of improving access by other developing countries to these markets. Furthermore, this study has to identify measures and the means of their implementation with a view to encouraging investment among developing countries on the basis of mutual benefits and sound commercial practice, as recommended in Part IV, 25, of the Mexico City Conference report.

(c) The UNCTAD secretariat should continue to assist developing countries to strengthen the existing multilateral financial institutions by reinforcing their mutual links and co-ordinating their activities in order to enable them to identify, prepare, promote and finance large-scale projects in all fields of economic co-operation among developing countries (Part I, 2 and IV, 23(e) and (g) of the Mexico City Conference Report).

(v) Preference in procurement

International financial institutions should give preferential treatment to procurement from developing countries in implementing projects in other developing countries.

(vi) Monetary co-operation: The monetary authorities of developing countries should strengthen their mutual exchange of information on monetary and financial matters in accordance with the rules and regulations of the concerned countries, as well as on subjects dealing with the general monetary situation and its effects on developing countries.

150

18.  The Ministers are of the view that member Governments of the Group of 77 should avail themselves of the occasion of the Bank/Fund meeting in Belgrade in 1979 to convene a meeting of the Group of 77 at the level of Ministers of Finance or Economy and in this connexion request the Government of Yugoslavia to make appropriate arrangements for such a meeting in consultation with the Chairman of the Group of 24.

J.  Multinational production enterprises among developing countries (MPEs)

19.  The Ministers recognize the need for:

(a)  The formulation of long-term issues and policy guidelines for the identification and selection of multi-country production projects among developing countries, taking into consideration current trends and prospects in the international economy;

(b)  co-ordinating the supply of technical assistance from UNCTAD and other international organizations of the United Nations system, within their respective fields of competence, in support of the developing countries' efforts for strengthening their mutual co-operation for the establishment of multinational production enterprises;

(c)  UNCTAD to formulate a clear definition of the concept of multinational production enterprises among developing countries and formulate any other proposals which might serve developing countries to promote production of multinational production enterprises, and to submit its report to a meeting of representatives of developing countries for consideration and action;

(d)  co-operation in production drawing significant benefits from (i) barter arrangements, i.e. payments by products obtained through joint enterprises; (ii) long-term contracts for the provision of goods essential for the national economies; and (iii) technical co-operation.

20.  The Ministers recommend that on the basis of past experiences and existing situation, the identification and establishment of multinational production enterprises could be based on the following:

(a)  projects physically located in one or more countries of significant economic interest to two or more countries;

(b)  projects which have either significant input or output linkages with new or existing facilities in more than one country and/or projects involving the location of complementarity and similar facilities in one or more countries, and

(c)  projects which could only be economically and efficiently developed on the basis of markets larger than any single country could provide.

21.  The Ministers recommend that:

(i)  consideration be given to the following indicative list of sectoral investment possibilities:

(a)  the production, marketing and distribution of social goods based on complementarities and suitable for the establishment of modular projects;

(b)  the rational development and processing of non-renewable resources, with special emphasis on petroleum projects and unwrought non-ferrous metals;

(c)  the optimal exploitation of natural resources for the efficient development of agro-business projects through the processing of primary products;

(d)  the development of basic industries;

(e)  the development of the engineering industries, with special emphasis on capital goods;

(f)  the development of industries belonging to sectors with long-term growth and rapid growth potential.

151

(ii) The nature of an institutional arrangement for the promotion of multinational production among developing countries should be left to the decision of the participating governments.

(iii) Regional development banks and private development financing institutions should play an important role in providing financing for the feasibility studies of selected projects, as well as equity and long-term financing.

(iv) UNCTAD in collaboration with regional economic commissions and subregional economic groupings should concentrate its activities as follows:

(a) in the formulation and evaluation of sectoral studies leading to the identification and selection of multi-country projects among developing countries within the order of priorities established by interested countries;

(b) in providing a forum for devising intergovernmental framework agreements for working out trade and related measures facilitating the negotiation and operation of industrial collaboration agreements among interested parties, and

(c) in formulating sectoral studies in the field of basic industries, of which those on fertilizers, rubber products and pulp and paper should be completed at an early stage and should constitute a basis for consultation with interested governments and intergovernmental bodies, in close collaboration with UNIDO, FAO and the regional commissions; and

(d) the overall promotion of trade expansion and development through multinational production enterprises among developing countries and the linking of the latter with multinational marketing enterprises, joint ventures, integration arrangements and financial institutions.

K. Other substantive items contained in the Mexico City Programme on Economic Co-operation among Developing Countries and in the programme of work established in resolution 1 (I) of the UNCTAD Committee on Economic Co-operation among Developing Countries

22. As regards the other items included in resolution 1(I) of the Committee on Economic Co-operation among Developing Countries and in the Mexico City Programme, procedures should be adopted to ensure that, where necessary, after the Governments have studied them there is a wide regional and interregional examination of those items, so that the appropriate measures may be recommended.

L. Support measures

23. In view of the fact that the programme of meetings on economic co-operation among developing countries, proposed by the Group of 77, 1/ was not agreed on at the eighteenth session of the Trade and Development Board, nor at the second session of the Committee on Economic Co-operation among Developing Countries, due to the opposition of the developed countries, and considering that the United Nations General Assembly, at its recent thirty-third session, instructed the Secretary-General of UNCTAD to continue consultations to decide on said programme, and taking into account paragraphs 81 and 82 of the Provisional Report of the Preparatory Committee of the Group of 77;

The Ministers recommend that:

(i) the position formally adopted by the Group of 77 be ratified and that the need for this programme be stressed and the intention to execute it be fully expressed.

(ii) the developed countries be urged to abandon the negative attitude adopted up to the present and contribute to the implementation of the relevant resolutions of the United Nations General Assembly, thereby taking the first steps towards compliance with the concept of support measures, as stated in UNCTAD resolution 92 (IV) and resolution 1(I) of the Committee for Economic Co-operation among Developing Countries.

---

1/ For the programme of meetings, see the appendix to the present item.

(iii) the role of UNCTAD's ECDC Committee be strengthened to enable it to be
a forum for the negotiation of support measures from developed to
developing countries since such measures constitute a basic element
of the whole process of economic co-operation among developing countries
to which developed countries are expected to make meaningful contributions.

(iv) (a) UNCTAD should upon request of developing countries, subregional,
regional and interregional economic groupings of developing
countries assist in preparing specific proposals for support
measures as need arises;

(b) developed countries respond positively to such requests when they
are made;

(c) any assistance extended on a subregional, regional or interregional
basis should be in addition to assistance extended to individual
developing countries.

24. The Ministers strongly recommend that:

1. the United Nations system, in particular UNCTAD and the regional and
economic commissions, should strengthen and increase its assistance
to economic co-operation among developing countries. In this regard,
the UNDP should intensify its assistance to subregional, regional
and interregional projects, taking also into account the role foreseen
for UNDP by the World Conference on Technical Co-operation among
Developing Countries. To this end, adequate resources should be made
available.

2. Specifically the Ministers recommend that:

(a) measures should be taken by the United Nations to intensify the
role of UNCTAD within the United Nations system in the promotion
of economic co-operation among developing countries and its
co-ordination and co-operation with other members of the
United Nations system, as well as to strengthen its working
arrangements with UNDP, with a view to enhancing joint operational
strategies, taking into account the strong co-relation between
economic and technical co-operation among developing countries;

(b) as a matter of priority, each developing country should consider
drawing up, with the assistance of UNCTAD, a full national inventory
of its own requirements and resources and contribute to the updating
of the general inventory that UNCTAD should compile in order to
match inputs and needs at the global level;

(c) developing countries should support, through individual or
collective endorsement, project proposals addressed to UNDP in
support of economic co-operation among developing countries. To
this effect, they may wish to consider special contributions,
including as appropriate earmarking of a proportion of their own
UNDP Indicative Planning Figures (IPF);

(d) acknowledging that economic co-operation among developing countries
is an important element of the New International Economic Order and,
as such is based on interdependence, common interest and co-operation
among all States, developing countries should invite, through the
United Nations development system, contributions from developed
countries for the implementation of economic co-operation among
developing countries projects whose objectives are of interest to
both categories of countries;

(e) developing countries should urge the United Nations system, and
particularly UNDP, to devote increasing the IPF resources to
result-oriented activities in support of economic co-operation
among developing countries, with special stress on the need for
substantially increasing UNDP's resources for subregional, regional
and interregional projects in this field;

(f) developing countries should request UNCTAD to intensify both its

rôle within the United Nations system in the promotion of economic
co-operation among developing countries and its co-ordination and
co-operation among developing countries and co-operation with other
members of the United Nations system, as well as to strengthen its
working arrangements with UNDP, with a view to joint operational
strategies given the strong correlation between economic and technical
co-operation among developing countries;

(g) the restructuring process of the United Nations system should ensure
that UNCTAD is strengthened and provided with all its necessary
human and financial means to effectively carry out its tasks on
economic co-operation among developing countries, which have
increased significantly without any meaningful additions to its
resources nor appropriate changes in its institutional set-up that
could enhance its role as a lead agency in the establishment of the
New International Economic Order;

. (h) the UNCTAD secretariat, in carrying out its tasks on Economic
Co-operation among Developing Countries, should work in close
consultation and co-operation with the regional economic commissions
since they have a vital role in promoting and implementing subregional,
regional and interregional economic co-operation among developing
countries.

## M.  Institutional matters

25.  The Ministers recommend that consideration should be given to the nature of
institutional arrangements for the organization and administration of economic
co-operation among developing countries at national, subregional, regional and
interregional levels.  Further, the Ministers consider that the institutional
profile needed to implement the Economic Co-operation Programme among Developing
Countries could take the following forms:

1. Periodic meetings at the ministerial level for the Group of 77:  Such
meetings would fall within the framework of the provisions of
resolution No. 1 of the III Ministerial Meeting of the Group of 77,
held at Manila, and paragraphs 41, 42 and 43 of the Final Report of
Conference on Economic Co-operation among Developing Countries held
in Mexico, for the purpose of defining economic co-operation, policy
sectors and priority areas.  Further the Ministers consider that to
carry out the studies recommended by the Ministerial Meeting, the
secretariats of the United Nations agencies, especially UNCTAD, UNDP,
the regional commissions and the regional and subregional organizations
for economic co-operation and integration of the developing countries,
should give the necessary support to the Group of 77;

2. Action committees:  It is necessary to find a formula for participation
open to all those developing countries interested in one specific aspect
or area that will enable a project to be implemented among the interested
countries.  For the consideration of developing countries a novel formula
for co-operation called Action Committees is presented.  These are organs
which could be established within a limited time to analyse and launch
projects of common interest to three or more member countries but providing
the opportunity for other developing countries to participate subsequently.
The Group of 77 takes note with interest of the significant experience of
one developing region concerning this instrument.

## N.  Technical co-operation and economic co-operation among developing countries

26.  The Ministers recall that technical co-operation among developing countries,
as conceived by the developing countries on several previous occasions and by the
United Nations Conference on Technical Co-operation among Developing Countries,
is a fundamental instrument in promoting economic co-operation among developing
countries.  They consider that:

(i) prompt and effective implementation of the Buenos Aires Plan of Action
and resolutions approved by the above-mentioned Conference is required;

(ii) among the many important provisions contained in the Buenos Aires Action
Plan in this context is the need to promote in the developing countries

national research and training centres of multinational scope in the developing countries.  This is also the subject of one of the resolutions adopted by the Conference.

(iii)    in support of the implementation of the Plan of Action, the importance of the contribution of developed countries and international organizations to the increased national and collective self-reliance of developing countries, needs to be stressed, in order to implement, inter alia, the recommendations relating to agriculture and industry.

(iv)    as the first meeting of the United Nations intergovernmental forum, which has been assigned the responsibility of the overall review of TCDC, as agreed in Buenos Aires, will take place in 1980, the Group of 77 must take the necessary measures to adequately prepare for this meeting, so as to reach a common position prior to the above-mentioned meetings.  To this end the Group of 77 should hold a preparatory meeting preceded by regional preparatory meetings.

Appendix

Programme of meetings to be convened by the UNCTAD secretariat by the end of 1979 for the Group of 77 as follows:

1.    Regional meetings of subregional and regional economic co-operation groupings to consider action in pursuance of the objectives of the Mexico City Programme on Economic Co-operation among Developing Countries.

2.    A meeting of the secretariats of economic co-operation groupings of developing countries on subregional, regional and interregional economic co-operation and integration among developing countries.

3.    Three meetings of governmental experts of developing countries to examine and make proposals, bearing in mind the studies undertaken by the UNCTAD secretariat in compliance with paragraph 2(a) of resolution 1(I) adopted at the first session of the Committee on Economic Co-operation among Developing Countries.

4.    A meeting of secretariats of economic co-operation groupings and multilateral financial institutions of developing countries on inter-country projects.


III.  FRAMEWORK FOR NEGOTIATIONS

Item 8
of the provisional agenda for UNCTAD V

Evaluation of the world trade and economic situation and consideration of issues, policies and appropriate measures to facilitate structural changes in the international economy, taking into account the interrelationships of problems in the areas of trade, development, money and finance with a view to attaining the establishment of a new international economic order and bearing in mind the further evolution that may be needed in the rules and principles governing international economic relations and UNCTAD's necessary contribution to a New International Development Strategy for the Third United Nations Development Decade.

I.    Evaluation of the world trade and economic situation

1.    The world economy is currently in the most serious crisis since the end of the Second World War.  The continuing economic malaise in the international economic system is not simply a phenomenon of cyclical nature, but primarily a symptom of underlying structural maladjustments.  The inability of the developed market economy countries to control their chronic balance-of-payments imbalances, persistently high levels of inflation and unemployment, and the new market rigidities manifested in rising protectionism, that prohibit the structural changes needed for an efficient path of production, all point to new developments that do not augur well for a well-balanced and prosperous world economy in the coming decade.  It is these new developments originating in the developed countries that raise new and profound

155

concerns for the developing countries.  Not only is the progress towards resolving
those issues that have long been of concern to developing countries likely to be
retarded, the fundamental problems themselves are currently being exacerbated by many
of the new imbalances that have emerged in recent years.  Not only have domestic
inflationary pressures been strengthened with a loss of potential GDP, developing
countries are being penalized as prospective markets of the developing countries
are closed off by over protectionism and industrial subsidies.

2.    The international economy, after a series of events in the 1970s including the
breakdown of the Bretton Woods monetary system in 1971, the world economic crisis of
inflation/recession, the rising tide of protectionism in developed countries, is in a
state of fundamental disequilibrium.  Decisions are being made on an ad hoc basis
and the specific policy measures which are taken in developed countries to protect
their domestic producers, have resulted in their structural adjustment difficulties
being transferred to developing countries.  This transference, inter alia, manifests
itself in disrupted markets for the developing countries and new balance-of-payments
difficulties.    Their deficits themselves are largely a reflection of the failure of
developed countries to adjust;  unless effective adjustment measures are taken by
developed countries the developing countries would continue to bear the burden of
adjustments.  Contemporary institutional and other arrangements have done little to
alleviate the burden for developing countries and in fact in some cases have
contributed to aggravate it.

3.    The failure of the existing international economic order to provide adequate and
equitable support to the international development process has had serious
repercussions on the economies of the developing countries especially on the
economies of the least developed countries.  The volume and value of trade of the
developing countries and the real value and purchasing power of their foreign
exchange earnings have been adversely affected.  At the same time a disproportionately
large share of burden of adjustment in the world economy has been thrown on the
economies of these countries.

4.    Moreover, recent developments in the world economy clearly demonstrate that the
existing international economic order is not only inequitable but also is functioning
inefficiently.  Accelerated development of the developing countries and efficient
functioning of the world economy requires a fundamental restructuring of the
international economic order.

5.    Also, in the existing international economic order developing countries have
little say in the manner of its functioning.  This is not surprising, in as much as
the decision-making related to the management of the world economy, the designation
of the rules of the game for international economic transactions and the power to
initiate changes in such rules have been the exclusive domain of the major developed
countries.

6.    It is worth pointing out in this context that in the current economic crisis
developed countries are wholly preoccupied by short-term economic policies aimed at
their own economic recovery.  A perception is emerging within some developed countries
that the crisis cannot be resolved without structural changes in their own economies.
But their actions so far have failed to demonstrate that for these changes to be
viable, they must be consistent with the broader objectives of establishing the
New International Economic Order and mindful of the causal link between the policies
of developed countries and the development of developing countries.  The emphasis
should shift to concerted measures for restructuring as the primary means to achieve
stable and sustained economic recovery.  This also requires a recognition by the
developed countries of the interrelationship between structural changes and measures
designed to generate growth in aggregate demand and production capacities in the
developing countries, to thus revive the process of growth in the global economy.
A recognition of this interrelationship by the developed countries would greatly help
towards injecting a new dynamism into the international negotiation process.

II.    Issues, policies and measures to facilitate structural changes

7.    In considering issues, policies and measures to facilitate structural changes in
the international economy it is important, however, to recognize that the concept of
structural change covers several distinct, though interrelated elements.  First,
structural change covers shifts in the patterns of production, consumption and trade
in the world economy.  A second element, related more specifically to the
international context, concerns the pattern of effective national control over the use

156

of their own resources. The third element relates to restructuring of the institutional framework including creations of new institutional framework, if necessary, to promote and support both the aspects of structural change referred to. One of the requirements of structural change would, of course, be larger share of developing countries in the international decision-making process.

8. Since increased economic and technical co-operation between the developing countries constitute a key element in the restructuring of the present international economic order, further efforts must be made, on the principle of collective self-reliance, to strengthen and develop the economic links between the developing countries. A new dimension in a restructured international economy exists in the field of trade and economic co-operation between the developing countries and the socialist countries of Eastern Europe and these important links should be nurtured and further strengthened.

9. Furthermore, the various aspects of structural change in the economies of both developed and developing countries, which are called for in different areas under other items, are related to supporting changes in the international institutional framework. The Common Fund and international commodity agreements under the integrated Programme for Commodities, the evolution of principles and policies to promote long-term industrial adjustments in developed countries, a reform of the international monetary system and an effective system of international financial co-operation for development, the code of conduct on transfer of technology, principles and rules on restrictive business practices are some of the elements of a new international institutional framework necessary to support and promote the structural changes that are required in the international economy.

10. There are, however, some further aspects of the international institutional framework which require careful consideration. Because of the close interrelationship that exists between the problems and issues in the areas of trade, development, money and finance, the rules and principles governing international relations in these areas as well as policies and measures in these areas need to be mutually supportive, and directed to the same basic objective. To ensure this, there are issues which require particularly urgent attention of the international community:

    (a) there is a need for global consultation in the fields of trade, development, money and finance, in order to ensure not only their mutual consistency but also that short-term policies promote, and do not obstruct, the movement towards long-term restructuring of the international economy.

    (b) how to set in motion further evolution of the rules and principles governing international trade and economic relations.

11. Generally speaking, the existing principles, rules and procedures governing international economic relations in the area of trade, money and finance, though they have been variously adapted to meet on an ad hoc basis changing conditions in the world economy and make provisions for accommodating some of the needs of the developing countries, have not yet been restructured in order to provide firm support for the development process in the developing countries.

III. Further evolution of the rules and principles governing international trade and economic relations

12. It is worth noting that under the pressure of imbalances in the world economy the framework established in the post-war period to govern international economic relations is threatened with disintegration and it is becoming increasingly difficult for governments of even developed countries to solve their problems within the existing principles, rules and procedures. The most apparent evidence of this disintegration was a collapse in 1971 of the Bretton Woods System. Equally important are the increasing strains being placed on the GATT principles and rules. In the recent past there has been a clear tendency of many developed countries to adopt commercial policies that are against the spirit and letter of GATT.

13. In addition to the requirements for the reform of the international monetary system, there is also a need to revise the existing principles, rules and procedures governing international trade. Rules and procedures having origin in GATT were originally negotiated in early post-war period without the participation of the present developing countries. Changes since then do not affect the underlying philosophy of the rules which are not responsive to the trade, development and financial needs of the developing countries.

14. To sum up the existing rules and principles governing international trade have become largely outmoded and ineffective. There is need for thorough revision, based on the new realities of the world economy to establish a system in which the development of the developing countries is a principal goal, with appropriate mechanisms to ensure that the system operates equitably and efficiently.

15. The existing trading rules need revision so as to extend them to cover the new protective devices falling outside the scope of the existing rules, intra-firm trade of transnational corporations, which is now a major segment of world trade and of the trade of developing countries, and which in effect, also evades the existing rules.

16. While the satisfaction of basic human needs of the people, and the eradication of mass poverty must have a high priority in economic and social development, the idea is unacceptable and erroneous that these goals can be achieved without the all round and comprehensive economic development of the developing countries and the establishment of the New International Economic Order. It is necessary for developing countries to guard against the introduction of new concepts by developed countries, norms and principles, such as "basic needs" access to supplies, graduation, selectivity, etc. which are being suggested but are in fact totally incompatible with the development requirements and aspirations of developing countries. Initiatives seeking piecemeal solutions or fragmentary measures for international co-operation would not be substitutes for the urgent need to rewrite, in the light of current world realities, the rules and principles governing international trade.

17. The need for concerted action for inducing structural changes and for reformulating and renegotiating the present unfair "rules of the game" is now fully recognized. This should not, however, divert the attention from serious issues requiring immediate implementation of the International Economic Order.

18. The Group of 77 recommend that the UNCTAD V request the Secretary-General of UNCTAD, according to the relevant resolutions of the Conference and the Board, to set up a high level intergovernmental Group of Experts:

    (a) to examine the problems relating to the management of the world economy, especially policies in the fields of trade, development, money and finance.

    (b) to recommend the adoption of concerted measures that would ensure that the policies of the developed countries are consistent with the requirements of the structural changes in the context of the New International Economic Order.

19. The Secretary-General of UNCTAD is requested to submit the reports of the abovementioned Group of Experts for consideration at the Trade and Development Board and special attention should be given to these reports at the regular sessions of the Board to be held at ministerial level.

IV. New international development strategy

20. The central element of the international development strategy of the Third United Nations Development Decade should be the implementation of the Programme of Action for the establishment of the New International Economic Order and in this context action needs to be taken to enhance the share of developing countries in the international decision making for management of the world economy.

21. The new strategy should also stress that:

    (i) The international economic policies of the developed countries, including economic groupings of the developed countries and their national policies having international implications, should contribute towards promoting the growth of the developing countries, taking into account their long-term and short-term development requirements.

    (ii) An important objective of industrial, social, trade, monetary, financial and regional policy initiatives by the developed countries should be to maintain and increase the production capacity and real purchasing power of the developing countries.

    (iii) The situation of the least developed countries should be given particular attention in the programme of action for the 1980s.

    (iv) Adequate attention should be paid to the eradication of mass poverty and to raising the living standards of people in the developing countries.

Item 9
of the provisional agenda for UNCTAD V

DEVELOPMENTS IN INTERNATIONAL TRADE

Item 9(a): Protectionism: trends and short-term and long-term policies and
actions needed to deal with the problems

The Group of 77, alarmed by the wave of protectionist measures introduced in
the recent years by developed countries and affecting particularly exports of
developing countries in the sectors based on their own raw materials and skills where
the comparative advantage shifted in their favour and opened up important perspectives
of growth of their industries, express their deep concern about the adverse effects
of such measures on the process of restructuring of the world industrial production
and trade consistent with their economic interests. The wave of protectionist
measures taken by the developed countries with growing frequency over the past years
is particularly affecting the developing countries by retarding the process of
structural change in the industrial sectors referred to above and making it more
difficult to achieve the substantial increase in the exports of manufactures and
semi-manufactures by developing countries that would be required inter alia, to
attain the Lima Target and developments of the economies of the developing countries.
The Group of 77 expressed their concern at the emergence in developed countries of
cartels and use of new devices such as "trigger price mechanisms", voluntary export
restraints and orderly marketing arrangements to restrain trade. They further
expressed concern at attempts by the developed countries to find solutions to
sectoral trade problems in exclusive fora instead of bodies with widest international
representations. Viewing these developments with deep concern, the Group of 77
decides that at UNCTAD V effective action should be taken to deal with this problem
and to agree on a programme of co-ordinated international action focusing on the
formulation of short-term policies and actions that curb protectionism and on
long-term policies for world industrial restructuring.

1.   To this end the Group of 77:

     (a)  deplores the new protectionist trends in the developed countries, which
have serious consequences for the developing countries;

     (b)  reaffirms the conviction that the proper solution is to be found in world
industrial restructuring consistent with the development objectives of the
developing countries;

     (c)  declares that when faced with proposed or adopted protectionist measures
by a developed country or group of developed countries, that affect the exports of
the developing countries, including the conclusion or the extension of voluntary
export restraints, the developing country or countries affected, without detriment
to any bilateral action that it deems or they deem advisable, may consult with other
interested developing countries, with a view to determining appropriate joint action.

     This joint action would include, inter alia, voluntary measures of economic,
financial or commercial policies with a view to counteracting the protectionist
measures imposed by any developed country or a group of developed countries against
developing countries.

2.   At UNCTAD V agreement should be reached on the following measures and actions:

A.   Long-term policies and actions for world industrial restructuring

     Long-term policies for world industrial restructuring in the interest of an
optimal over-all growth requires conscious efforts by the international community to
establish rational production patterns in the world. In this connexion there is need
to follow closely the evolution of the patterns of production and trade in the world,
identifying in developed countries the sectors requiring adjustment in order to
facilitate the movement of factors of production out of such sectors and in developing
countries the sectors deserving special encouragement and support with a view to
achieving the most effective international inter-industry and intra-industry
specialization. The following policy measures and actions should be agreed to this
effect:

     (a)  The setting up of a mechanism within UNCTAD which would allow for periodic
review of the patterns of production and trade in the world economy and identify

159

sectors needing structural adjustment with a view to achieving a better international division of labour and transference of production capacities to developing countries in the light of their comparative advantage and need to promote processing of their raw materials.

(b) An agreement on a framework for negotiations within UNCTAD to formulate, in co-operation with UNIDO and ILO, the measures and policies that need to be adopted by developed countries for encouraging the process of adjustment in the sectors so identified, and to facilitate the movement of factors of production out of such sectors.

(c) Constant monitoring should be undertaken,

(i)  to avoid development of excessive and uneconomical capacities in the developed countries which may lead to demand for protection, and

(ii)  to ensure the implementation of policies and measures as referred to in sub-paragraph (b).

(d) The agreement on world restructuring should be linked _inter alia_ to the target of 25 per cent share in world production of and 30 per cent of world trade in manufactures for developing countries by the year 2000. This should be based not only on inter-industry specialization which would leave labour intensive goods for production by developing countries but also on intra-industry specialization for different sectors and branches of an industry.

(e) UNCTAD should intensify its work on compiling and up-dating the inventory of barriers faced by exports of both agricultural and processed and manufactured products of developing countries in developed countries, with a view to holding consultations and negotiations for the dismantling of such barriers within a time bound frame.

(f) Sectoral agreements which lead to restrictions on trade of developing countries should not be formulated and those in existence should be dismantled to provide for free access to the products of developing countries. Developed countries should not find solutions to trade problems of different sectors in exclusive forums without participation of developing countries and outside bodies with widest international representation. They should take steps to effectively discourage setting up cartels and for dismantling the existing ones which are having a restrictive effect on the trade of developing countries.

B.  Policy measures and action needed to deal with the immediate short-term problems

Agreement should be reached with the developed countries, aimed at:

(a) The removal of existing restrictions imposed by developed countries against exports of developing countries within the shortest possible time bound frame and the adoption of measures to attain a considerable increase in the imports of products exported by developing countries presently subject to restrictions;

(b) There should be a reaffirmation of the "standstill" by developed countries and a decision should be taken at UNCTAD V to set up an effective intergovernmental body of experts to examine _suo moto_ in each specific case of protective action by developed countries against imports from developing countries whether there are "compelling reasons which make it impossible" to avoid such an action against imports of developing countries. In this connexion, arrangements should be made to inform UNCTAD of such protective actions which do not take into account the developing countries' interests in foreign trade or are injurious to such trade.

(c) The safeguard action by developed countries when impossible to avoid, should be under strictly defined conditions as outlined below and arise out of unforeseen and sudden development.

(i)  In any case, the restrictions imposed must be considered emergency action taken on a specific product and must be preceded by notification and subsequent negotiations with the developing countries which this affects;

(ii)  Any restriction should be temporary and degressive over an agreed time period and should include provision for the increase of the imports affected and allow the entry of new suppliers of the imports affected from the developing countries;

   (iii)   The restrictions will be accompanied by appropriate adjustment measures that ensure the temporary nature of such restrictions;

   (iv)   Moreover, the restrictions imposed should under no circumstances be such as to result in reduction in exports or output of the developing countries and thereby have adverse effects on their economies;

   (v)   The developing countries whose exports are adversely affected as a result of safeguard action should be adequately compensated;

   (vi)   Safeguard action should be non-discriminatory. In no case shall the exports of developing countries be singled out for action, through various devices, particularly on grounds such as that they are low cost exports.

   (d)   Measures should be taken to ensure the elimination of tariff escalation so as to provide more improved access to exports of manufactures and semi-manufactures from the developing countries.

   (e)   A strategy for surveillance of the protectionist actions by the developed countries which will facilitate the organization of concerted action, must be defined. For this, it would be desirable to make intensive use of and strengthen the present mechanisms, and those which may be established, within the framework of UNCTAD, with a view to examining the problem of protectionism in its general and particular aspects in order to formulate recommendations for its reduction or elimination.

## Item 9(b): Multilateral trade negotiations: evaluation and further recommendations arising therefrom

1. The Group of 77 reviewed the progress made in the MTNs so far and noted with grave concern that the developed countries have devoted most of their attention to their mutual trade and have failed to respond to the interests and concerns of the developing countries including the least developed countries consistent with the commitments undertaken in the Tokyo Declaration. The Group of 77 apprehend that unless corrective measures are taken at this stage, the results of the negotiations for the developing countries would be negative. It was stressed that, in their present form the draft codes for establishing the new rules for international trade responded basically to the interests of the developed countries, did not give due consideration to those of the developing countries, including the least developed among developing countries, and tended to institutionalize the protectionist policies presently being applied by the developed countries. The Group of 77 calls upon the developed countries participating in the MTN, to comply with the commitments undertaken in the Tokyo Declaration with respect to granting the developing countries special and more favourable treatment in each of the areas of negotiations. It emphasized that the developing countries, whose interests have so far received limited attention in the MTN, should thoroughly examine the consequences which the results of the MTN will have on their participation in future world trade and on the establishment of the New International Economic Order.

2. The Group of 77 expressed their disappointment with the deep concern over the mechanics of the negotiations which have led to a lack of transparency in the MTN, compromised their multilateral character and afforded little scope for participation by the developing countries. Further, the developing countries are being asked to make concessions not consistent with their trade, development and financial needs. This makes it necessary to make a thorough evaluation of the process of negotiation for the future.

3. Decisions in the MTNs shall be taken by consensus and agreement of participating developing countries, especially in the case of codes which are sought to be adopted. No code should be considered to have been adopted in the MTN or in the GATT without the agreement of developing countries participating in the negotiations. No additional obligations should result for the developing countries from the codes to be adopted in the MTN or in the GATT without the agreement of developing countries participating in them.

4. In this context the Ministers of the Group of 77 stress the following:

## (a)    Tropical products

Developed countries should respond favourably in conformity with the commitments in the Tokyo Declaration to request on tropical products from developing countries to improve the developed countries' offers. Developed countries which have not implemented their offers should do so immediately. All barriers to trade faced by all tropical products, including their processed forms, in developed countries should be removed. To the extent that this objective will not be achieved in the Tokyo Round, further endeavours will be needed and negotiations will have to be continued for the removal of these barriers.

## (b)    Other agricultural products

Developing countries note with concern that no results have been realized in the field of agricultural products, especially concerning the most stable and favourable treatment for the suppliers from developing countries.

## (c)    Tariffs and non-tariff barriers

The products of interest to developing countries should not be excluded from tariff-concessions especially in sectors like textiles, leather, rubber and wood products. However, developing countries having a substantial interest and which may be affected by tariff reductions may seek the exclusion of any specific products.

There should be advanced implementation of tariff cuts for products of particular interest to developing countries.

Developing countries also note with deep concern that no action has been taken by developed countries for the removal of quantitative restrictions faced by products of developing countries and that quantitative restrictions in certain sectors like textiles have not even been discussed in the negotiations. Therefore measures should be taken for the removal of such barriers immediately.

## (d)    Safeguard

Action should continue to be taken on a most-favoured-nation basis, under strictly defined conditions of market injury or threat thereof, and shall not be used to discriminate against exports of developing countries. Developing countries view with deep concern the continuing discriminatory treatment of their exports on grounds of lower costs or prices. They urge that the new code on safeguards should call for very early termination of all such discriminatory measures whether national or under multilateral arrangements. They reject attempts at giving legitimacy to such discriminatory treatment. The concept of unilateral selective action even on a provisional basis should be rejected. The so-called "voluntary export restraints" and "orderly marketing arrangements" should be brought under the discipline of the Code being evolved in the area of safeguards and be subjected to multilateral review. There should be special and differentiated treatment for developing countries in the context of the safeguard code. As a measure of such differential and more favourable treaement in favour of developing countries the newcomers and small supplier developing countries should be excluded from safeguards. The safeguard action by developed countries against imports of developing countries should be time bound and accompanied by adjustment measures. Safeguard action should in no case result in the roll back of the exports of the developing countries.

## (e)    Subsidies and countervailing duties

The right of developing countries to use export and other subsidies to diversify their economies and to achieve their socio-economic objectives of development shall be recognized. The developing countries have the right to use export subsidies to overcome structural disadvantages from which their economies and export sectors suffer. Countervailing duties may be levied against subsidized imports of developing countries only in exceptional cases and only after determination of "material injury" on the basis of objective criteria and when all bilateral and multilateral consultation procedures have been exhausted. No action shall be taken on the basis of displacement of exports of developed countries by subsidized exports of developing countries in relation to a third country market, by developed countries. The use of subsidies by developed countries on products directly competing with products of developing countries should not be allowed.

(f)   Graduation

The Group of 77 rejects the concept of "graduation" sought to be introduced by developed countries in the trading system, which would, *inter alia*, allow developed countries to discriminate among developing countries in a unilateral and arbitrary manner.

(g)   Legal framework

Improvements in the legal framework of international trade should respond directly and meaningfully to the trade interests and economic development needs of the developing countries and should in no case impose on the developing countries additional burdens or constraints.

Bearing in mind that a principal objective of developing countries in this area was to establish a new legal framework for differential treatment in trade between developed countries and developing countries and thus to preserve the commitments of the Tokyo Declaration, the Group of 77 reiterates that it is necessary to obtain effective progress in this area before the end of the negotiations.

5.   UNCTAD V will present a very appropriate opportunity to analyse the economic and commercial effects of the MTN on the developing countries and the extent to which the agreements contained in the Tokyo Declaration have been fulfilled.

UNCTAD V should underline the need that after the end of the MTN the developing countries would have the possibility to negotiate on a multilateral basis with the developed countries with a view to promote on a permanent basis the interests of developing countries in accordance with the requirements of the New International Economic Order.

6.   Before the close of the MTN, the developing countries should make an assessment with the assistance of UNCTAD as to what additional benefits would flow for their trade from the negotiations and how far the objectives of the Tokyo Declaration have been achieved with a view to taking further steps for the achievement of those objectives before the negotiations are closed and final instruments are drawn.

7.   The Group of 77 stressed the need that further technical assistance be provided for by relevant international organizations to help the developing countries to fully assess, and assist developing countries in realizing, any additional benefits that would flow for their trade from the MTNs.


Item 10
of the provisional agenda for UNCTAD V
COMMODITIES

Item 10(a):   Integrated Programme for Commodities

Three main lines of action can be identified within the Integrated Programme for Commodities.

The first one relates to the measures to achieve the dynamic stabilization of commodity prices, thus avoiding excessive fluctuations.

The second which follows from the first is to obtain more security and stability for income derived from the export of commodities by developing countries, using additional measures such as complementary financing.

In the third place, greater participation by the developing countries in the economy of their commodities, presupposes measures to increase local processing, as well as the participation of those same countries in marketing, transport and distribution and to secure for them a greater and sure access to markets.

Consequently, it seems necessary to expedite the implementation of the strategy of the Integrated Programme for Commodities to achieve effective integration of the negotiations on the different measures which can be applied and thus achieve mutually harmonized solutions.  To this end,

163

The Ministers decide

To promote joint action by the developing countries in negotiating the Common Fund and individual commodities, expediting any pending agreements and ensuring the implementation of the new institution within a specific period.

Common Fund

The Ministers affirm:

1.    That the Common Fund, as a new entity, should serve as the key instrument for the attainment of the agreed objectives of the IPC as embodied in UNCTAD resolution 93(IV).   It should be an effective and economically viable institution for the financing of stocking arrangements and other measures relevant to commodities as provided in that resolution, whether those aiming at stabilizing commodity markets or those of a developmental nature.   The overall purpose of this institution should be to help to improve market structures and international trade in commodities which are of interest to the developing countries, and to secure stable conditions in the commodity trade at price levels which are remunerative and fair to producers and equitable to consumers, taking into account, inter alia, movements in prices of imported manufactured goods, production costs and world inflation, and changes in the international economic and monetary situation.

2.    That the Common Fund is one integral entity and there should be organic and functional links between its two windows which perform complementary functions and are established only for accounting purposes.

3.    That the capital of the Common Fund should be of a magnitude adequate to enable it to effectively attain the objectives for which it is established.

4.    That the main source of capital for the Common Fund should be mandatory direct government contributions (cash and on call) with a meaningful minimum equal amount of $US 1 million to be paid by each country and an assessed additional contribution based on an appropriately modified United Nations formula.   The allocation of contributions should be in accordance with the principle of equitable burden sharing as between developed and developing countries.

5.    That the Common Fund should have the necessary instruments to enable it to borrow on favourable terms from the capital market.   Callable capital would be pledged directly to the Fund by ICA members to the value of each ICA's borrowing entitlements and on modalities to be agreed.

6.    That both the first and the second windows should be endowed, from the start, with adequate resources to allow them to provide appropriate finance for their respective measures.   In particular, mandatory direct government contributions should be allocated in an appropriate proportion between the two windows.

7.    That the proportion of direct government contributions to the second window be complemented by voluntary contributions for which a minimum target figure should be set for the establishment of the Common Fund and mechanisms for frequent and regular replenishments should be considered and agreed upon in due time.

8.    That the second window, singly or jointly with other financial institutions, should finance activities such as research and development, both quantitative and qualitative improvements in production, market promotion, marketing and distribution, and diversification.

9.    That the Common Fund should also finance under specific conditions, national stocks of commodities in developing exporting countries with a view to improving their market staying power and avoiding distress sales.

10.  That cash deposits of ICAs with the Common Fund should not be higher than 30 per cent of their total financial requirements for stocking, in order to facilitate the conclusion of new ICAs, be attractive for ICAs to join the Common Fund, and minimize the financial burden on the part of developing member countries.   At the same time, the terms and conditions for the granting of

loans by the Common Fund to the ICAs should be such as to be financially
attractive for ICAs to join the Common Fund.

11. In its operations, the Common Fund shall respect the autonomy of ICAs and
commodity organizations.

12. That the criteria for the definition of international bodies for commodities
eligible for financing by the Common Fund should take into consideration the
importance of adequate coverage of commodities of export interest to developing
countries.

13. That developing countries should secure a decisive voice in the voting
structure of the Common Fund, in particular by ensuring that as high a percentage
as possible of total votes would be allocated to member countries on the basis
of the equality principle.

14. That the forthcoming Conference in March 1979 should be held at a high
level, including Ministerial level, from all participating countries in order
to facilitate agreement and decision on the basic and fundamental elements of
the Common Fund before the convening of UNCTAD V in Manila. They urge all
participating Governments, in particular the developed countries, to exercise
the requisite political will to ensure the successful outcome of the negotiating
Conference.

15. The Ministers note that some of the measures provided in resolution 93(IV)
are still outstanding and in this regard they affirm the importance they attach
to the measures contained in the resolution including paragraphs 3 and 4 in
section III.

## Action on individual commodities as contained in resolution 93(IV)

16. The Ministers urge Governments to move from the stage of commitment to that
of action and implementation, and in particular:

(a) Request the convening as soon as is practicable of negotiating
conferences for commodities now in their preparatory phase and for which the
technical stage of problem identification has made enough progress, on the
basis of action programmes on the price stabilization and other measures; these
negotiating conferences should be concluded within the extended time-frame of
the IPC. To facilitate the negotiating process, assistance should be given to
developing producing countries in their efforts to strengthen and harmonize
their negotiating positions through meetings among these countries or through
the framework of commodity associations.

(b) Invite member governments of existing ICAs, in accordance with the
appropriate decision-making procedures of these ICAs, to consider including
other IPC measures which may be relevant to such commodities and to consider
the association of these ICAs with the Common Fund, with a view to using the
financial facilities available on its first and second windows as appropriate.

(c) Urge that early steps be taken for effective application of appropriate
measures and procedures for stabilizing and improving in real terms the price of
commodities exported by developing countries taking account of world inflation,
and changes in the world international economic and monetary situation including
exchange rates, terms of trade, return on investment and other relevant factors.

(d) Request the inclusion, where the developing countries deem appropriate,
in the studies and specific negotiations of the processed and semi-processed
products, which are manufactured with the raw materials on the indicative list
contained in Conference resolution 93(IV).

(e) Decide to promote "horizontal" action which will enable agreements to
be reached on specific products among producing countries. The agreement
formulas which the producer associations provide could provide this type of
guidelines.

(f) Request that the preparatory meetings on the remaining perishable
commodities be convened as soon as possible so that concrete aspects can be
identified which will make it possible to hold negotiating Conferences on these
products, in view of the special importance which they have for the economies

of the producing developing countries and also in view of the fact that, although significant progress has been made on the respective studies, discussion of them has been postponed for a long time.

## Other elements of the IPC

### Complementary facility for commodity shortfalls

#### The Ministers

17. Request the Secretary-General of UNCTAD, in consultation with the IMF, to prepare a detailed study for the operation of a complementary facility to compensate shortfalls in earnings of each commodity, taking account of its financial requirements, possible sources of financing, its financial feasibility, institutional arrangements and the modalities and considerations that would provide adequate compensation in real terms to developing countries, paying attention to the situation of the least developed countries. This facility should be additional to the improvement of the IMF Compensatory Financing Facility and to actions taken under the IPC to deal with the problem of price stabilization in real terms. The study should be completed at the earliest possible date with a view to facilitating its consideration by the Committee on Commodities and the Trade and Development Board after the completion of the negotiations on the Common Fund.

### Processing and product development

#### The Ministers

18. (a) Urge that a commitment be taken to the establishment of "a comprehensive framework for international co-operation for expanding in developing countries the processing of primary commodities and the export of processed goods" taking into account the on-going work and negotiations on related issues. Consideration should be given, inter alia, to the following elements:

(i) Adoption and strengthening by developed countries of adjustment assistance policies and measures which would encourage their domestic industries to move progressively out of lines of production in which they are less competitive internationally, leading to re-deployment of productive capacities for such industries to developing countries. In this respect, a first step could consist of commitment by developed countries not to grant new subsidies to industries directly competing with developing countries' exports and to phase out existing subsidies;

(ii) Establishment of guidelines to regulate production and investment of synthetic substitutes competing with natural products;

(iii) Multilateral commitments from importing developed countries, wherever appropriate within the framework of individual commodity negotiations, to import from developing countries increasing quantities of commodities in their processed or semi-processed forms, or to reserve for developing countries outlets created by future increases in demand for such processed or semi-processed commodities.

(iv) Commitment to an increasing and progressively more balanced allocation of financial resources, both loan and equity capital, through international financial institutions for the development of primary commodity processing in developing countries; such an allocation should include and meet specific sub-targets for the least developed among the developing countries.

(v) Periodic review and examination by the Committee on Commodities of market access provided to primary and processed products from developing countries.

(b) In this context, request the UNCTAD Secretariat, in consultation with UNIDO, FAO and other competent agencies of the United Nations system, to undertake a systematic and thorough study of the prospects regarding the commodities included in the indicative list of resolution 93(IV), including the amount of investment required, the required action by developing countries themselves and the support measures by the developed countries and the

international financial institutions; the conclusions of this study should be considered by the Committee on Commodities, which will forward them to the Trade and Development Board with the relevant observations and recommendations.

### Marketing and distribution

The Ministers recommend:

19. A commitment to the establishment of a framework for international co-operation in the field of marketing and distribution of primary commodities, with a view to increasing the share of developing countries in the marketing and distribution of commodities exported by them, including, inter alia, the following:

(a) Improvements in the functioning of commodity exchanges through appropriate regulations, including removal of discrimination in the structure of membership, control, and management of commodity exchanges to ensure the equitable participation of export interests from developing producing countries in the management of the commodity exchanges.

(b) Increased technical and financial support from developed countries, and international financial institutions for the development of indigenous marketing and distribution systems of developing countries, including, inter alia, financing national stocking, storage facilities, market intelligence, the establishment of joint marketing boards and State-trading organizations, securing representation on commodity exchanges, and establishment and strengthening of commodity exchanges in territories of the developing countries to deal with their export commodities.

(c) Standardization of marketing practices and arrangements.

(d) Support for detailed investigations of:

(i) the market structures of all primary commodities of export interest to developing countries. To this end, they reiterate the need for the UNCTAD Secretariat to conclude or undertake, where appropriate, studies on transport, marketing and distribution for each of the commodities on the indicative list contained in Conference resolution 93(IV). These studies should be submitted by a certain date to the Committee on Commodities which will submit them to the Trade and Development Board with the relevant observations and recommendations.

(ii) Long-term contracts and agreements in commodity trade, particularly minerals and metals, with a view to exploring the possibility of establishing international agreed principles and standards governing such contracts, particularly the major clauses dealing with the fixing of prices and renegotiations of their terms.

(e) Elimination of barriers to fair competition between marketing enterprises of developed and developing countries, in particular the practice of dumping and excessive brand advertising, through adequate fiscal or other measures.

### Research and development, market promotion and horizontal diversification

The Ministers recommend

20. That a medium-term investment programme of the needs in these fields of commodities on the indicative list contained in resolution 93(IV) should be prepared by the Secretary-General of UNCTAD, and submitted to the Trade and Development Board through the Committee on Commodities.

### Follow-up action

The Ministers recommend

21. That the existing machinery of UNCTAD should be utilized and strengthened to monitor the implementation of decisions reached at UNCTAD V in the field of the developmental aspects of the Integrated Programme for Commodities.

Item 10(b): Other elements

Food production and trade

The Ministers recommend

22. A commitment to substantially increase, with the support of the developed countries and the concerned international organizations, investment and technical assistance to accelerate food production in developing countries, to expand the share of developing countries in exports of food and food products, to ensure stable and equitable prices and access to adequate supply of food and to strengthen world food security, including, _inter alia_, the following:

   (i)   Adoption in developing and developed countries of policies and measures that would encourage food production and exports of developing countries.

  (ii)   Adoption of appropriate schemes among developing countries for expanding and diversifying food production and trade.

 (iii)   Early conclusion of international commodity agreements on food commodities with arrangements for establishing adequate reserves where necessary.


Item 11
of the provisional agenda for UNCTAD V

MANUFACTURES AND SEMI-MANUFACTURES

Item 11(a): Comprehensive measures required to expand and diversify the export trade of developing countries in manufactures and semi-manufactures

1. Developing countries will continue to be hampered in their efforts aimed at expanding their production and exports of manufactures and semi-manufactures unless effective short-term and long-term policies and measures are taken to permit greater access for the developing countries to the markets of the developed countries and to restructure world production and trade patterns. The restructuring of world trade in manufactures and semi-manufactures calls for changes in the industrial policies of the developed countries (developed market economy countries and centrally planned economies) supported by action with regard to transnational corporations which are a dominant factor in world production, marketing and distribution of manufactures and semi-manufactures, supplemented by measures to increase intra-industry trade, to remove the supply constraints on developing countries, to control the operations of TNCs, and to improve access for the manufactured exports of developing countries. Accordingly, there is urgent need for a concerted set of policies and measures for attaining the objectives of expanding the industrial base of the developing countries, resulting in greater participation by the developing countries in world trade in manufactures.

2. Up to now, industrial restructuring has been proposed by the developed countries almost exclusively for industries which are not capital intensive and use simple technology, and abundant manpower. To accept this policy line would mean qualitatively freezing our development and consolidating an unjust and progressively ineffective international division of labour.

3. The Group of 77 emphasizes that there is an urgent need for the reshaping of the structure of the world industrial production and trade patterns in order to ensure a substantial increase in the share of the developing countries, including the least developed and landlocked countries, in world export of manufactures and semi-manufactures. The Group of 77 recognize that an expansion of production and diversification of international trade in manufactures and semi-manufactures of developing countries is necessary for attainment of the generally accepted goals for their accelerated economical industrial development. This requires efforts to build up and expand production capacities, establishment and strengthening of distribution and marketing organizations, development of industrial and commercial infrastructure and a better access for the products of developing countries in the developed countries' markets and adoption of appropriate policies by the developed countries.

168

4.    A target of 25 per cent share in world production of manufactures for the
developing countries by the year 2000 has already been agreed.   In order to attain
this target there would have to be substantial improvement in the share of developing
countries in the world trade in manufactures from the present extremely low level of
eight per cent.   The increased share in manufactures should also in consequence be
reflected in a corresponding increase in the share in world trade of developing
countries which should account for 30 per cent of the total world trade in
manufactures by the year 2000.   The UNCTAD secretariat in co-operation with UNIDO
should identify the growth sectors and the input requirements for the achievement of
the targets taking into account the particular circumstances and development
requirements of the various developing regions and the special needs of the least
developed countries.

5.    A major restructuring of production is essential to achieve these objectives
and developed countries should evolve policies which would promote such adjustment
through movement of factors of production from the areas where dynamics of
comparative advantage is shifting in favour of developing countries and to enable
developing countries to process their commodities and raw materials.   Such policies
should also promote greater intra-industrial specialization and give impetus to
orderly transfer of industries to developing countries.   In this context,
establishment of appropriate joint ventures and sub-contracting of production within
a sector, in developing countries should also be undertaken.

A.    Production of manufactures and semi-manufactures

6.    The following measures should be undertaken to improve the supply capability
of the developing countries in the field of manufactures and semi-manufactures.

   (i)    International organizations and developed countries should assist
          developing countries in setting up and strengthening financial,
          commercial and other infrastructure for developing countries and
          promoting their exports of manufactures and semi-manufactures.

  (ii)    New financial facilities should be set up by international financial
          institutions to provide additional financing for the manufacturing
          sector of the developing countries.   In this context particular
          attention should be given to the least developed countries.

 (iii)    Facilities should be established to provide long-term export credit
          refinancing for developing countries.

  (iv)    The processing of raw materials in developing countries should be
          encouraged, by inter alia, participation of developing countries at
          the appropriate stages in the vertical integration prevalent in raw
          materials industries and the developed countries should not maintain
          or introduce tariff escalation by degree of processing for imports
          from developing countries in their markets.

   (v)    Developing countries should be encouraged to move to establish and
          expand industries which have a dynamic world demand and particularly
          capital goods industries.

  (vi)    Elimination of  obstacles to exports of manufactures of developing
          countries arising from standardization motivated by domination and
          share of markets of developing countries by the developed countries.

 (vii)    Technological capabilities of developing countries should be expanded
          with a view to their greater participation in industrialization and
          world trade in manufactures.

B.    Marketing and Distribution

7.    In order to become true partners in the world trade, developing countries and
their trading organizations should be effectively involved in the marketing and
distribution of their export and import products.   International organizations and
developed countries should provide technical and financial assistance and help
develop technical and financial expertise in developing countries to enable them to
optimize their gains from manufacture trade.   The developed countries should evolve
policies which would encourage and facilitate the operation of developing countries;
marketing and distribution organizations in the markets of developed countries.

The developing countries should also be assisted in establishing and promoting other commercial infrastructure necessary for effective and efficient trading. In order that the developing countries are able to optimize the earnings from their imports and exports the following further action should be taken:

(i) The establishment or promotion of trading houses at the national level, engaged simultaneously in import and export activities.

(ii) The establishment of multinational procurement and marketing enterprises of developing countries to enable them to derive maximum trading benefits and to secure economies of scale.

(iii) The establishment by firms in developing countries of their own direct marketing channels in principal foreign markets. Policies should be adopted to promote greater use of their own trade marks or brand names to establish consumer acceptance.

(iv) The activities of transnational corporations should be reoriented, inter alia, towards more complete manufacture in developing countries and further processing therein of raw materials for both domestic and foreign markets. Transnational corporations should take positive steps for promotion of exports of developing countries in semi-manufactures and manufactures.

## C. Market access

8. Developed countries should evolve trade policy measures and adopt other positive policies in such areas as government procurement in these countries which would assist in promoting the exports of developing countries in manufactures and semi-manufactures and attainment of the target in the Lima Declaration and Programme of Action for production of manufactures in developing countries. This should be reflected in their trade policy régimes and the schemes evolved under the GSP should be geared towards the attainment of these objectives. In particular, protection afforded to industries in developed countries processing commodities and raw materials of developing countries or where the comparative advantage lies in favour of developing countries should be removed within an agreed time frame. There should be no prolongation of arrangements regulating trade in textiles, which restrict development of textile exports of developing countries. The barriers arising out of restrictive practices in services and invisibles or unfavourable freight structures against developing countries' exports should be removed. Developed countries should establish a separate classification in their tariff régime for products of developing countries so as to distinguish from similar products of developed countries with a view to allowing a more favourable treatment to the former. Special treatment should be accorded by developed countries to handicraft products of developing countries including handloom products, through duty free and quota free entry to this market.

## D. Services sector

9. The Group of 77 noted with concern that protectionist devices employed by developed countries against developing countries are spreading to the services sector, particularly in transport, banking and insurance.

10. The Group of 77 expresses special concern with new proposals in the field of civil aviation such as the introduction of a new régime of air traffic on an end-to-end basis between developed countries with insistence on excluding stopovers in intermediate developing countries. This scheme provides for a system of duopoly whereby special fares become an exclusive arrangement between two developed countries. Under this scheme, the growth of the airlines of developing countries will be curtailed.

11. The implementation of this duopolistic system in civil aviation would further hamper the development of tourism in developing countries, particularly those categories of countries recognized by the United Nations as requiring special treatment. This is particularly serious as the tourism industry makes a vital contribution to the development of many developing countries.

12. The Group of 77 therefore calls upon UNCTAD to request the Secretary-General to initiate as a matter of urgency, an examination and analysis of the effects of the discriminatory civil aviation practices employed by the developed countries on the growth of air transport, including air cargo and tourism in developing countries.

13. The Group of 77 further calls upon the developed countries to immediately eliminate all discriminatory practices in transport, banking and insurance employed against developing countries.

E. Collective efforts of developing countries

14. To accelerate their economic and industrial development developing countries should intensify their collective efforts to establish and expand industries based on development of local resources, build necessary infrastructure allowing more meaningful absorption of external capital and technology and to widen their national and regional markets and to increase substantially their shares in world trade through better access for their manufactured products.

Item 11(b): Principles and rules and other issues relating to restrictive business practices

1. The restrictive business practices notably those of the transnational corporations have adverse effects on the economic development of the developing countries, particularly in the field of production and marketing of manufactures and semi-manufactures.

2. Through practices such as licensing, patent and cartel arrangements, price fixing, transfer pricing, exclusive dealing arrangements, consignment selling and so-called voluntary quotas etc., not only do they restrict trade but they also prevent appropriate transfer of technology needed by developing countries to accelerate their industrialization so as to expand their production of manufactures and to realize an increased share of manufactures in export markets.

3. The Group of 77, therefore, deems it necessary that specific measures be taken to control the restrictive business practices including those of the transnational corporations, through inter alia the enactment of appropriate and effective national legislation.

4. They also feel that efforts should be made to promote co-operation among developing countries to co-ordinate measures in this field.

5. The Group of 77 took note of the fact that the United Nations General Assembly has decided that a conference to negotiate a set of multilaterally agreed equitable principles and rules for the control of restricted business practices should be convened between September 1979 and April 1980 for this purpose. The Group of 77 requests the Secretary-General of UNCTAD to convene the above-mentioned conference in the latter part of 1979.

   (i) They expressed the hope that the principles and rules should provide for differential treatment for developing countries. They also felt that transactions between the various institutions of TNCs which impose RBPs and which adversely affect the interest of developing countries should also be subject to such principles and rules. The principles and rules to be evolved concerning the restricted business practices should also extend to the field of trade in invisibles and services which adversely affect the trade and economies of the developing countries.

  (ii) The Group of 77 urges that the greatest possible effort be made to find solutions to outstanding problems such as the scope of application of the exceptions, preferential treatment, institutional agreements and the legal nature of the principles and rules in a spirit which will enable the principles and rules to be universally applied and bearing in mind that the system must be clearly oriented towards monitoring restrictive practices which adversely affect international trade and especially those having a negative effect on the developing countries and their economic development.

6. The Group of 77 urges the UNCTAD Secretariat to undertake in-depth studies and intensify the ongoing work on these practices in preparation for the above-mentioned conference which should adopt measures aimed at controlling restrictive business practices particularly in respect of the import and export transactions of transnational corporations such as:

  (i) transfer prices for intra-firm transactions;

  (ii) arrangements within TNCs for the territorial allocation of markets and products;

    (iii)  acquisitions by TNCs of domestically-owned enterprises in both developed and developing countries;

    (iv)  formal and informal marketing and distribution arrangements in respect of exports and imports of TNCs with other enterprises, including TNCs;

    (v)  exclusive dealing arrangements and abuses of market power through the use of trademarks.

7.    In the meanwhile the role of UNCTAD in the area of restricted business practices should be strengthened and an appropriate machinery should be established within UNCTAD for effective notification and dissemination of information on restricted business practices adversely affecting the trade of developing countries, for controlling the implementation of the principles and rules as well as for making recommendations on possible revisions and improvements; and for technical assistance to developing countries for control of such practices and evolution of appropriate consultation procedures.

8.    The Group of 77 reaffirms that any model law on restricted business practices to be elaborated in UNCTAD would be only a model made by experts of developing countries to assist in formulation of their national legislations.

## Item 11(c):  Review and evaluation of the generalized system of preferences

The introduction of the GSP has made some contribution to the improvement of market access for exports of the developing countries during the seventies. While the preference-giving countries have repeatedly made commitments to maintain and improve the GSP, recent years have witnessed a slackening of efforts to ensure improvements in its operation.  The Group of 77 notes this development with concern and urges that the following specific measures be decided at UNCTAD V.

1.    A positive formal decision should be taken extending the duration of the system beyond the initial period ending 1981.  The GSP should be given a legal character for increasing the certainty and permanence of its application.  The possibility of unilateral withdrawal of concessions under the GSP inhibits investments in production for export and thus hampers fulfilment of the long-term objectives of the system, i.e. to promote the industrialization of developing countries and accelerate the rate of their economic growth.  There should, therefore, be provision for binding of negotiated rates under GSP.  Withdrawal of concessions should not be unilateral but subject to prior consultations with the developing beneficiary countries, on the basis of mutually agreed objective criteria and procedures. Also in case of withdrawal under such conditions, offsetting trade advantages should be granted.  Further, withdrawal of concessions shall not be made except in the context of conditions justifying safeguard type of action.

2.    The consultation and participation mechanism within UNCTAD should be improved for the implementation and renegotiation of the various GSP schemes, in order to ensure that the best use is made of the system.

3.    Among other things, the schemes under GSP should be geared towards attainment of a share of 25 per cent for developing countries in world production of manufactures by the year 2000 and the need for corresponding increase in share of developing countries in world trade in manufactures to 30 per cent.

4.    Some preference-giving countries have not recognized as beneficiaries all developing countries, members of the Group of 77.  Discriminatory features and utilization of these schemes as an instrument for political and economic coercion or of retaliation continue to be incorporated in the schemes of GSP despite Resolution 96(IV) specifically calling upon concerned countries to rectify the situation.  Also, certain preference-giving countries have incorporated conditions for eligibility to preference in their schemes which indirectly imply certain reciprocity of concessions.  These constitute a departure from the conditions which are applicable to the system.  The principles of non-discrimination and non-reciprocity are reaffirmed and all developing countries should be recognized as beneficiaries without any conditions or discrimination.  Devices such as competitive need criteria which lead to such discrimination should also be eliminated.

5.    Agreement should be sought for a time-bound programme of expansion of product coverage so that the GSP covers all dutiable imports from developing countries, particularly products of interest to least developed countries, taking into account

the need for compensating adequately the developing countries enjoying special preferential treatment. The programme should include in particular also those products which are of special interest to developing countries, i.e. those in Chapters 1 through 24 of the CCCN. All preference-giving countries which have not yet done so should extend immediately preferential duty-free entry to all industrial products particularly those based on procession of their commodities and raw materials and all agricultural products originating in developing countries.

6. In increasing the amount of tariff reductions account should be taken of their erosion suffered by the system in the multilateral trade negotiations.

7. To eliminate non-tariff measures, such as quotas, maximum limits, exclusions because of competition requirements which restrict the full use of the different schemes for products of special interest to the developing countries.

8. The safeguard mechanism should be prevented from stopping the exports from the developing countries without justification thus invalidating the objective of the GSP. Escape-clause-type safeguard provided under the GSP should be taken after prior consultation with interested countries and only when it is established that preferential imports are the direct cause of serious injury to domestic industry. The action should be temporary in nature and subject to multilateral surveillance and review and linked to adjustment measures.

9. The preference-giving countries should liberalize and simplify their GSP rules of origin. These countries should also harmonize their GSP rules of origin into the greater advantage of preference-receiving countries and with the aim of enabling preference-receiving countries to enjoy greater benefits under the GSP.

10. In the improvement of the GSP schemes higher priority should be given to the products of interest to the least developed countries. Technical assistance should also be extended to them to enable them to utilize better the trade advantages offered under various schemes, including assistance with regard to the rules of origin and their application. Financial and technical assistance for the establishment and development of industries in the area of products covered by the GSP should also be made available to the least developed countries.

11. Agreement should be reached for extending the activities of the second phase of the UNCTAD/UNDP technical assistance project for enabling the developing countries to improve utilization of the benefit of the schemes.

Item 11(d): Review of the implementation of Conference resolutions 96(IV) and 97(IV)

1. UNCTAD V will be an opportune time for the evaluation of the extent to which the developed countries have complied with the different provisions of Conference resolutions 96(IV) and 97(IV), and for taking the necessary steps for their effective implementation.

2. The process of implementation of these two important resolutions has been extremely slow and discouraging. The principle of a standstill on barriers to imports from developing countries has not been adhered to and new restraints have been imposed on exports from developing countries without any multilateral surveillance of such measures and any compensation contrary to the provisions of resolution 96(IV). Also various systems of so-called voluntary export restraints, orderly marketing arrangements, minimum price arrangements, measures to prevent disruption of the market, etc., continue to be applied on an increasing scale.

3. While separate recommendations are made on the problems related to GSP, growing protectionism of the developed countries, adjustment assistance, restrictive business practices and related matters, the progress in the implementation of the resolution 96(IV) as a whole, containing a set of interrelated and mutually supporting measures for expansion and diversification of exports of manufactures and semi-manufactures of developing countries should be kept under constant review by the UNCTAD Committee on Manufactures.

4. The Group of 77 notes that the Arrangement regarding the international trade in textiles was extended for a further period of four years from 1978. The Protocol of extension allowed "for jointly agreed reasonable departures" from the provisions of the Arrangement. Such departures have tended to nullify the basic objectives of the Arrangement and have seriously affected the textiles exports of developing countries. The developed countries which have utilized these departures should take steps to bring them into full conformity with the objectives and provisions of

the Arrangement as soon as possible.  They should adopt policies of adjustment so that it will be possible to introduce a liberal trade régime with regard to textiles after the expiry of the Arrangement.

5.  The technique of tariff re-classifications should continue to be applied to facilitate the accordance of a differential treatment to the products of developing countries.

6.  The Group of 77 stresses particularly the need to strengthen and increase co-operation between UNCTAD and UNIDO in order to carry out joint analysis and make policy recommendations on industrialization and trade in manufactures and semi-manufactures from the developing countries.  The prompt establishment of the ad hoc UNCTAD/UNIDO Group of Experts on Industrial Collaboration Arrangements is urged.

7.  With regard to resolution 97(IV) special attention should be paid to reorienting the activities of the transnational corporations in the developing countries towards more complete manufacturing in the developing countries and the further processing of domestic raw materials and bringing about greater control by the developing countries over the processing, marketing and distribution of their manufactures and semi-manufactures.  Moreover, efforts should be continued with a view to strengthening the participation of national enterprises of developing countries in the activities of TNCs, controlling the restrictive business practices of such corporations and to ensure that they are a positive factor in the export efforts of the developing countries.  Decisions should be taken at UNCTAD V to give an early start to negotiations for the establishment of adequate norms for the regulation and control of the activities of the transnational corporations, so that their way of operations coincides and is compatible with and not contrary to the specific interests of recipient countries.

## Item 12
## of the provisional agenda for UNCTAD V

### MONETARY AND FINANCIAL ISSUES

### Introduction

The Group of 77 focused its attention at the outset on certain vital interrelationships between trade, financial and monetary issues at the global level.  The Group noted that the surest way of resisting the rising tide of protectionism -- and indeed of turning it back -- was to revive the process of growth in the global economy.  Needed structural adjustments in the pattern of production and trade would be facilitated in both developed and developing countries alike by a climate of economic expansion rather than of stagnation.

It was in this context that they observed that the extent and persistence of considerable underutilization of resources leading to unemployment in the developed world should no longer be seen as an exceptionally prolonged trough to the business cycle with a more or less automatic recovery to follow.  This situation inhibits an effective international adjustment process.  What would be required to restore full employment is a new impulse on a historic scale comparable for example with the transfer of resources to Europe for post-war reconstruction; this time, meeting the needs of the third world would have a decisive role to play in a situation where purely domestic reflation in developed economies would be no substitute against the existing background of production capacities geared to export markets that have been developed over three decades of export led growth.

For the resulting revival of effective demand to lead to the restoration of investment and growth initially in the developed world, international monetary stability was an essential prerequisite.  Excessive volatility in currency values would otherwise dampen the inducement to invest; and this cannot be eliminated without a major reform of the international monetary system along the lines spelt out below.  Regional arrangements contemplated by some developed countries are at best a partial solution which all the same underscores the deficiencies of the present system and the beginning of concern with the problem of reviving investment. Paripassu with movement towards a fundamental monetary reform, a massive transfer of resources to meet the needs of the third world becomes today the necessary precondition for the revival of the growth process in the developed world and more generally in the world economy.  If excess production capacity in the developed world is reckoned to be of the order of at least

174

$200 billion, an initial _additional_ financial transfer in the range of $35 billion to $50 billion would help launch the process of fully utilizing this excess capacity and help bring about the necessary structural changes in the world economy. In this regard, special attention should be given to the needs of the least developed countries and the most seriously affected countries. The mechanism would analytically imply the raising under the collective guarantee of the international community of monies in international capital markets and their disbursement to developing countries over a long term period, with an interest subsidy element as appropriate, in the form of both project and programme lending for structural change.

It is axiomatic that recourse to these mechanisms should in no way prejudice the expansion of ODA to meet the accepted international targets for which, again, specific proposals are formulated below.

Item 12(a):  Consideration of requirements of the international monetary system which would foster world trade and development, compatible with the needs of a satisfactory international adjustment process, taking account of the adverse effects of fluctuating exchange rates and world inflation, and in particular, taking into account the development of developing countries and their needs for balance-of-payments support

1.  Since the breakdown of the Bretton Woods System in 1971, international monetary relations have been marked by unusually high and persistent inflation and a high degree of instability in the exchange rates of major currencies. Despite the _ad hoc_ measures undertaken since then, the international adjustment process has not been satisfactory and large payments imbalances have persisted. This is of special concern in the context of an international economy which seems to be in permanent state of stagnation, with low production and trade growth rates occurring simultaneously with high unemployment, underutilization of resources and inflation rates. The burden of correcting these imbalances has fallen disporportionately upon developing countries, which have borne the weight of the adjustment measures. It has to be emphasized that in this situation a major proportion of the balance-of-payments disequilibria of developing countries have been caused by external factors arising in the developed countries such as the world recession/inflation. In the absence of adequate offsetting finance developing countries have had no choice but to limit their development programmes and incur an extremely high external debt compared with their economic capacity. There is now clear and urgent need for a fundamental reform of international monetary arrangements to make them more effective in fostering world trade and development, and in particular, to make them supportive of the development of developing countries in the over-all context of the establishment of the New International Economic Order.

2.  Although within the International Monetary Fund certain decisions have been taken recently increasing the quotas, establishment of the supplementary financing facility, and new allocation of SDRs, there is still a need for improvements in their characteristics. They only partially meet the demands of the developing countries. Among other things these decisions do not go far enough in making the SDRs the principal reserve asset of the International Monetary System nor in ensuring equitable distribution of international liquidity. Moreover, the allocation of SDRs received by developing countries would be reduced by their contribution for the reserve tranche of the seventh increase in quotas. In this context the Group of 77 recognizes the merit of the proposal made in connexion with the seventh general review of quotas that the SDR component of the quota increase of developing countries should be financed by developed countries. Unfortunately this was not implemented at that time but it should be done in future increases in quotas.

3.  The severe impact of the erratic exchange rate movements of major currencies on developing countries' trade and foreign reserves have contributed to the slowing down of the economic growth rate of these countries. To overcome this problem the international community should move towards a system based on the SDRs as the principal international reserve asset with a minimum of conditions for their use. Moreover, developed countries, in addition to intensifying their

efforts to control inflation, 1/ should provide financial instruments to protect
the real value of the financial assets of the developing countries. Furthermore,
in exercising its surveillance over exchange rate, and balance-of-payments 1/
policies the IMF should intensify its surveillance over the major currencies
and pay due regard to the special circumstances and needs of the developing
countries. In this context the Fund should recognize the structural character
of balance-of-payment disequilibria of developing countries and accordingly apply
appropriately flexible conditionality in the use of IMF resources designed to
stimulate the recovery of world economic activity, the expansion of trade and
employment and facilitate a more balanced adjustment process.

4.    Many other issues of importance are relevant in a discussion of the reform
of the monetary system. These include inter alia ways of ensuring a better and
more balanced international adjustment  process including measures which would
make surplus developed countries and reserve currency countries accept an
equitable share of the burden of adjustment and to promote the transfer of real
resources to developing countries and the establishment of a link between SDRs
creation and development financing which could take one of the two forms
viz. (i) a direct link whereby the share of developing countries in SDR allocation
would be increased above their share in the IMF quotas; (ii) an indirect link
whereby a specified proportion of newly created SDRs allocated to developed
countries, would be channelled to multilateral development finance institutions.

      The Group of 77 emphasizes that an essential precondition for effective
monetary reform is an equitable decision-making process in the Bretton Woods
institutions.

5.    The Group of 77 emphasizes these issues along with the following as being
of immediate importance at UNCTAD V:

      (a)  In order to enable developing countries to maintain their development
programmes in the face of continuing inflation and recession in developed
countries, a facility should be established to provide balance-of-payments
support to finance their externally-induced deficits. As noted above a major
part of the present deficits have arisen from imbalances in the international
economy, in particular recession/inflation as well as mounting protectionism in
developed countries which has adversely affected both the volume and purchasing
power of developing country exports. Since the causes of these deficits are
external to the developing countries themselves, the balance of payments should
not be dependent on "conditionality" of the type imposed on present upper credit
tranche support. Rather it should be related to broader development targets.
For the facility to be meaningful it must be able to provide financing that is
significant in relation to present levels of deficits. Bearing in mind that
these deficits are largely the counterparts of structural surpluses in developed
countries - requiring in their own view a substantially long period of
adjustment to eliminate - the facility should provide support on longer-term
maturity that would enable the concerned developing country to carry out
structural adjustments that would facilitate the attainment of its development
objectives.

      (b)  The international economic situation is adversely affecting developing
countries and a more flexible conditionality in the use of IMF resources would
stimulate the recovery of world economic activity, the expansion of trade and

_____

      1/ The available empirical evidence supports the observation that, contrary
to expectations, floating has not generally succeeded in isolating domestic
economies from foreign inflationary shocks. This is especially true when these
shocks emanate from the reserve currency country. In particular, developing
countries, mainly pegging their currencies to the United States dollar (which is
also their main foreign reserve asset), experience both direct price effects and
indirect price effects through constant pressures on their domestic monetary
bases. These countries cannot easily sterilize such imported inflation due to
either their underdeveloped financial markets or commitments of credit policy to
long-run credit objectives. Furthermore, their trade pattern may not permit
changes in their currency peg, since such changes can have an impact on their
competitive positions. Differences in national inflation rates when superimposed
on exchange rate changes result in wide divergence in real exchange rates. This
is perhaps a major reason for the need of exchange rate surveillance under a
system of managed float.

employment and facilitate the adjustment process. The rules of the game for balance-of-payments adjustment should be fair and balanced so that the burden of adjustment falls not only on deficit countries but also on persistent surplus countries. Balance-of-payment support in general must not be used to exercise political pressure on developing countries and should not be dependent on acceptance by the developing country of measures and programmes which involve social costs which hinder its basic aims, objectives and priorities.

(c) The existing compensatory financing facility should be improved and liberalized to compensate fully for shortfalls in the purchasing power of exports of developing countries resulting from changes in relative price or shortfalls in volume measured according to a trend rate of growth. Repayments should be set in the light of the factors giving rise to the shortfall and should be required to be made when the purchasing power of export rises above the trend rates. In this connexion, the Group of 77 should urge for the acceptance of the following recommendations:

(i) the limit on outstanding drawings under the facility should be increased from 75 per cent to 100 per cent of a member's quota. Drawings in any 12-month period should be increased from 50 per cent to 100 per cent;

(ii) the repayment period should be lengthened from the present three to five years to one of five to seven;

(iii) countries should have the choice of basing the calculation of their shortfalls on their total receipts from merchandise exports or the combined receipts from merchandise exports andsservices;

(iv) in the calculation of shortfalls, account should be taken of the increase in the price of imports;

(v) increased import volume resulting from climatic or other factors beyond the control of the country concerned should also be taken into account in calculating the shortfalls;

(vi) drawings under the facility should not be subject to any credit tranche conditionality; and

(vii) even when the charges for the Compensatory Financing Facility are lower than the commercial rate, the annual rate of 4-3/8 per cent should be maintained for the period during which this service is being provided.

(d) The Group of 77 urges that a subsidy account to enable developing countries, in particular the least developed, to borrow from the IMF supplementary facility be created.

6. The Group of 77 emphasizes that a genuine and fundamental reform of the international monetary system is necessary and that such a reform should be consistent with the trade and development requirements of the developing countries.

7. The Ministers of the Group of 77:

(i) Call on the Group of 24 to intensify its work in accordance with its mandate and to do preparatory work on the fundamental reform of the international monetary system, and invite the Chairman of its Deputies to convey reports of all its meetings to the Chairmen of the Group of 77 in Geneva and New York; further call on the above-mentioned Groups to collaborate with each other on these matters and make arrangements for continuing co-operation. The Ministers of the Group of 77 are of the view that member Governments of the Group of 77 should avail themselves of the occasion of the Bank/Fund meeting in Belgrade in 1979 to convene a meeting of the Group of 77 at the level of Ministers of Finance or Economy and in this connexion request the Government of Yugoslavia to make appropriate arrangements for such a meeting in consultation with the Chairman of the Group of 24;

(ii) Recommend that UNCTAD V establish an ad hoc intergovernmental high level group of experts within UNCTAD to examine fundamental issues concerning the evolution of an international monetary system that is

consistent with the long-term trade and development requirements of
the developing countries;

(iii)  Call for examination of the possibility of holding an international
conference on monetary reform at an appropriate time.

## Item 12 (b):  Measures to augment the net flow and improve the conditions of resource transfers from developed to developing countries

### ODA - Bilateral

(a)  The Ministers of the States Members of the Group of 77 note with concern
(i) that the actual performance of the developed countries belonging to the DAC
has fallen far short of the 0.7 target; (ii) that ODA as a percentage of DAC GNP
has fallen steadily from 0.34 per cent in 1971 to 0.30 per cent in 1977;
(iii) that the three largest developed market economies - the United States,
Federal Republic of Germany and Japan - have allowed a continuing decline in ODA
as a proportion of their GNP; (iv) that concessional flows from socialist
countries of Eastern Europe are below the international target.  The Ministers
of the Group of 77 record with appreciation that three developed donor countries
Netherlands, Norway and Sweden - have passed the 0.7 per cent ODA target, and
have stated that they intend to try to reach the level of 1 per cent of their
GNPs.

(b)  Without prejudice to whatever target that may be set for the
Third Development Decade, the Ministers of the Group of 77 call for a programm
of immediate measures by each developed donor country in the form of binding
commitments for an annual growth rate of ODA disbursements for each of the next
three years.  In particular, the Group of 77 calls on the United States, the
Federal Republic of Germany and Japan to raise their ODA disbursement at least by
25 per cent per year for each of the next three years in real terms so as to
double their disbursement by the end of the period.  In this connexion the
Group of 77 notes that the Government of Japan has announced its intention to
double its ODA disbursement in three years and expresses its view that this
increase should be in real terms.  They also call on the socialist countries of
Eastern Europe to increase their development assistance to satisfactory levels
and provide full information on such flows.

(c)  There should be a general increase in real terms in the present total
ODA flows to all developing countries and in the context of this general increase
the quantum in real terms of ODA flows to least developed countries, most
seriously affected countries, land-locked and island developing countries should
be doubled.

The increases to these categories of countries should be achieved within
the shortest possible time and in any event not later than in 1981.

(d)  The transfer of resources should be depoliticized and placed on an
increasingly assured, continuous and automatic basis and achieve a rational and
equitable distribution among developing countries taking into account different
levels of development.  The quality of ODA should be improved so that:

(i)  ODA to least developed countries should be in grants and to other
countries at least at 95 per cent concessionality.

(ii)  Definition of ODA should be modified to be net of amortization and
interest.

(iii)  Loans with less than 50 per cent grant element should not qualify
as ODA.

(iv)  ODA should be untied and programme assistance should be increased as
against project assistance.

(v)  Local cost financing should be provided.

(vi)  Greater preferential margins should be allowed to developing countries'
suppliers in the context of international bidding for projects
financed by multilateral financial institutions.

(e) There are now substantial ODA funds which have been committed but remain undisbursed. Consideration should be given to the possibility of using these for developmental purposes and particularly to provide balance-of-payment support by having the developed donor countries deposit ODA resources in a revolving fund as soon as they are committed. They would be drawn down by the developed donor country as and when they are disbursed.

(f) Developed countries should keep their public opinion informed about the importance of accelerating the transfer of resources to developing countries.

(g) Implementation of immediate increases should be monitored regularly by the Trade and Development Board.

## Multilateral assistance

The Ministers of the Group of 77:

(i) In view of the size and increasing financial needs of developing countries, stress the need of an urgent and substantial general increase of the capital base of multilateral financial institutions provided by developed countries so as to ensure that their commitments in favour of developing countries increase in real terms at a satisfactory rate and are consistent with the needs of those countries. The increase in capital base should be made for both the World Bank and the regional development financial institutions.

(ii) Urge IBRD and regional development banks to modify their rules and procedures in granting loans to developing countries in order to avoid delays in implementation and disbursements.

(iii) Urge the IBRD and the regional banks to provide increasing technical assistance both for project development and execution.

(iv) Since IDA plays a major role in the transfer of resources to the least developed countries and other low income countries, call for the sixth replenishment to be effected without delay so as to result in a significant real increase in resources. In this regard the replenishment of the soft windows of the regional development banks should be co-ordinated so as to result in increased lending capacity in real terms.

(v) Urge the reviving of the Third Window of the World Bank.

(vi) Considering the multiyear nature of the programme of the operations of UNDP and other related United Nations agencies, urge that the financing of these operations should be planned also to cover several years.

(vii) Agree that the proposal for the establishment in the World Bank of a long-term facility to finance purchases of capital goods by developing countries should be considered as quickly as possible with a view to taking a positive decision at the earliest possible date.

(viii) Call for an increase in programme lending of the multilateral financial institutions to make it equal to at least 25 per cent of total loans and also to stress in this context that the lending programmes of the multilateral financial institutions should become increasingly responsive to the over-all priorities and in particular to sectoral priorities of the recipient developing countries. Call for adequate local cost financing to be provided.

(ix) Call for a massive transfer of resources to developing countries which would enable them to accelerate their pace of development and thus contribute to inflation-free growth of the global economy. Such a massive transfer of resources for project development and execution and programme finance purposes to developing countries will be successful only if it is compatible with the development priorities of developing countries and its terms and conditions consistent with their debt servicing capacity over the longer term.

(x) Support the establishment of clear and coherent objectives for the transfer of resources from developed creditor countries and multilateral institutions as well as to the creation of operative mechanisms that effectively verify the additionality of resources.

(xi) Reject the principle of arbitrary "financial graduation" which is being established in IBRD and other international financial institutions providing non-concessional finance. With this principle, developed countries also seek on the one hand to reduce or cease loans to these countries, which have achieved progress in their economies and on the other hand to avoid their responsibility with regard to the transfer of real resources. The problem should be resolved by establishing objective criteria through negotiations where developing and developed countries will have equal representation and voice.

## Private flows

The Ministers of the Group of 77:

(i) While acknowledging the need for private flows, stress that these should not in any way undermine the targets set for concessional flows.

(ii) Call for expeditious implementation of the Manila recommendations to help remove the present administrative and institutional obstacles impeding the developing countries' access to national capital markets. Call for a preferential treatment for developing countries to enable them to make floatations or placements on schedule in developed countries with national capital markets; and raise in favour of developing countries the ceilings on foreign floatations especially in countries whose currencies are in high demand. Charges should be carried out rapidly with a view to facilitating the developing countries' access to international capital markets. In this regard, the Group of 77 hopes that the contemplated European monetary system will not lead to realignment of currencies that would result in imposing a cost on developing countries incurring liabilities in these currencies.

(iii) Welcome direct private investments which are compatible with their national legislation and development priorities while at the same time allowing them to enjoy an increased local participation in management, administration, employment and on-the-job training for local manpower, as well as local participation in ownership. The Group of 77 Ministers recall the urgency of defining a code of conduct governing the activities of the transnational corporations which meets the interests of all parties concerned.

(iv) Call on multilateral financial institutions to consider undertaking co-financing arrangements, after study and detailed examination in accordance with the priorities of the countries concerned.

## Multilateral guarantees

Whereas multilateral financial institutions (MFIs) have the capacity to extend guarantees to enable their members to mobilize resources from the private capital markets, they have not so far provided guarantees in any significant volume since such guarantees are considered by their articles of agreement as being equivalent to loans. In seeking multilateral guarantees, the Group of 77 stress the need to ensure that such guarantees bring additional capital flows to the developing countries concerned and do not in any way adversely affect the access to capital markets already enjoyed by some developing countries. The guarantees must be established in such a way as to avoid the possibility of existing borrowers being asked to go to the facility for guarantees even if they do not wish to do so. In this context the Group of 77 countries urge that attention be given to: (1) a recommendation to establish a separate multilateral guarantee facility for the interested developing countries; (2) a recommendation to amend the articles of agreement of multilateral financial institutions to allow them to provide guarantees more easily, including partial guarantees.

## Item 12 (c): Other financing issues related to trade

The Ministers of the Group of 77 considered the proposal for the establishment of the multilateral export credit guarantee facility which was examined and recommended by a group of international experts in UNCTAD. The Ministers of the Group of 77 call for UNCTAD V to agree on the establishment of such a facility in favour of developing countries that wish to enhance their access to international capital markets and diversify their exports.

Item 12 (d): (i) Review of implementation and further action that may be required pursuant to Trade and Development Board resolution 165 (S-IX), part A

The Ministers of States members of the Group of 77 while recognizing the efforts of some developed countries in taking steps to alleviate ODA debts of some developing countries, regret that the efforts so far have not been fully consistent with the relevant provisions of Part A of resolution 165 (S-IX). In this regard, the Ministers:

-- Invite the developed countries which have already taken some actions in favour of some developing countries affected by the resolution to extend these actions to cover the ODA debt of all the poorer developing countries described in the resolution without discrimination on any ground. In the case of developed donor countries which grant relief measures to only a limited group of countries the Group of 77 would not consider such developed countries as having implemented resolution 165 (S-IX);

- Urge the developed countries which have not yet done so, to take, as early as possible, the necessary steps to fully implement Part A of the above-mentioned resolution; to benefit all the poorer developing countries covered by the resolution without discrimination;

- Recall that the initial aim was to succeed in alleviating the ODA debt of the developing countries affected by resolution 165 (S-IX) within the framework of international co-operation.

Item 12 (d): (ii) Detailed features for future operations related to debt problems of interested developing countries (Trade and Development Board resolution 165 (S-IX), part B)

The Group of 77 calls for:

(a) The completion of negotiations on detailed features for future debt operations by UNCTAD V in the light of the basic concepts contained in resolution 165 (S-IX). In this connexion the preamble, objectives and initiative procedures as drafted by the UNCTAD intergovernmental group of experts are satisfactory. In "analysis", the Group of 77 rejects any effort to bifurcate debt problems into "acute" and "long-term". In "action", the Group of 77 stresses the need to ensure that domestic measures correctly reflect the responsibility of the debtor and do not give external authorities the right to infringe on the sovereignty of States.

(b) The establishment of an International Debt Commission, comprising eminent public figures with recognized knowledge and experience of debt problems and economic development. Any interested developing country which believes it has, or may have a debt problem could address itself to the Commission.

The Commission will:

(i) examine the debt and development problems of the requesting country;

(ii) in the light of such examination and in accordance with the modalities of the detailed features, make recommendations on measures required to deal with the debt problem in the broader context of development including measures of debt reorganization and additional bilateral and multilateral finance, and

(iii) convene a meeting of all parties concerned with a view to implementing the recommendations under (ii).

In carrying out its work, the commission will be assisted throughout by relevant international organizations including UNCTAD. This procedure and the detailed features drawn up in terms of resolution 165 (S-IX) will assure a global approach in which countries in similar situations will be treated similarly.

The Ministers of the Group of 77 note with dismay that explicit provisions in two UNCTAD consensus resolutions, namely 132 (XV) and 165 (S-IX) calling for UNCTAD to attend the creditors clubs were not honoured by the Paris Club in a recent instance. This was so in spite of an invitation by the debtor developing country concerned. In future debt negotiations interested developing countries using creditor clubs should be entitled to full assistance and participation from UNCTAD and other relevant international institutions.

Item 12 (e): Review of the present system of international financial co-operation in the context of world trade and development and consideration of ways and means within this context to make it more effective in contributing to the development of developing countries

1.    Past experience has shown that various aspects of international financial co-operation have been dealt with in an ad hoc manner by a multiplicity of fora and institutions which often operate along lines which are not mutually supportive of, or even consistent with, each other. This has led to a lack of predictability which has prevented individual developing countries from planning their development with confidence and it has also resulted in a failure to achieve the targets for the development of developing countries despite the fact that these have been universally accepted. Basically the problem has been that there is no meaningful commitment in respect of the total transfer of resources required to achieve these targets and the contributions necessary from individual developed countries and multilateral financial institutions in order to ensure that the total is reached. The need for a coherent system of international financial co-operation is becoming increasingly evident and the Group of 77 endorses the following basic elements of such a system.

2.    In order to become fully supportive of internationally accepted targets for the development of developing countries the Group of 77 should seek from developed countries commitments to co-operate more effectively in evolving in a comprehensive manner an effective and equitable system of international financial co-operation, which must inter alia meet the following objectives:

    (a)  Ensure the transfer of real resources to developing countries adequate to meet the external capital needed to achieve these development targets.

    (b)  The form and composition of these capital flows should be consistent with the development plans of recipient developing countries and fully responsive to their investment and development priorities including sectoral allocations: the characteristics of the capital flows should be such - quickly disbursing, untied, programme, etc., so as to enable their rapid and effective utilization.

    (c)  This transfer of real resources should be on terms commensurate with the debt servicing capacity of the developing countries and their own development objectives. This would imply that notwithstanding the importance of private flows the bulk of the resource transfer should be in the form of concessional flows.

    (d)  In order to achieve this, the developed countries that have failed so far to reach the ODA target, should sharply increase their ODA to reach this internationally accepted target.

    (e)  Private capital flows to developing countries should be sustained on improved terms and conditions. Capital market regulations in developed countries should be liberalized in order to ensure the improved access of developing countries to these markets.

    (f)  In the context of transfer of resources to developing countries the need for more concessional transfers to least developed, MSA and other special categories of developing countries should receive special attention.

    (g)  In addition to securing adequate long-term capital flows the system of international financial co-operation should provide necessary financial resources including fund quota increases, longer-term balance-of-payments financing and compensatory finance to offset shortfalls in the purchasing power of exports and to meet unforeseen import needs of individual developing countries. These financial resources should be available on appropriate terms and conditions and should be fully supportive of the country's development programme.

    (h)  This system of financial co-operation would also provide for a

multilateral framework for future debt operations of interested debtor
developing countries that safeguards their development programmes on the basis
of Trade and Development Board resolution 165 (S-IX).

(i) The transfer of real resources should be placed on an increasingly
assured, continuous and automatic basis, providing reasonable certainty to
recipient countries in making their development and investment programmes. There
should be an assessment at an international level of the necessary contributions
of developed donors and multilateral financial institutions. Means should be
found in the form of an international covenant to ensure that transfer of
resources take place in a way consistent with this international assessment.

(j) The policies of multilateral financial and monetary institutions and
their treatment of individual countries should be fully consistent with the
priorities and development objectives established by the international community
in the United Nations General Assembly.

(k) Developing countries should enjoy an equitable share in the decision-
making process at the international level on matters affecting the international
monetary and financial systems including decision-making in specialized agencies
competent in these areas.

(l) There should be regular monitoring to ensure that inadequate functioning
of any of the components of the system of international financial co-operation is
remedied promptly.

(m) The transfer of resources should be adequate in volume, terms and
conditions to meet the development finance needs of all developing countries.

The Group of 77 calls for agreement at UNCTAD V on these basic elements of a
system of international financial co-operation in the firm belief that it would
be in the interest of the international community as a whole. Further detailed
work on the elements should then be entrusted to appropriate intergovernmental
machinery within UNCTAD, beginning with the convening of a group of experts.

### Item 13
#### of the provisional agenda for UNCTAD V

TECHNOLOGY

## Item 13 (a): International code of conduct on the transfer of technology

1.   In view of the crucial importance of technology to the economic and industrial
growth and development of countries, the Group of 77 reaffirms that the basic aims
in the negotiation on the code of conduct on the transfer of technology are to
eliminate restrictive and unfair practices affecting their technological
transactions and to strengthen their national technological capacities in order
to accelerate the process of their technological transformation and development
while increasing the international flow of all forms of technology under favourable
terms.

2.   The United Nations Conference on an International Code of Conduct for the
Transfer of Technology was held from 16 October to 10 November 1978, pursuant
to resolution 89 (IV) of UNCTAD and General Assembly resolution 32/188. The
draft code of conduct upon which the negotiations at the United Nations Conference
were held had been prepared by the Intergovernmental Group of Experts, which had
itself met in six sessions over a period beginning in November 1976 and ending
in June 1978.

3.   The Group of 77 was not satisfied with the progress made at the negotiating
Conference. The Group of 77 had unreservedly accepted various proposals put
forward by the Committee Chairmen. This was done in the spirit of compromise.
Despite the great flexibility and political will displayed by the Group of 77
in an attempt to secure progress, it was clear that other Groups lacked the
political will to move forward. Some Groups had done nothing to advance the
negotiations. The Group of 77 could not accept a text that endorsed the
status quo, which was unfavourable to developing countries. The Group of 77
emphasizes that the progress which had been achieved had been made possible by
the virtually unilateral concessions of the Group of 77. The Group of 77 views

183

the situation with concern and invites developed countries to show evidence
of more co-operative spirit so as to resolve the outstanding fundamental issues
at the resumed United Nations Conference on International Code of Conduct in
February/March 1979. What is needed is political will on the part of other
groups to move forward.

4.     The United Nations Conference will meet again in February/March 1979, at which
time it will continue the negotiations leading to the adoption of the code of
conduct. While some progress has been made in negotiating some provisions, a
significant number of issues remain to be  resolved.

5.     The Group of 77 maintains that all international transfer of technology
transactions must be within the scope of application of the code, and that such
transactions occur either when the parties are from different countries or when
they are located in the acquiring country if one of the parties is either owned
or controlled by a foreign entity in accordance with the relevant national
legislation.

6.     The code must be applicable in transactions or arrangements between parent
enterprises and their subsidiaries in the acquiring country, or between subsidiaries
or affiliates of the same enterprise wherever they are located.

7.     The Group of 77 affirms that the aim of the chapter on restrictive practices
must be to eliminate practices which have an adverse effect on the social and
economic development of countries, and particularly of developing countries.

8.     The Group of 77 further affirms that any mention in the code of conduct of
industrial property rights must be balanced by reference  to the national needs
of economic and social development, as defined by each country, particularly of
the developing countries.

9.     The Group of 77 considers that the law applicable to transfer of technology
transactions must be the code of conduct and the law of the acquiring country,
particularly with respect to issues involving public policy.  Moreover, public
policy issues, as determined under the law of the technology acquiring State,
should normally be decided by national courts and tribunals of the technology
acquiring State.  Arbitration is recognized as a means of the settlement of
disputes if the manner of selection of arbitrators and the procedure is of a
type which will be fair and equitable, and if the code and national law provided
for under the provisions of the code is the law applied by the arbitrator.

10.    The Group of 77 reaffirms the need to adopt a legally binding code of conduct
as one of the key instruments which will contribute to the establishment of the
New International Economic Order.

11.    The Group of 77 therefore urges the resumed session of the United Nations
Conference to take necessary steps to conclude work on the elaboration of a
universally applicable international code of conduct which incorporates the
positions of the Group of 77 as stated in paragraphs 5 to 9 above, and to achieve
the objective stated in paragraph 10 above in the shortest possible time.

12.    The United Nations Conference should also take the necessary measures to
consider and establish appropriate international machinery for its effective
implementation.

13.    It is the firm conviction of the Group of 77 that at the resumed session the
Conference should concentrate on the fundamental issues.  If these fundamental issues
are tackled successfully the Code could be completed and finally adopted.

14.    The Group of 77 recommends further that the outstanding issues be resolved
at the resumed session of the United Nations Conference in February/March 1979
and those issues that may still remain unresolved be considered at the fifth session
of the United Nations Conference on Trade and Development.

Item 13(b):  UNCTAD's contribution to the economic, commercial and development
aspects of the industrial property system in the context of its on-going revision

1.     The revision of the Paris Convention for the Protection of Industrial Property
Rights taking place in the World Intellectual Property Organization should reflect
the historical and economic changes which have taken place, and

the new trends in national legislation and practices of developing countries. The process of the revision should culminate in the establishment of a fair balance between the public interest and the broader needs of development, on one side, and the industrial property holders rights on the other.

2. The Declaration of Governmental Experts from developing countries members of the Group of 77 on the role of the industrial property system in the transfer of technology of October 1977 (see document TD/B/C.6/24/Add.1, annex IV) should be one of the main bases for subsequent negotiations, particularly at the Diplomatic Conference scheduled for February 1980.

3. The Group of 77 reiterates that the new Article 5A of the Paris Convention should reflect the main concerns particularly of developing countries, promote the actual working of inventions in each country and enable member countries to take all appropriate measures to prevent abusive practices in the field of industrial property. Therefore, the Group of 77 urges all developed countries to live up to their commitments taken and agreed at the second session of the Preparatory Intergovernmental Committee on the revised Article 5A of the Paris Convention.

4. In order to serve as a useful tool for facilitating the transfer of technology to developing countries, and the development of indigenous technology, and to respond to the historical and economic changes which have been taking place in the last few decades, the current revision of the Paris Convention should recognize that all rights granted by a patent should be related to the working of the patent and guided by the considerations and concerns expressed by the experts from developing countries in their Declaration of October 1977 (see para. 2 above).

5. The process of revision of the Paris Convention as regards trade marks should be guided by the Declaration of the Objectives of the Revision of the Paris Convention (December 1975), giving "full recognition to the need for economic and social development of countries", to redress the present imbalance between rights and obligations of trade mark owners, and by the considerations and concerns expressed by the experts from developing countries in their Declaration of October 1975 (see para. 2 above).

6. The Group of 77 reiterates its position on all aspects of the revision of the industrial property system as contained in the above Declaration. The Group of 77, therefore, expects that its concerns find a place in the on-going process of the revision of the Paris Convention.

7. UNCTAD should continue developing its activities, including technical assistance, in providing its valuable contribution to the function of the industrial property system in the transfer of technology and the main lines of its revision, related to the economic, commercial and developmental aspects on the basis of the results of the meetings held on this subject in 1975 and 1977, respectively, seeking preferential treatment for the developing countries.

8. The Group of 77 urges the World Intellectual Property Organization to publish, before the end of 1979, the new Model Law on Inventions for Developing Countries.

Item 13(c): Strengthening the technological capacity of the developing countries including accelerating their technological transformation

1. In the implementation of resolution 87(IV) in relation to "Strengthening the Technological Capacity of the Developing Countries", while some positive steps have been taken at the national, regional and subregional levels, a comprehensive strategy is yet to be worked out and put in motion to bring about the technological transformation of the developing countries.

2. The review the progress made so far in the efforts to strengthen the technological capacity of the developing countries reveals the following:

    (i) A large number of developing countries have established national centres or institutions.

    (ii) At the regional level, an Asian Centre has been established in

Bangalore and an African Centre in Dakar, while decisions have been taken to establish a Regional Arab Centre and a Latin American mechanism for technological information (RITLA).

(iii) At the subregional level, the decision has been taken to establish a subregional centre on pharmaceuticals for the Caribbean region.

3.    While the establishment of some national centres and the decisions to set up regional and subregional centres are indicative of steps in the right direction, there is need for further assistance to ensure that when these centres become operational they would have the capacity to fulfil their objectives.  Financial assistance is required from UNDP, other international financial institutions and from voluntary contributions.  These centres would need to be complemented by interregional centres as appropriate in order to re-enforce the bargaining power and economies of scale of developing countries.

4.    What is needed in the implementation of resolution 87(IV) is the assistance of the international community to the developing countries in their technological plans and policies (at the national, regional and subregional levels); the development of local manpower (policy makers, planners, and technologists); the creation of institutions as well as the technological infrastructure; and the type of regional centres which would assist and co-operate with national centres in the fulfilment of their objectives.

5.    There is an urgent need to strengthen the technological capacity of the developing countries and to move towards the acceleration of their technological transformation.  Measures towards these ends might include:

(a)  the formulation and implementation of a technology plan as one of the fundamental instruments of national development strategy for technological transformation;

(b)  the formulation and implementation of policies, laws and regulations on the transfer and development of technology in all its aspects;

(c)  the formulation and implementation of technology policies and plans concerning specific sectors of critical importance to these countries;

(d)  the establishment and functioning of institutional mechanisms, including technology centres, the establishment and strengthening of Technological Training of Research Centres or Institutes and other arrangements at national subregional, regional and sectoral levels;

(e)  the increased training and exchange of personnel and experience among developing countries including co-operative exchange of skills among these countries and establishment of appropriate institutional arrangements for them;

(f)  the elaboration of special arrangements for the transfer and development of technology;

(g)  the promotion and intensification of R and D activities on problems of critical importance to developing countries, particularly undertaking them in developing countries.

6.    The problems faced by developing countries in the technology field vary not only from country to country, but from sector to sector in these countries. Technology plans should therefore be based on concrete policies for each individual sector and should integrate those policies on individual sectors into a coherent technology strategy as part of a national development strategy.

7.    Preliminary work has been carried out by UNCTAD in sectors of critical importance to developing countries such as pharmaceuticals, food, energy, electronics, design engineering and consultancy, iron and steel, standardizations and quality control, and control of transfer pricing.  The Group of 77 emphasizes that it is important to examine at an expert level specific sectors of critical concern to all developing countries in order to evolve an appropriate common strategy in these sectors so that a phased programme can be drawn up for increasing production in developing countries of manufactured products in the light of the Lima Declaration and the Plan of action and of the MTNs.  Such a strategy should fully take into account the technology inputs required for the

formulation of global production plans by the joint UNCTAD and UNIDO Expert Group in these sectors.

8.    In paragraphs 13, 16 and 18 of Conference resolution 39(III), and in paragraphs 10 and 11 of Conference resolution 87 (IV) as well as in the chapter on Special Treatment for Developing Countries and International Collaboration in the draft Code of Conduct on Transfer of Technology, developed countries have accepted to undertake several measures to co-operate with the developing countries in strengthening their technological capacity.

9.    Very little, however, is known about the implementation by developed countries of the international obligations they have thus assumed.  Nor is much known about the institutional structures they have created and the new policies they have adopted to implement these obligations.  The Secretary-General of UNCTAD is requested to obtain information from member States an implementation of these commitments and to report to the Committee on Transfer of Technology.

10.   It is important, therefore, that UNCTAD V decide on the concrete modalities through which the action agreed to by the developed countries is undertaken and the manner in which such implementation is kept under continuous review.

11.   The UNCTAD Advisory Service on Technology has played a significant role in assisting developing countries to strengthen their technological capacity. However, much more is required to ensure that the Advisory Service on Technology becomes an effective tool in helping developing countries in carrying out a programme of action towards their technological transformation.

12.   The Advisory Service on Technology is, however, handicapped by its lack of resources.  The Secretary-General of UNCTAD should, therefore, make concrete proposals for consideration at the Fifth Conference concerning the ways and means of making the Advisory Service on Technology more effective in meeting the increasing requirements of developing countries for technical and operational assistance in strengthening their technological capacity, individually and collectively, and paving the way for their accelerated technological transformation. For this purpose enlarged financial assistance is required from UNDP, other international financial institutions and through voluntary contributions, particularly by developed countries.

Item 13(d): Development aspects of the reverse transfer of technology

1.    The first serious consideration of the development aspects of reverse transfer of technology took place from 27 February to 7 March 1978.  The Intergovernmental Group of Experts had before it three types of studies which were prepared by the UNCTAD Secretariat.  The studies were:

   (i)   studies focusing on international issues;

   (ii)  case studies of four Asian countries examining some of the main
         issues at the national level;

         and

   (iii) a study on the conceptional and empiric basis for co-operative skill
         exchange among the developing countries themselves.

2.    Pursuant to the report of the Intergovernmental Group there had been areas of agreement.  For example, agreement had been reached on the following:

   (i)   that the problem of reverse transfer of technology is a multifaceted
         one, embracing social, economic and development issues as well as
         other aspects;

   (ii)  that in order to have a balanced understanding of the issues and
         improving the policy responses, there was need for studying the
         experience of countries belonging to different geographical areas;

         and

   (iii) that there is a need for a comprehensive approach to reverse transfer
         of technology.

3.   The report of the Intergovernmental Group of Experts also emphasized the fact that action was needed by the developed countries, the developing countries, and UNCTAD.   Concerning the participation of UNCTAD the Group suggested that further work was needed on the subject of reverse transfer of technology. Reaffirming General Assembly resolution 33/151, the Group of 77 requests the Secretary-General of UNCTAD in collaboration with other agencies concerned, to continue within the work programme of UNCTAD his studies, particularly on the following three main areas:

(i)    the experience and policy of individual countries to and from which flows of skilled manpower take place;

(ii)   the modalities of co-operation at the national, regional and international level;

and

(iii)  the examination of the feasibility of various proposals made hitherto regarding co-operative exchange of skills among developing countries.

<br>

Item 14
of the provisional agenda for UNCTAD V

SHIPPING

Item 14(a):  Developments pertaining to the Convention on a Code of Conduct for Liner Conferences

1.   The Code of Conduct for Liner Conferences was adopted at a diplomatic conference held in Geneva in March 1974.  The Code has not yet come into force because of non-fulfilment of the 25 per cent tonnage requirement.  The industrialized countries, who own the majority of the world tonnage, have not ratified the Code.  Some developing countries have demonstrated their political will by signing, ratifying and acceding to the Code.  To date, 34 developing countries have signed the Code. Of these, 20 come from Africa, seven from Asia, and seven from Latin America. Meanwhile, developing countries are mainly users rather than providers of shipping services.  Whilst efforts are being made to rectify this anomalous position, vital problems arising therefrom continue unabated.  These relate, in particular, to the provision of adequate and reliable shipping services, undue escalation of freight rates and dubious surcharges.

2.   The Ministers take note of the above developments and urge:

(i)    that other developing countries should endeavour to ratify or accede to the Code, if they have not already done so;

(ii)   that developing countries initiate steps to bring the provisions of the Code into operation in their respective liner trades;

(iii)  that developing countries seek assistance from their regional commissions and UNCTAD as to the most harmonious and effective way in which they could implement provisions of the Code in co-operation with, whenever possible, like-minded States and shipping lines;

(iv)   that continued political pressure be put on the developed countries with a view to their ratifying the Code and thereby bringing up the total tonnage requirement for the Code to enter into force;

(v)    that, in the event that at the time UNCTAD V convenes the Code has come into force, developing countries should urge all States to initiate without delay the implementation procedures contained in the Code;

(vi)   that UNCTAD, in co-operation with regional United Nations agencies, conduct in-depth studies of level and structure of conference tariffs to help establish rational, realistic and non-discriminatory relationships between the freight rates and commodities traded by developing countries;

(vii)  that developing countries establish or strengthen shippers' councils or any other similar institutions and devise an effective programme at global, regional and national levels with a view to counter-balancing the monopolistic power of liner conferences;

(viii) that the application of any increase in freight rates as well as the imposition of surcharges by liner conferences be subject to prior consultation among governmental authorities, groups of shippers, national shippers' councils, or similar institutions. These consultations must be based on a formula to be jointly worked out among the parties concerned, and must also take account of the economic realities of developing countries.

3. In order to further improve the position of the developing countries, the Group of 77 requests the Secretary-General of UNCTAD, after the Code comes into force, to conduct studies so that in future the Code can be further strengthened.

Item 14(b): Participation of developing countries in world shipping and the development of their merchant marines

1. Despite the recognition by the third session of the United Nations Conference on Trade and Development that developing countries should have an increasing and substantial participation in the carriage of maritime cargoes, the situation to date remains far from satisfactory. It is noted, again, that no progress has been made in the area of shipping under the International Development Strategy for the Second United Nations Development Decade and the Programme of Action for the Establishment of a New International Economic Order.

2. The introduction of new systems of transportation like international multimodal transport may bring its own train of problems particularly for developing countries. It is also noted that the insignificant share of developing countries in the carriage of all types of bulk trades, including refrigerated cargoes, is a matter for serious concern. In particular, there is need to ensure that the monopolistic power existing in international shipping is controlled.

3. The Ministers, aware of the above considerations, urge:

(i) that action be taken to enable developing countries to transport an equitable share of all cargoes generated by their own foreign trade;

(ii) that regular bulk cargo movements between a pair of exporting and importing countries should, in principle, be transported on an equitable basis by vessels of the national lines of the respective trading countries, or by vessels otherwise operated by them. However, where a developed country is trading with a developing country in this regard and the developed country is incapable of operating national carriers as economically as the developing country, the developed country should leave transport arrangements in the hands of developing countries;

(iii) that sales and purchases of bulk and refrigerated cargoes and transportation provisions in relation thereto are shared in accordance with bilateral or commercial agreements which will ensure the principle of equitable participation.

4. The Ministers call for co-operation among developing countries in relation to the following:

(i) Discussions should be opened, followed by negotiations where appropriate, between developing exporting countries and developing importing countries with a view to taking measures which would ensure that, as far as feasible, all cargoes shipped between developing countries should be shipped on vessels of the national lines of the respective trading countries or by vessels otherwise operated by them;

(ii) Discussions should be opened between developing bulk importing countries which import less than shipload quantities of bulk products with a view to examining the possibilities of joint bulk operation in co-operation with developing exporting countries;

(iii) Developing countries which are situated within the same liner service area should pool information on cargo movements and movements and service requirements with a view to developing joint sailing arrangements to increase the competitiveness of their liner fleets vis-à-vis that of the liner fleets of the traditional maritime countries;

(iv)  Developing countries should establish regional associations of shipowners and joint ventures in shipping and shipyards.

5.   The Ministers, taking note of the desire of many developing countries to phase out open registry operation, call on the UNCTAD secretariat, in consultation with other related agencies, to undertake further studies in respect of the repercussions of phasing out open registries, its economic and social impact on the economies of developing countries, its effect on world shipping, and how the phasing out of open registries would ensure simultaneous development of the merchant fleets of developing countries, with a view to taking a decision on the desirability of phasing out, and also to study the feasibility of establishing a legal mechanism for regulating the operations of open-registry fleets during the corresponding period, stressing the need to adopt such legislative measures as might enable them to ensure that substandard vessels do not operate to their disadvantage.

6.   The Ministers urge that action be taken to facilitate financing of the ship acquisition 1/ ship-building and port development

(i)  Developed countries extending credit for ship financing to developing countries should be urged to make these credits available on favourable terms.  In particular the maximum loan duration should not be less than 12-14 years, including an adequate period of grace.  Similarly down payment should not be more than 10-20 per cent of the contract price.  Such loans should be at the most favourable rate of interest.  Concessionary credit should also be extended to developing countries obtaining their ship requirements in ship-building yards located in other developing countries;

(ii)  Technical and financial assistance should be provided to developing countries for the development of their shipyards;

(iii)  Developed and developing countries should explore together thoroughly the possibilities of using bilateral and multilateral development aid for the acquisition of second-hand ships.  International financial institutions should give re-financing facilities to national financial institutions of developing countries in their lending for ship acquisitions;

(iv)  Developing countries which have the required management and operational expertise in shipping should be encouraged to participate in joint ventures with other developing countries.  Joint ventures among developing countries would provide the required collateral for the financing of vessels as a result of the larger scale of operations and pooling of cargoes.  Joint ventures between developed and developing countries can also offer possibilities for developing countries to acquire vessels as well as management and operational expertise;

(v)  Lack of competently prepared feasibility studies is sometimes an important restricting factor for ship finance.  To assist developing countries with feasibility studies for ship acquisition a special ad hoc unit should be established within UNCTAD;

(vi)  Similar facilities should be extended for financing projects for port development in developing countries;

(vii)  Similarly credit on easy and favourable terms should be made available to developing countries for acquisition of freighter air craft;

(viii)  The Committee on Shipping should keep the subject of ship finance on its agenda, review the matter at regular intervals, and recommend measures which may be necessary, including the establishment of a consultative group;

---

1/  These proposals are in line with recommendations made by the UNCTAD Group of Experts on improved methods of financing ship acquisition by developing countries which met from 29 May to 2 June 1978 (see TD/B/C.4/179).

(ix) Developed countries, particularly those with ship-building industries should be urged to refrain from adopting protectionist measures which will have the undesirable effect of both raising the prices of ships and denying to developing countries the opportunity to establish and expand their shipbuilding industry in which they enjoy comparative economic advantage.

7. The Ministers urge further work to be undertaken by UNCTAD

(i) Having identified in broad outline the possibilities for expanding the tanker and bulk carrier fleets of developing countries the UNCTAD secretariat should now proceed with in-depth studies of the possibilities in specific bulk trade routes, examining the manner in which cargo is currently tied to trading partner countries or transnational corporations and the means whereby it may be re-tied to the developing countries concerned.

(ii) In co-operation with the Centre for Transnational Corporations, the UNCTAD secretariat should investigate the controls which are exercised by transnational corporations over bulk movements of commodities such as iron ore, coal, grain, phosphate and bauxite/alumina;

(iii) Development of containerization and multimodal transport should receive the closest possible attention of the developing countries so that these countries can derive full benefits from new technologies. UNCTAD, in co-operation with ICAO, should carry out appropriate studies, including those on air cargo movements, so as to increase the air transport fleets of developing countries and to facilitate the export of goods by air as desirable. To this end, modernization and improvement of port facilities should also be necessary. The Committee on Shipping, in the context of its new terms of reference covering the subject of multimodal transport, should undertake intensive work to prepare guidelines for developing countries, as well as consider ways and means for assisting developing countries in the physical development of such facilities and further surface transport.

(i) The Committee on Shipping should review at its regular session the whole question of the participation of developing countries in world shipping and the development of their merchant fleets, with particular emphasis on problems with which developing countries are confronted. In this regard,

(a) The UNCTAD secretariat should give the necessary technical support to the Committee on Shipping to enable the Committee to discharge its responsibilities.

(b) The UNCTAD secretariat should undertake in-depth studies on the refrigerated trades of developing countries.

(ii) UNCTAD should extend technical assistance and training to developing countries in shipping matters such as:

(a) fleet development, including projections for the fleet and service requirements of developing countries and the acquisition of vessels.

(b) ship operations, including liner operations, container control, cargo handling and forwarding;

(c) chartering and brokering;

(d) financial management, including ship accounting systems;

(e) ship maintenance and management.

Item 15
of the provisional agenda for UNCTAD V

LEAST DEVELOPED AMONG DEVELOPING COUNTRIES

The Ministers urge the immediate implementation of an action programme in favour of the least developed countries, additional to the measures in favour of all developing countries, as well as effective implementation of the measures contained in Conference resolutions 62(III) and 98(IV) with respect to the least developed countries, taking into account the interests of all developing countries and the responsibilities of the international community as expressed in those resolutions.

1.    The Ministers therefore recommend that the fifth session of the Conference, as one of its major priorities, launch a radically expanded programme, in two phases:

Phase One: An emergency effort for the immediate future in the form of a Crash Programme (1979-1981) of greatly expanded assistance for the least developed countries, aimed at providing an immediate boost to their economies, immediate support for projects for the provision of the most pressing social needs, and paving the way for much larger longer-term development efforts; and

Phase Two: A substantial New Programme of Action for the 1980s for the least developed countries with the objective of transforming their economies toward self-sustained development and enabling them to provide, as part of this process they have established by themselves, at least minimum standards of nutrition, health, transport and communications, housing and education as well as job opportunities to all their citizens, and particularly to the rural and urban poor, by the end of the decade.

This New Programme of Action for the 1980s would be undertaken within the framework of International Development Strategy for all developing countries during the Third Development Decade.

I.    Crash Programme (1979-1981)

2.    The Crash Programme for the least developed countries should contain, inter alia, the following:

(a)  Greatly expanded assistance resources for projects, especially those which have been identified, and programmes which can be executed quickly and bring substantial immediate benefits to the least developed countries, including:

(i)    Immediate expansion of resources to strengthen efforts to improve nutrition, health, education, transport and communications, housing and job problems, and thus to provide immediate support for projects for the provision of social needs;

(ii)   Massive supply of inputs necessary for agricultural and rural development, such as fertilizers, pumps etc., in order to increase production and productivity, especially of foodstuffs;

(iii)  Provision of assistance for overcoming urgent bottlenecks in management, maintenance, repair and physical facilities in order to obtain better use of existing infrastructure and industrial plant;

(iv)   Financial and commodity support for activities at the Community level which create jobs, including support for local small-scale labour-intensive rural public works projects;

(b)  Emergency help, as necessary, to meet balance-of-payments needs, disaster, relief, etc.

(c)  Speed up of approval and implementation of all assistance projects already in the pipeline;

(d)  Immediate financial support for preparations for the substantial New Programme of Action for the 1980s, including identification of planning bottlenecks and steps to correct them, survey of resources, feasibility studies and detailed preparation of investment projects, as well as projects to meet social needs;

(e)  Major immediate efforts to mobilize the skilled personnel (both domestic and foreign) which will be urgently needed to support the planning efforts for the 1980s as well as other aspects of the Crash Programme (1979-1981).

II.  New Programme of Action for the 1980s

3.   The substantial New Programme of Action for the 1980s for the least developed countries will require support from donors for a much wider range of actions than have been typical of such flows in the past, and they will need to be provided under far more flexible criteria and conditions.  They should cover four main areas:  social needs, structural change, emergency support and the search for transformational investments.

### Fields of immediate financial support

4.   The New Programme of Action should provide direct and indirect financial support for the improvement of nutrition, health, housing, education, transport and communications, and employment in each of the least developed countries. Such expenditure should accelerate economic progress by providing needed income in rural areas and among the urban poor, and should bring tangible benefits to the poorest and subsistence sectors of the population even before the structural changes needed can take place.  The aim should be to provide fully adequate minimum standards for the poor as soon as possible, and in any event by the end of the decade.  As the decade progresses, the better working of the economic system in the least developed countries should itself provide increasing support for such standards.

### Structural change

5.   The substantial New Programme of Action for the 1980s must aim to transform the main structural characteristics of the least developed countries, which are the sources of their extreme economic difficulties, as well as to adjust to their natural handicaps.  The characteristics to be overcome are:

(a)  Very low income per head, with the bulk of the population far below a minimum standard of social needs;

(b)  Very high proportion of the population in the subsistence sectors;

(c)  Extremely low agricultural productivity and weak agricultural support institutions;

(d)  Extremely low level of exploitation of natural resources -- minerals, energy, water, etc. (because of lack of knowledge or lack of financing and skills for their development);

(e)  Very limited development of manufacturing industry;

(f)  Extremely low level of exports per head of population and even with aid inflows, very limited absolute availabilities of imports;

(g)  Acute scarcity of skilled personnel at all levels;

(h)  Very weak institutional and physical infrastructure of all kinds (including administration, education, health, housing, transport and communications, etc.);

(i)  Most of the least developed countries suffer from one or more major geographical or climatological handicaps, such as land-lockedness, drought and desertification, or high exposure to cyclone or flood disaster or locusts.

### Emergency support

6.   The New Programme of Action should make full provision for emergency assistance to meet unexpected problems as they arise, and thus to permit the programme as a whole to go forward, despite fluctuations in export earnings, natural disasters, etc.

### The search for transformational investments

7.   High priority should be given within the New Programme of Action to identify and support the major investment opportunities in the least developed countries, because of their high potential for leading the way to the substantial transformations that are necessary if more ambitious growth and welfare targets

are to be realized.  Existing international financial institutions should allocate increased financial resources in support of these activities.

III. Detailed steps for the planning and approval of the New Programme of Action for the 1980s

8.    The substantial New Programme of Action for the 1980s on behalf of the least developed countries requires, in the first place, a global planning effort, aimed at launching the programme and mobilizing international support.  This should be paralleled by commencement, as soon as possible, of planning efforts for a greatly expanded programme by each least developed country itself, with full support from bilateral and multilateral assistance institutions to complement each country's own more intensive work in the identification, preparation and implementation of such a major new programme, and reflecting its own specific needs and priorities.

9.    The stages of the global planning effort should include:

(a)    Preparation, by the UNCTAD Secretariat, of an outline for a substantial New Programme of Action for the 1980s to be given full consideration at UNCTAD V.

(b)    Launching of the New Programme of Action by decision of the fifth session of the Conference, with details to be worked out as indicated below;

(c)    Studies being undertaken by the UNCTAD Secretariat of the requirements, special measures and other detailed elements of an improved strategy to assist the least developed countries should, inter alia, be geared specifically to providing detailed recommendations for the operation of the substantial New Programme of Action for the 1980s;

(d)    The results of these detailed studies are to be considered by a group of high-level experts to be convened by the Secretary-General of UNCTAD late in 1979;

(e)    The  recommendations of the group of high-level experts, as well as the background studies should be reviewed by the Intergovernmental Group of the Least Developed Countries at its third session, called especially for this purpose, early in 1980, and by the Trade and Development Board, as part of its preparations for the Third United Nations Development Decade.  This work should lead to the adoption of precise recommendations to meet the objectives of the New Programme of Action for the 1980s, with commitments by the international community, and particularly developed countries and international institutions, as well as the least developed countries themselves with respect to:  (i) targets for growth; (ii) external financial requirements; (iii) priority areas for support; (iv) institutional arrangements; and (v) provision for reviews of progress.

10. The studies to be undertaken by the UNCTAD Secretariat should take account of the  similarities of the economic situations which exist in the least developed among the developing countries within the same geographical region.

IV. Financial assistance requirements and policies

11. The massive efforts needed for the New Programme of Action for the 1980s will require much more ambitious planning and preparation on the part of the least developed countries themselves, with the full support of the international community.  However, such plans can only seriously be drawn up if there is assurance that substantial additional resources are indeed committed to the least developed countries.  Thus serious planning must start with such assurances.

12. The Ministers therefore call upon the fifth session of the Conference to take the following steps in support of the Crash Programme (1979-1981) and the New Programme of Action for the 1980s, described above:

(a)    To urge the developed countries and international institutions to support these programmes to a maximum extent and, in particular, to call upon:

(i)    each developed country to at least double the quantum of ODA in real terms currently being made available to the least developed countries. Such doubling should come through as part of an increase in the present total ODA flows in real terms to all developing countries.  These increases should be achieved within the shortest possible time, and, in any event, not later than 1981;

. (ii) Developed countries which now provide substantially less than the average flow of concessional assistance to the least developed countries, expressed as a per cent of each donor's GNP, to agree to reach at least the average flow by 1981;

(iii) Donors to take immediate steps to plan for the provision of the much larger flows to be required in order to implement the New Programme of Action for the 1980s, and as part of the process of working out the details for the Programme, to provide specific assurances of the size and continuity of such resources during the decade;

(iv) Governments of developed countries to provide some resources in form of automatic or semi-automatic transfers, to meet the needs of the least developed countries, particularly for programmes to combat poverty and improve the social infrastructure in such areas as health, education and housing, transport and communications;

(v) Donors to provide assistance in real terms, offsetting, as necessary, the effects of inflation.

(b) To call upon the developing countries in elaborating their programme for greater collective self-reliance and economic and technical co-operation among themselves, to pay particular attention to the special difficulties of the least developed countries and to expand support for the latter substantially as a further important contribution to the above programmes.

(c) With respect to the terms and conditions of assistance, to urge developed countries to implement immediately the following steps:

(i) Provision of all financial assistance in the form of 100 per cent grants;

(ii) Removal of all kinds of tying stipulations from all financial assistance;

(iii) Conversion of all past official debt into grants.

(d) As a major contribution to expanding the capacity of the least developed countries to put external assistance to immediate use, donors to provide for up to 100 per cent local cost financing in connexion with financial and technical assistance projects, where considered necessary by a least developed country.

(e) Donors, in providing expanded assistance to meet the needs of the least developed countries, to make full use of the more flexible modalities agreed upon in the UNCTAD donor/recipient meeting in November 1977 (see part two of TD/B/681), and in particular are urged:

(i) To provide more flexibility in the types of financing made available, so as to include not only project assistance, but also programme and sector assistance, balance-of-payments assistance, budgetary support, etc

(ii) To provide assistance in support of social objectives, minimum standards of consumption and human welfare and minimum levels of public services;

(iii) To provide for recurrent costs wherever appropriate;

(iv) To give urgent attention to making administrative improvements in the planning and implementation of assistance programmes;

(v) To increase the volume and to improve the quality of technical assistance.

(f) To invite governments of individual least developed countries to organize meetings with bilateral and multilateral donor institutions to examine the report of the donor/recipient meeting (TD/B/681) in detail and to consider the specific follow-up steps that might be taken to implement the recommendations in each country. The UNCTAD secretariat should stand ready to assist least developed countries in organizing such meetings, in collaboration with the Regional Economic Commissions and with support from UNDP.

(g) To call upon bilateral and multilateral donor agencies to co-ordinate their efforts with the objective of ensuring that at least an adequate minimum flow of assistance is provided to each least developed country. Specific arrangements for this purpose should be worked out as part of the process of specifying detailed institutional arrangements for the New Programme of Action for the 1980s.

## V. Commercial policy measures

13. The extremely low absolute level of export receipts for the least developed countries and the resulting sharp limitation on the capacity to import, is one of their major structural handicaps. Special efforts will therefore be needed to ensure adequate markets for the expanded production which the New Programme of Action for the 1980s will bring about. The Ministers therefore recommend the following:

(a) Within the integrated Programme of Commodities, adoption of appropriate differential and remedial measures as called for in paragraphs 3 and 4 of Part III of Conference resolution 93(IV);

(b) With respect to the multilateral trade negotiations, effective implementation is urgently needed of paragraph 6 of the Tokyo Declaration, which states:

"The Ministers recognize that the particular situation and problems of the least developed among the developing countries shall be given special attention, and stress the need to ensure that these countries receive special treatment in the context of any general or specific measures taken in favour of the developing countries during the negotiations."

(c) With respect to the Generalized System of Preferences:

(i) In the continuous improvement of their GSP schemes, developed countries to give special attention to the least developed countries;

(ii) Improvement, liberalization and simplification of the Rules of Origin in respect of export products of the least developed countries;

(d) Provision for waiver of interest on present IMF compensatory financing facilities to stabilize export earnings, in the case of the least developed countries;

(e) Provision of assistance for the expansion of exports of the least developed countries, wherever possible, in an integrated manner, covering all the relevant stages, including planning, production, transportation, promotion and sales;

(f) Provision of longer-term purchase arrangements for the products of the least developed countries by the developed countries wherever possible;

(g) Provision of especially favourable treatment to imports from the least developed countries in the case of government procurement by developed countries. In this context the least developed countries should be given the benefits of the Code being negotiated in the MTN without being required to make reciprocal concessions;

(h) Developed countries and international organizations should adopt special measures in favour of the least developed countries to foster the creation of industries for on-the-spot processing of raw materials and food products, as one of the bases for diversification of exports;

(i) Where there are projects to expand exports of the least developed countries, special consideration should be given by developed countries, as part of the programme, to temporary removal of tariff and non-tariff barriers to market access for such products, taking into account the interests of other developing countries;

(j) In the effort to increase export earnings in real terms for all developing countries within the context of individual commodity agreements, special attention should be paid to the peculiar situation of least developed countries; consideration should also be given for exemption from pre-financing of buffer stocks and payments of dues and subscriptions;

(k) Establishment of special arrangements to assist the least developed countries in the sale of their exports in developed country markets, including the creation of especial sections within import promotion centres in the developed countries for this purpose.

## VI. Transfer of technology

14. The developed countries and competent international institutions should:

(i) assist the institutions of least developed countries to obtain under preferential terms and conditions and at a minimum cost, the results of scientific and technological developments appropriate to their requirements;

(ii) in order to overcome the technological and negotiating weaknesses of the countries, assist in the establishment of transfer of technology centres designed to obtain necessary technological information, to select from available alternatives and to negotiate proper terms and conditions for external collaboration;

(iii) make arrangements for the grant of patented, patent-related and non-patented technologies, including know-how, suited to the economic conditions of the least developed countries;

(iv) provide the necessary assistance for establishing institutions of applied technology, with the aim of developing indigenous technologies and promoting the adaptation of imported technologies to national requirements;

(v) in order to compensate for the reverse transfer of technology through the brain-drain from the developing countries, now amounting to several billion dollars, make arrangements for the provisions to the least developed countries on a cost-free basis, of skilled manpower suited to the requirements of accelerated development of the least developed countries.

15. The Ministers urge developed countries and competent international institutions to strengthen their efforts to assist the least developed countries in the field of transfer of technology and to implement fully the provisions of paragraph 34 of Conference resolution 98(IV).

## VII. Shipping

16. The governments of developed and developing countries should invite shipowners and liner conferences to establish freight tariffs for the least developed countries which will encourage and assist in expanding the export and import trade of these countries, and to develop promotional rates for exports of the least developed countries which will facilitate the opening of new markets and the development of new trade flows.

17. The developed countries and the international financial institutions should give high priority to giving financial and technical assistance to the least developed countries to help them in acquiring and expanding their national merchant fleets and in improving the port facilities.

## VIII. Other special measures

18. The fourth session in the Ministerial Meeting of the Group of 77 urges developed countries and international institutions to implement the especial measures on behalf of the least developed countries in other fields, as contained in Conference resolutions 62(III) and 93(IV), and in particular call upon UNCTAD, the UNDP and other relevant agencies to strengthen their assistance to the least developed countries in the field of insurance and reinsurance and to implement fully the provisions contained in paragraphs 31-33 of Conference resolution 98(IV).

19. All the above measures should be applied to all the least developed among developing countries without discrimination.

## IX. Further work by UNCTAD

20.   The Ministers call upon the Secretary-General of UNCTAD to take primary responsibility, with full participation by other appropriate institutions, for detailed preparation of the Crash Programme (1979-1981) and the New Programme of Action for the 1980s on behalf of the least developed countries, and for the detailed arrangements at the global level for their implementation, co-ordination, and monitoring of progress.    To meet the urgent needs of the least developed countries under the programmes, the work of the UNCTAD secretariat should be strengthened, and necessary additional resources should be made available.

21.   The Secretary-General of UNCTAD should continue and intensify the work programme of UNCTAD on behalf of the least developed countries as contained in Conference resolution 98(IV), paragraph 37(b) and, in preparation for the New Programme of Action for the 1980s, along the lines indicated in TD/B/AC.17/7, paragraph 52.    Further work should be undertaken, with particular attention to the need for in-depth study of the circumstances of individual least developed countries, in the following areas:  (such studies, in the form of pilot studies and individual country case studies, should provide the basis for necessary policy changes, at the international or country level, and should identify promising areas for technical and financial assistance).

    (a)  Study of longer-term export potentials, import substitution potentials, and alternative strategies for their realization;

    (b)  Study of import cost-savings potential;

    (c)  Evaluation of the role of foreign financial and technical assistance and potential for expanding the capacity to use aid effectively;

    (d)  Survey of the internal trade and distribution network, including its relations to foreign trade;

    (e)  Survey of the adequacy of credit facilities for small farmers and artisans, and the possible role of foreign assistance.

22.   In view of the importance of improving the foreign economic sector performance of the least developed countries, the Ministers request the Secretary-General of UNCTAD to establish an advisory service in the field of planning and policies for the foreign economic sector of the least developed countries, to be financed from the regular budget of UNCTAD.

23.   The requirements for preparation by individual least developed countries of their own specific proposals under the Crash Programme (1979-1981) and the New Programme of Action for the 1980s will require strong technical assistance support.    The UNDP and bilateral assistance institutions are urged to support UNCTAD in strengthening its technical assistance activities in support of such efforts.

24.   In order to effectively discharge its responsibilities in this area, and in recognition of the importance of these issues, the unit of the UNCTAD dealing with the least developed among the developing countries should be adequately strengthened and urgent consideration should also be given in the context of the restructuring of the institutional machinery of UNCTAD, to transforming it into a separate division of the secretariat.

### Item 16
#### of the provisional agenda for UNCTAD V

### LAND-LOCKED AND ISLAND DEVELOPING COUNTRIES

Item 16(a):  Specific action related to the particular needs and problems of land-locked developing countries

1.   Reiterate the special measures and specific actions related to the particular needs and problems of the land-locked developing countries envisaged in Conference resolutions 63(III) and 98(IV), part IV, and in Trade and Development Board resolution 109(XIV), as agreed, and urges their full implementation by the international community.

2.   Recognize that land-locked countries are generally among the least developed among the developing countries;  that their lack of territorial access to the sea, aggravated by great distances to seaports, by remoteness and isolation from world markets, and in the case of one of them devastation by a long war, and by the greater difficulties and costs of their international transport services, acts as a major impediment to their foreign trade and one of the serious constraints to their further economic and social development;  that their difficulties often include inadequacy of physical facilities along the transit routes and in the seaports, delays and uncertainties in transit-transport operations, complications related to the commercial aspects of transiting a foreign territory, as well as very high real costs of access to world markets.

3.   Stress the need for financial and technical assistance from the international agencies and developed countries as a means to solve the common transit and transport problems relating to land-locked countries and their neighbours.

4.   Recognize that specific action related to the needs and problems of land-locked countries must aim to:

(a)   reduce the costs of access to and from the sea and to world markets of land-locked countries;

(b)   improve the quality, efficiency and reliability of transit-transport services taking into account the needs and means of both the land-locked countries and their transit neighbours;

(c)   restructure the economies of the land-locked countries to overcome their geographic handicaps;

(d)   offset the costs of improvements through especially favourable terms and conditions of assistance;

(e)   construct dry ports as an additional facility.

Co-operation between land-locked countries and transit countries

5.   Recognize that measures to deal with the transit problems of land-locked countries require effective co-operation and close collaboration between land-locked countries and their transit neighbours. Where any study is to be undertaken in any transit country, such study shall be undertaken with the approval or consent of the transit country concerned. Where any programme or action is to be undertaken in or in relation to any transit country, such programme or action will be undertaken with the approval or consent of that transit country. Any proposals in relation to special measures to reduce the transit costs shall be given due consideration by the transit country.

Integrated planning approach

6.   An integrated planning approach recognizes the need for close co-operation between the land-locked and transit developing countries concerned. Such co-operation, between these countries, including the establishment of high-level consultative committees, should include the following key elements:

(a)   the need for close co-operation between land-locked developing countries and their transit neighbours concerning all aspects of transit facilities in accordance with agreements between the land-locked and transit countries;

(b)   clear recognition that major efforts to reduce the cost of access to the sea and to world markets facing land-locked developing countries may necessitate improved procedures and new investments not only within the land-locked developing countries, but also within the neighbouring transit developing countries as well;

(c)   the supportive role of needed financial assistance by the international community as a whole. Transit transport infrastructures need to be effectively improved both in the land-locked and transit countries. Financial arrangements must be provided by all members of the international community which take fully into account the fact that the improvements would be beneficial to both land-locked and transit countries. Such assistance should normally be on especially concessional terms;

(d)  the need to take into account all aspects of the problem of transit and transport of land-locked and transit countries bearing in mind the relevant arrangements and evolving policies of the concerned countries and including: procedures and regulations, documentation, management, training, organizational and institutional arrangements, maintenance of existing facilities and infrastructure, new facilities and infrastructural requirements, possibilities for joint ventures, the effects of delays and uncertainties on the cost and quality of transit services.  Improvements in each of these factors can lead to lower transit costs, and several complementary improvements will normally be needed to achieve maximum reduction in these costs;

(e)  the importance of studying the possibilities of providing each land-locked country with alternative routes wherever this is feasible, in order to ensure against any difficulties that may arise on other transit routes;

(f)  the need for detailed planning and costing studies on all available options.  Such studies should aim to provide decision-makers with a clear picture of what improvements are likely to have the highest pay-offs, and a clear guide to the priorities for more detailed follow-up projects;  they could form a concrete basis for attracting needed assistance from the international community.

## Integrated, regional and subregional transport planning

7.  Consider the following as key elements of integrated, and where necessary, regional and subregional transport planning:

(a)  the land-locked and developing transit countries can derive substantial long-term benefits from the improvement and development of integrated transport infrastructure, and, where necessary, regional and subregional transport infrastructure.  The international organizations and financial institutions should give high priority in their assistance programmes for such projects;

(b)  land-locked and developing transit countries would benefit substantially from the harmonization of transport planning and the promotion of joint ventures in the field of transport, where necessary at the regional and subregional levels;

(c)  interested land-locked countries, in co-operation with other countries, might consider creating a co-operative air transport development project, which might provide more economical, balanced and effective airfreight and passenger services, based upon a central organization which could undertake the necessary planning studies with appropriate technical assistance;

(d)  all possible efforts should be made to apply accepted international conventions to facilitate transit traffic of the land-locked countries to promote and diversify trade of land-locked countries.  In view of the above, the question of revising any of the existing multilateral conventions so as to bring them in closer conformity to the need to promote the trade and development of the land-locked and developing transit countries should be examined.

## Priority areas for action and assistance

8.  Urges the international community to give strong financial and technical assistance support in the following areas:

(a)  development of all-weather through-road transport routes connecting land-locked and developing transit countries with terminals of ports (sea/air) roadways and railways as the case may be, including adequate provision for heavy vehicles and maintenance;

(b)  the extension or connexion of the rail system of transit countries into land-locked countries and the provision of adequate rolling stock without the need for transshipment;

(c)  development or improvement of navigability of inland waterways including existing waterways so that continuous year-round use is possible;

(d)  to ensure that each land-locked developing country has at least one airport fully equipped in accordance with international standards and to provide for the purpose of aircraft and other equipment related to air transport on favourable terms;

(e)  to provide for the early introduction of new, more efficient or more
économical forms of transport, such as pipelines (for oil, natural gas and other
suitable products) and containerization system;

(f)  to provide fast and reliable communication links between the commercial
centres of the land-locked countries and transit points;

(g)  development and improvement of transit and port facilities especially
for the use of any land-locked country, including the establishment of berth,
transit shed, transit storage, and exclusive transit areas in transit ports
including related facilities at necessary breakpoints;

(h)  to establish TIR 1/ warehouses in land-locked countries on a
preferential basis;

(i)  the governments of developed and developing countries should invite
and urge shipowners, members of liner conference and insurance companies, as far
as feasible, to establish freight rates and premiums for the land-locked
developing countries which will encourage and assist the expansion of the export
trade of the land-locked countries and to develop promotional rates for
non-traditional exports of these countries, which will facilitate the opening up
of new markets and the development of new trade flows.

9.  Where the projects are related to, or have a bearing on, transit-transport
infrastructures (roads, railways, waterways, ports, etc.) in the transit countries,
a joint request by the concerned land-locked and transit countries would have to
be made for financial and technical assistance.

Restructuring and diversification of the economies of land-locked developing
countries

10.  Urge the provision of concessional assistance by the international community
to help diversify the economies of the land-locked developing countries, with
particular priority to the establishment of import-substitution industries and
export-oriented industries, as well as to the development of natural resources.

Special Fund for land-locked developing countries

11.  Keeping in view the meagre resources available to the Fund.

(a)  urge the international community and particularly developed countries
and other countries in a position to do so, to contribute generously to the
United Nations Special Fund for land-locked developing countries;

(b)  endorse the interim arrangements by which the Special Fund is managed
by the Administrator of the UNDP in close collaboration with the
Secretary-General of UNCTAD;

(c)  invite the Administrator of UNDP to ensure that the resources of the
Special Fund are used in ways which are in addition to, and generally different
from, the types of activities which the UNDP normally finances;

(d)  welcome the growing support of UNDP for technical assistance projects
aimed at improving the transit and transport situation of land-locked developing
countries.

Further action

12.  Requests the Secretary-General of UNCTAD to continue and intensify the work
programme of UNCTAD in relation to the special problems of developing land-locked
countries, including:

(a)  review of the special economic problems deriving from the geographical
situation of the land-locked developing countries, and consideration of possible
further recommendations for action in their favour, with a view to reducing the
real cost of their access to and from the sea and to world markets;

---

1/  TIR = Transport international routier.

(b) studies of the transit-transport situation, facilities and arrangements in different areas with a view to facilitating government action aiming at:

(i) improvement, where required, of transiting procedures and regulations;

(ii) international joint ventures in the field of transit-transport;

(iii) charges in the transit-transport sector.

13. Requests the UNDP to increase their financial and technical assistance to land-locked countries and further requests the international community and international financial institutions to continue to provide and increase their assistance to land-locked developing countries at concessional rates.

14. Recommends intensified activities relating to conducting necessary studies, implementation of special measures and action programmes, including those under ECDC, as well as those under UNCTAD, and at regional and subregional levels, in co-operation with regional commissions; and further recommends that financial and technical assistance be provided for this purpose by the international community, international financial institutions and UNDP.

## Item 16(b): Specific action related to the particular needs and problems of island developing countries

1. The Ministers reiterate the specific actions related to the particular needs and problems of island developing countries as contained in Conference resolution 98(IV), part III, and in the relevant General Assembly resolutions and urges full compliance with them by the international community.

2. They also endorse the recommendations of the UNCTAD expert group on feeder and inter-island services by air or sea for island developing countries (TD/B/687), and urges their early implementation by the international community.

3. Further specific action is needed in the case of island developing countries to off-set the major handicaps in transport and communications, great distances from market centres, highly limited internal markets, lack of marketing expertise, low resource endowment, lack of natural resources, heavy dependence on a few commodities for the foreign exchange earnings, shortage of administrative personnel and heavy financial burdens. The developed countries and international organizations should be prepared to adjust their programmes and policies to ensure that the full benefit of general measures in favour of developing countries are generally shared by these island countries.

## I. Priority areas for action and assistance

4. The Ministers urge the international community to give strong financial and technical assistance support to the efforts of the island developing countries in the following areas:

(a) In order to lower their vulnerability to economic instability, every effort should be made to diversify their economies;

(b) Island economies, particularly those with limited domestic markets, rely heavily on exports for their foreign exchange earnings. Access to markets should therefore be facilitated by:

(i) assistance in trade promotion efforts;

(ii) simplification of preference procedures, so that small administrations and enterprises can take advantage of preferential access to markets where it is in principle available;

(c) Many of these countries are actively seeking private foreign investment for export processing industries, other industries, tourism, etc. Such efforts should be supported by assistance from the international community, including:

(i) investment in infrastructure - water, electricity, industrial estates, transport;

(ii)  establishment of appropriate technical education and training programmes, including the areas of marketing and management;

(iii)  design of incentive packages;

(iv)  establishment of joint ventures upon request by developing island countries;

(v)  assistance in negotiating with foreign private investors.

(d)  Migrant workers from the island developing countries make an important economic contribution to their own countries and to the host countries. For this reason, the host countries are urged to assist the island developing countries in their economic and social development by financial and technical assistance. Studies to examine the means of maximizing the social and financial benefits to the source island countries should be undertaken; these studies could consider also alternative measures to migration. Governments of host countries should take the necessary action to prevent exploitation of migrant workers, in particular by assuring that housing and remuneration for the specific type of work undertaken equate with the standard and rates obtained in their respective countries.

(e)  Feeder and inter-island transport services for the island developing countries generally need to be subsidized. UNCTAD and other appropriate agencies should stand ready to respond to requests from island developing countries for assistance in designing appropriate subsidy schemes, and bilateral and multilateral donors of assistance should stand ready to respond to requests from such countries to help finance them.

(f)  Islands are often subject to natural disasters (hurricanes, volcanic eruptions, earthquakes, tidal waves). Efforts should be made at the regional or global level to improve methods of mitigating or preventing damage from natural disasters. The scope for setting up or improving regional or interregional disaster insurance schemes or funds should be explored.

(g)  Assistance procedures should be simplified, in recognition on the one hand, of the small total amounts to be disbursed and which cannot support heavy administrative overheads, and on the other, of the limited time available to the few civil servants of small governments. Modifications in policy which donors might consider specifically for island developing countries include:

(i)  moving away from project aid to programme aid;

(ii)  investing aid missions with greater authority to commit the donor governments;

(iii)  adjustment of normal aid procedures to lighten the burden on the administrations of island developing countries.

(iv)  UNDP should convene a meeting of donors of island developing countries to discuss assistance procedures.

(h)  Often in island developing countries there are tasks requiring the attention of specialists, which, though essential, are not sufficient to keep the specialist fully occupied. In such cases, it can be sensible to recruit an expert whose services can be made available to a number of such countries. It is often desirable that he serves a limited region so that he can become conversant with the local context. Donors should consider such arrangements sympathetically.

(i)  A major element for improved conditions for island developing countries can be provided through co-operation arrangements in a variety of fields, as well as through broader integration schemes. For example, the island developing countries will greatly benefit from co-operation arrangements among themselves in areas such as the development of shipping, air services, telecommunications, tourism, insurance and re-insurance. These countries cannot afford to maintain expertise with respect to many services and, therefore, can particularly benefit from sharing arrangements amongst themselves. Minimum services will often require assistance which could be of a financial, technical, administrative and marketing nature and support from the international community will be necessary.

(j) Financial, manpower and geographic constraints have often restricted the ability of Governments of some island developing countries to have adequate participation in international conferences. The international community should assist them in overcoming such difficulties.

(k) Increased utilization of islands' harbours by international shipping for servicing, refuelling, ship repair and transshipment.

(l) Greater utilization of airports of islands ideally situated for such purposes as transit, refuelling and servicing.

(m) Compensatory finance arrangements covering not only shortfalls in export earnings but also unexpected increases in import bills should be made available to island developing countries.

## II. Further work by UNCTAD

5. The Ministers request the Secretary-General of UNCTAD to continue the work programme of UNCTAD on behalf of island developing countries as contained in Conference resolution 98(IV), including the review of the special economic problems deriving from the geographical situation of island developing countries and consideration of possible further recommendations for action in their favour, with a view to reducing the geographical handicaps.

With this objective in mind a global project should be launched to support the need to identify special measures in favour of developing island countries. The project will be phased into two stages:

(i) In the first phase, the project will produce an in-depth study analysing the uniqueness of island economies and the constraints inhibiting their economic growth, in particular their distance from market centres, the smallness of their economies and markets, low resource endowment and heavy dependence on few commodities for foreign exchange earnings.

(ii) In the second phase, the outcome of the above-mentioned study will form the basis for a conference of planners from island countries that will propose specific measures for external assistance, recognizing, inter alia, the traditional island life and institutions, physical environment, development priorities and the problems of island countries in the international economy.

6. The UNDP, international financial institutions and bilateral assistance institutions are requested to increase the assistance to island developing countries. These institutions are urged to support UNCTAD in strengthening its technical and advisory services on behalf of island developing countries. This can be achieved by identifying specific programmes of technical assistance which will meet the requirements of island developing countries. The criteria, terms and conditions governing the flow of bilateral and multilateral financial and technical assistance to the island developing countries should be geared to the special needs and problems of the countries concerned. A major proportion of such aid should be made on a grant basis.

7. Since the regional economic commissions have identified the special needs of island developing countries in their respective regions UNCTAD should, in carrying out its task, co-ordinate its activities and co-operate with regional and subregional economic commissions in the implementation of programmes in favour of these countries.

8. Recognizing the importance of tourism as a major source of income, employment and foreign exchange for some island developing countries and the need for these countries to have an equitable share in international air passenger transport, it is deemed appropriate:

(a) To support the recommendations of the UNCTAD Group of Experts on inter-island and sea services and urges their immediate adoption and implementation by the international community;

(b) To support the efforts of these island developing countries to conclude as soon as possible equitable air services agreements both for scheduled and non-scheduled services by airlines of national designation;  and

(c)  To invite the UNCTAD in collaboration with appropriate regional institutions to undertake as a priority research subject studies on the policy issues involved in the development of air transport services.

Item 17
of the provisional agenda for UNCTAD V

TRADE RELATIONS AMONG COUNTRIES HAVING
DIFFERENT ECONOMIC AND SOCIAL SYSTEMS

Introduction

1.    This subject has been dealt with systematically since the First UNCTAD.
Progress has been made, but there can be no doubt that trade and economic relations between the developing countries and the socialist countries of Eastern Europe could be greatly increased and improved.  The present situation of the international economy and the phenomena of growing protectionism have made it necessary for the economic relations of both groups of countries to be increased and be linked to the efforts to establish a New International Economic Order.  Planning trade by means of long-term agreements and contracts; consideration of comprehensive approaches to economic relations instead of attention focused exclusively on trade; the greater capacity of the developing countries to formulate policies for foreign economic relations and to achieve their implementation; attaining a mutual expansion of trade based on the principle of non-reciprocity; and a greater impact of multilateral approaches, are among some of the elements which could contribute to the achievement of a greater and better economic relationship between the two groups of countries.

2.    In this context the socialist countries of Eastern Europe should play an increasingly more active role in bringing about the early establishment of the New International Economic Order.

3.    The Ministers propose that UNCTAD adopt a comprehensive programme on trade and economic relations among countries having different economic and social systems. Such a programme should embody the establishment and improvement of a series of instruments for the promotion of economic relations and should embody the following measures:

1.  Expansion and improvement of preference schemes

(i)   The socialist countries of Eastern Europe should expand and improve without delay their schemes of generalized preferences.  A preferential duty free entry should be granted to all manufactured products of developing countries, particularly those based on processing of their commodities and raw materials and on all tropical products.

(ii)  Action should be taken by the socialist countries of Eastern Europe to remove all forms of tariff and non-tariff barriers.  This should be done on the basis of non-reciprocity and non-discrimination.

(iii) Such improvements should, inter alia, recognize the need for increased imports of manufactured and semi-manufactured products from developing countries.

2.  Payments arrangements

Limited progress has been made in the field of payments.  In order to improve the situation the following measures should be implemented:

(i)   All payments should be made in convertible currency, unless in those cases where developing countries express a preference for or interest in other special arrangements like the clearing account system.

(ii)  Improvement in the CMEA payments arrangements by inter alia, the use of transferable roubles  so that developing countries can use their surplus balances in transactions with other CMEA countries, or transfer such

205

balances into convertible currencies.

3.  Trade development potentials for exports of developing countries

(i)  The socialist countries of Eastern Europe should take the necessary
measures to identify and accommodate in their medium and long-term plans
the potential areas of trade development with developing countries,
particularly in the field of manufactured and semi-manufactured products.
In this manner, developing countries would be aware of the import
potential that the socialist countries of Eastern Europe would have for
their exports, particularly in sectors where developing countries have a
comparative advantage. All effort would be made by developing countries
to utilize such areas of export interest.

(ii)  The socialist countries of Eastern Europe should adopt other policy
measures which would ensure the growth of demand in their countries for
products of developing countries and the consequent imports from
developing countries. These policy measures should result in reserving
and increasing share for the developing countries in the markets and
import programmes of the socialist countries of Eastern Europe, especially
in the import market for processed and semi-processed goods. Special
measures could also include sub-contracting and tripartite ventures.

4.  Establishment of joint ventures

(i)  Where developing countries consider it to be advantageous, joint ventures
should be promoted and established, particularly in the field of industry,
agriculture and trade, with individual developing countries, groups of
countries and tripartite corporations. The socialist countries of
Eastern Europe should encourage and participate in such efforts. Such
joint ventures should include effective participation of nationals of
developing countries and greater utilization of local materials.

(ii)  The objectives of such joint ventures should be to promote the
industrialization of developing countries and to increase the exports
of manufactured and semi-manufactured products from these countries.

5.  Financial assistance

(i)  The socialist countries of Eastern Europe should increase their financial
assistance to developing countries with a view to meeting the target of
0.7 per cent of ODA set out in the Second United Nations Development
Strategy before the end of 1980.

(ii)  They should adopt the necessary measures which would make the Special Fund
of the International Investment Bank effective. Through this Fund
resources should continue to be made available to developing countries
for the identification and financing of national, subregional and
regional projects directly or through the regional development banks.

(iii)  Through this bank, the socialist countries of Eastern Europe should be
able to arrange resources earmarked for financial assistance to
developing countries and a lowering of the rates of interest levied on
borrowings in convertible currency by developing countries.

6.  Technical assistance and training

It was considered desirable to provide incentives for multilateral approaches
which will make possible relations between one or several countries of one group
and one or several countries of the other group and with the corresponding
secretariats of their economic groups. For this it would be necessary to increase
mutual knowledge and develop contacts at every level. It was seen that there are
several multilateral mechanisms in the socialist countries of which the developing
countries could take advantage.

(i)  The socialist countries of Eastern Europe should increase the level of
technical assistance given to developing countries, in particular for
the training of high-level staff from the developing countries in the
technical and scientific fields and assistance in the establishment of
technical and scientific institutions or centres in these countries.

206

(ii)  The UNCTAD secretariat should assist developing countries through a study of the ways and means of effective utilization of technical co-operation agreements between developing countries and socialist countries of Eastern Europe.

(iii) The UNCTAD secretariat should submit concrete proposals on effective utilization of the Special Fund of the International Investment Bank for financing programmes of economic and technical assistance to developing countries.

In order to facilitate trade and economic co-operation, and the exchange of information, action should be taken to set up joint intergovernmental commissions between developing countries and socialist countries of Eastern Europe and to promote co-operation between their chambers of commerce.

## 7.  Institutional matters

(i)   The Intergovernmental Group of Experts on Trade Opportunities which met from 17 to 22 October 1977 should be reconvened to study, inter alia, the proposals of the Group of 77 submitted to the Group of Experts.

(ii)  The Intergovernmental Group of Experts to study a multilateral system of payments between socialist countries of Eastern Europe and developing countries should also be reconvened.  This Group met from 28 November to 2 December 1977.

(iii) UNCTAD should upon request continue to organize bilateral consultations not only at regular sessions of the Board, but also at other times.

(iv)  The Group of 77 recognizes the need to increase its capacity to formulate policies and to establish institutions for their implementation, so as to orient trade and co-operation with the socialist countries of Eastern Europe.  Both parties should be better informed of the characteristics and structures of their corresponding external sectors, thus creating and improving appropriate institutional arrangements between them to solve the difficulties which their economic relations might face as well as for promotion, considering broad participation of the economic agents involved.

(v)   The role which UNCTAD could play to support the developing countries in practically all the fields mentioned was stressed.  This support can take the form of studies, convening groups of experts, organizing training courses and direct technical assistance.  For this, co-ordination with the regional processes for co-operation and with the United Nations regional commissions and the UNDP would be very useful.

Item 18
of the provisional agenda for UNCTAD V

ECONOMIC CO-OPERATION AMONG DEVELOPING COUNTRIES

Support measures by developed countries and international organizations
for Economic Co-operation among Developing Countries (ECDC)

1. The Ministers of the Group of 77 reaffirm that strategy of collective self-reliance should be viewed as an integral part of a global economic system, specifically as an essential element of an overall strategy for development encompassing the restructuring of international economic relations, and that Economic Co-operation among Developing Countries is a key element in a collective self-reliant strategy and thus becomes both an essential part of and an instrument for the necessary structural changes required for a balanced and equitable process of world economic development,  ushering in a new set of relationships based on mutual interests and accommodations.  Therefore:

(a)  A first Short Medium-Term Action Plan for Global Priorities on ECDC is adopted, to be reviewed at the Fifth Ministerial Meeting of the Group of 77, calling for specific action in the priority areas of economic co-operation among developing countries.

207

(b)   Economic co-operation among developing countries is a basic component of their efforts towards the establishment of the New International Economic Order (NIEO).

(c)   Economic co-operation among developing countries is a matter that chiefly concerns the developing countries, and it should be formulated and implemented by them, at the subregional, regional, interregional and global levels.

(d)   In this context, the developed countries and the organizations of the United Nations system should give strong support to this process in fulfilment of the different General Assembly and UNCTAD resolutions.

2.   Recognized that the programme of meetings on economic co-operation among developing countries, proposed by the Group of 77, was not agreed on at the eighteenth session of the Trade and Development Board, nor at the second session of the  Committee on Economic Co-operation among Developing Countries, due to the opposition of the developed countries, and considering that the United Nations General Assembly, at its recent thirty-third session, instructured the UNCTAD Secretary-General to continue consultations to decide on said programme, and taking into account paragraphs 81 and 82 of the Provisional Report of the Preparatory Committee of the Group of 77;

The Ministers recommend that:

(a)   the position formally adopted by the Group of 77 be ratified and that the need for this programme be stressed and the intention to execute it be fully expressed, including in particular through the convening by UNCTAD, by the end of 1979, of the following:

(i)   Regional meetings of subregional and regional economic co-operation groupings to consider action in pursuance of the objectives of the Mexico City Programme on Economic Co-operation among Developing Countries.

(ii) A meeting of the  secretariats of economic co-operation  groupings of developing countries on subregional, regional and interregional economic co-operation and integration among developing countries.

(iii) Three meetings of governmental experts of developing countries to examine and make proposals, bearing in mind the studies undertaken by the UNCTAD secreratiat in compliance with  paragraph 2(a) of resolution 1(I) adopted at the first session of the Committee on Economic Co-operation among Developing Countries.

(iv) A meeting of secretariats of economic co-operation groupings and multilateral financial institutions of developing countries on inter-country projects.

(b) the developed countries be urged to abandon the negative attitude adopted up to the  present and contribute to the implementation of the relevant resolutions of the United Nations General  Assembly,  thereby taking the first steps towards compliance with the concept of support measures, as stated in UNCTAD resolution 92(IV) and resolution 1(I) of the Committee for Economic Co-operation among Developing Countries.

(c) the role of UNCTAD's ECDC Committee be strengthened to enable it to be a forum for the negoations of support measures from developed to developing countries since such measures constitute a basic element of the whole process of economic co-operation among developing countries to which developed countries are expected to make meaningful  contributions.

(d)

(i) UNCTAD should upon request of developing countries, subregional, regional and interregional economic groupings of developing countries assist in preparing specific proposals for support measures as need arises;

(ii) developed countries respond positively to such requests when they are  made;

(iii) any assistance extended on a subregional, regional or interregional basis should be in addition to assistance extended to individual developing countries.

3. **The Ministers strongly recommend** that the United Nations system, in particular UNCTAD and the regional economic commissions, should strengthen and increase its assistance to economic co-operation among developing countries. In this regard, the UNDP should intensify its assistance to subregional, regional and interregional projects, taking also into account the role foreseen for UNDP by the World Conference on Technical Co-operation among Developing Countries. To this end, adequate resources should be made available.

4. Specifically the Ministers recommend that:

(a) measures should be taken by the United Nations to intensify the role of UNCTAD within the United Nations system in the promotion of economic co-operation among developing countries and its co-ordination and co-operation with other members of the United Nations system, as well as to strengthen its working arrangements with UNDP, with a view to enhancing joint operational strategies, taking into account the strong correlation between economic and technical co-operation among developing countries;

(b) as a matter of priority, each developing country should consider drawing up, with the assistance of UNCTAD and other international organizations concerned, a full national inventory of its own requirements and resources as a basis for securing appropriate support measures from developed countries;

(c) developing countries should support, through individual or collective endorsement, project proposals addressed to UNDP in support of economic co-operation among developing countries. To this effect they may wish to consider special contributions, including as appropriate earmarking of a proportion of their own UNDP Indicative Planning Figures (IPF);

(d) acknowledging that economic co-operation among developing countries is an important element of the New International Economic Order and, as such is based on interdependence, common interest and co-operation among all States, developing countries should invite, through the United Nations development system, contributions from developed countries for the implementation of economic co-operation among developing countries projects whose objectives are of interest to both categories of countries;

(e) developing countries should urge the United Nations system, and particularly UNDP, to devote increasing the IPF resources to result-oriented activities in support of economic co-operation among developing countries, with special stress on the need for substantially increasing UNDP's resources for subregional, regional and interregional projects in this field;

(f) developing countries should request UNCTAD to intensify both its role within the United Nations system in the promotion of economic co-operation among developing countries and its co-ordination and co-operation among developing countries and co-operation with other members of the United Nations system, as well as to strengthen its working arrangements with UNDP, with a view to joint operational strategies given the strong correlation between economic and technical co-operation among developing countries;

(g) the restructuring process of the United Nations system should ensure that UNCTAD is strengthened and provided with all the necessary human and financial means to effectively carry out its tasks on economic co-operation among developing countries, which have increased significantly without any meaningful additions to its resources nor appropriate changes in its institutional set-up that could enhance its role as a lead agency in the establishment of the New International Economic Order;

(h) the UNCTAD secretariat, in carrying out its tasks on Economic Co-operation among Developing Countries, should work in close consultation and co-operation with the regional economic commissions since they have a vital role in promoting and implementing subregional, regional and interregional economic co-operation among developing countries.

Technical co-operation and economic co-operation among developing countries

5.   **The Ministers recall that** technical co-operation among developing countries as
conceived by the developing countries on several previous occasions and by the
United Nations Conference on Technical Co-operation among Developing Countries, is a
fundamental instrument in promoting economic co-operation among developing countries.
They consider that:

   (i)   prompt and effective implementation of the Buenos Aires Plan of Action
         and resolutions approved by the above-mentioned Conference is required;

  (ii)   among the many important provisions contained in the Buenos Aires Action
         Plan in this context is the need to promote in the developing countries
         national research and training centres of multinational scope in the
         developing countries.   This is also the subject of one of the resolutions
         adopted by the Conference;

 (iii)   in support of the implementation of the Plan of Action, the importance of
         the contribution of developed countries and international organizations to
         the increased national and collective self-reliance of developing countries,
         needs to be stressed, in order to implement, inter alia, the recommendations
         relating to agriculture and industry.

### Item 19
### of the provisional agenda for UNCTAD V

#### INSTITUTIONAL ISSUES

1.   The Group of 77 recognizes the evolving role of UNCTAD as a major forum for the
evaluation and review of world economic developments in the context of its mandate,
for initiating discussions on new concepts and policies and even more for negotiations
on a wide range of issues relevant to international economic relations and, in this
context, the need to enhance its capacity to perform its evolving functions
effectively.

2.   UNCTAD needs to be strengthened, especially in the following aspects:

   (a)   Clear recognition of UNCTAD as the principal instrument of the
General Assembly for international economic negotiations on international trade and
development, particularly in the context of negotiations on the establishment of the
New International Economic Order, and reaffirmation of this role;

   (b)   Reaffirmation of UNCTAD's role as the major instrument for review and
follow-up of international economic developments;

   (c)   The need to strengthen co-ordination between UNCTAD and other agencies and
organizations of the United Nations system in order to enable UNCTAD to perform its
role effectively;

   (d)   Urgent need to provide UNCTAD with sufficient resources and special
flexibility in its method of operations, so as to enable it to perform its role and
functions effectively, taking into account the logistic problems associated with the
increased workload of UNCTAD;

   (e)   The need for further adapting the permanent intergovernmental machinery of
UNCTAD to the new emphasis in the role of UNCTAD, in particular its increased
activity as a negotiating forum, while enabling it to continue to perform the full
range of tasks with which it has been entrusted;

   (f)   The need to maintain and strengthen UNCTAD's support to the developing
countries in the field of trade and development, particularly in the context of the
negotiations for the establishment of the New International Economic Order.

3.   The increasing activities and functions of UNCTAD also demand, particularly in
the present context, their harmonization, rationalization and co-ordination in a
systematic manner so as to maximize its effectiveness.   Consequently it is
recommended, inter alia, that:

(a)  Ways and means should be sought of grouping the specific issues and subjects to be addressed by special expert group meetings, in order to minimize the number of sub-meetings and to encourage the attendance of high level government experts.   Meetings of experts appointed in their personal capacity should be reduced in number;

(b)  Rather than have a whole Committee meet in routine formal sessions unless there are sufficiently important and large number of issues to be discussed, special sub-groups could be convened to deal with a specific number of issues within the competence of the Committee;

(c)  The practice by which each Committee, group or sub-group decides on when and how to meet should be reviewed by the Board with a view to ensuring minimum frequent disturbances in the schedule of meetings;

(d)  An appropriate mechanism to provide policy direction and co-ordination on certain issues and to harmonize and integrate activities of the secretariat on these issues;

(e)  Urgent need that documents in all working languages be made available at an appropriate time in accordance with the relevant rules.

4.    The strengthening of UNCTAD should be seen as an equally important element in the process of completing the restructuring of the social and economic sectors of the United Nations.

## C. Rules of Procedure of the Fourth Ministerial Meeting of the Group of 77, Arusha, 12-16 February 1979*

PREAMBLE

The Fourth Ministerial Meeting of the Group of 77,

Recalling the objectives set out in the "Joint Declaration of the seventy-seven developing countries at the conclusion of the United Nations Conference on Trade and Development", 1964, which is contained in the Final Act of that Conference,

Further recalling the recommendations made by the Group of 31 Developing Countries at the second part of the tenth session of the Trade and Development Board of the United Nations Conference on Trade and Development concerning the objectives, organization and level of the Ministerial Meeting of the Group of 77,

Taking into account the expressed wish of the Group of 77 to hold the Fourth Ministerial Meeting in Arusha, United Republic of Tanzania, in a spirit of mutual understanding, thus furthering international co-operation,

Further taking into account the Ministerial Meetings of the Group of 77 held in Algiers in 1967, in Lima in 1971 and in Manila in 1976,

Noting with appreciation the work done by the Senior Officials Meeting in preparation for the Ministerial Meeting,

Decides to adopt the following:

RULES OF PROCEDURE

### Rule 1

The accredited representatives of the Governments members of the Group of 77 shall participate in the Ministerial Meeting.

### Rule 2

All decisions of the Meeting shall be taken by consensus.

The Meeting shall elect a President, 10 Vice-Presidents and a Rapporteur-General who will constitute the Bureau of the Meeting, together with the Regional Co-ordinators and the Officers of Committees or Working Groups, as may be established in accordance with rule 4. The Chairman of the Senior Officials Meeting shall be an ex officio member of the Bureau.

### Rule 4

The Meeting may establish such Committees and Working Groups as may be necessary. The Committees and Working Groups shall submit their reports for examination by the plenary session.

### Rule 5

The Bureau shall examine the credentials of representatives and submit its report to the plenary session.

### Rule 6

The plenary sessions shall be held in public unless the Meeting decides otherwise.

---

*Reprinted from Sauvant, document V.2.D.2.

## Rule 7

Each Committee and each Working Group established shall elect a Chairman, a Vice-Chairman and a Rapporteur.

## Rule 8

For the purpose of oral statements in plenary the official languages of the Meeting shall be Arabic, English, French and Spanish. However, rule 53 of the General Assembly's rules of procedure will apply to oral statements in plenary in any other language other than the official languages of the General Assembly.

## Rule 9

The conclusions of the Meeting shall be published in a Final Document.

## Rule 10

In all matters not covered by these rules of procedure, the Meeting shall apply mutatis mutandis the rules of procedure of the United Nations General Assembly.

# ANNEX III
# CHRONOLOGY OF MEETINGS DOCUMENTED IN THIS COLLECTION

## Chronology of Meetings of the Group of 77 and Related Events*

| Date | Place | Title of meeting |
|---|---|---|
| 11 November 1963 | New York | Group of 75 at the Eighteenth Session of the United Nations General Assembly |
| 9-13 December 1963 | Niamey | Organization of African Unity, Economic and Social Commission, Preparatory Meeting for UNCTAD I |
| 24 February- 7 March 1964 | Alta Gracia | Inter-American Economic and Social Council, Special Committee on Latin American Co-ordination, Preparatory Meeting for UNCTAD I |
| 12 March 1964 | Teheran | Economic Commission for Asia and the Far East, Preparatory Meeting for UNCTAD I |
| 23 March- 16 June 1964 | Geneva | UNCTAD, First Session |
| 15 June 1964 | Geneva | Group of 77 at UNCTAD I |
| 30 December 1964 | New York | Nineteenth Session of the General Assembly of the United Nations, Establishment of UNCTAD |
| 23 September 1966 | Geneva | Group of 31, Preparations for UNCTAD II |
| 7 September 1967 | Geneva | UNCTAD, Trade and Development Board |
| 25-27 September 1967 | Bangkok | Ministerial Meeting of ECAFE Developing Countries Members of the Group of 77, Preparatory Meeting for the Algiers Ministerial Meeting |
| 25-30 September 1967 | Bogota | Ad Hoc Committee on Latin American Co-ordination, Fourth Meeting at the Expert Level, Preparatory Meeting for the Algiers Ministerial Meeting |
| 7-15 October 1967 | Algiers | Economic Commission for Africa/Organization of African Unity, Preparatory Meeting for UNCTAD II |
| 10 October 1967 | Algiers | Co-ordination Committee, Preparatory Meeting for the Algiers Ministerial Meeting |
| 10-25 October 1967 | Algiers | First Ministerial Meeting of the Group of 77 |
| 1-14 December 1967 | Geneva | Working Group of Fifteen |
| 1 February- 29 March 1968 | New Delhi | UNCTAD, Second Session |

* The Group of 77 normally meets to prepare for impending international conferences, meetings or major international economic negotiations with the developed countries. These events have also been included in this chronology. The documents pertaining to all meetings of the Group of 77 as well as to the related events are contained in Karl P. Sauvant, ed., The Third World without Superpowers, 2nd Ser., The Collected Documents of the Group of 77 (Dobbs Ferry, N.Y.: Oceana, 1981).

| Date | Place | Title of meeting |
|------|-------|------------------|
| 28 March 1968 | New Delhi | Group of 77 at UNCTAD II |
| 10 March 1971 | Geneva | Group of 31 |
| 10 March–<br>7 November 1971 | Geneva | Preparatory Committee for the Lima Ministerial Meeting |
| 1-8 June 1971 | Vienna | UNIDO, Special International Conference |
| 4 June 1971 | Vienna | Group of 77 in the Special International Conference of UNIDO I |
| 18 September 1971 | Geneva | UNCTAD, Trade and Development Board |
| 5-7 October 1971 | Bangkok | Ministerial Meeting of the Asian Group of the Group of 77, Preparatory Meeting for the Lima Ministerial Meeting |
| 8-14 October 1971 | Addis Ababa | Economic Commission for Africa and Organization of African Unity, African Ministerial Meeting Preparatory to UNCTAD III |
| 20-27 October 1971 | Lima | Twelfth Meeting of the Special Committee on Latin American Co-ordination (CECLA), Preparatory Meeting for the Lima Ministerial Meeting |
| 25-27 October 1971 | Lima | Senior Officials Meeting, Preparatory Meeting for the Lima Ministerial Meeting |
| 28 October–<br>7 November 1971 | Lima | Second Ministerial Meeting of the Group of 77 |
| 31 January 1972 | Geneva | Intergovernmental Group of Twenty-Four International Monetary Affairs, Preparatory Meeting of the Deputies |
| 6-7 April 1972 | Caracas | Group of 24, First Ministerial Meeting |
| 13 April–<br>21 May 1972 | Santiago | Group of 77 at UNCTAD III |
| 13 April–<br>21 May 1972 | Santiago | UNCTAD, Third Session |
| 24 September 1972 | Washington | Group of 24, Second Ministerial Meeting |
| 28 September 1972 | Washington | Committee of 20, First Meeting |
| 24 March 1973 | Washington | Group of 24, Third Ministerial Meeting |
| 26-27 March 1973 | Washington | Committee of 20, Second Meeting |
| 29 July 1973 | Washington | Group of 24, Fourth Ministerial Meeting |
| 30-31 July 1973 | Washington | Committee of 20, Third Meeting |
| 23 September 1973 | Nairobi | Group of 24, Fifth Ministerial Meeting |
| 23 September 1973 | Nairobi | Committee of 20, Fourth Meeting |
| 18-23 December 1973 | Cairo | Second Conference of African Ministers of Industry, Preparatory Meeting for UNIDO II |

| Date | Place | Title of meeting |
|---|---|---|
| 16 January 1974 | Rome | Group of 24, Sixth Ministerial Meeting |
| 17-18 January 1974 | Rome | Committee of 20, Fifth Meeting |
| 7-14 April 1974 | Tripoli | Third Conference on Industrial Development for Arab States, Preparatory Meeting for UNIDO II |
| 9 April-<br>2 May 1974 | New York | Group of 77 at the Sixth Special Session of the General Assembly of the United Nations |
| 9 April-<br>2 May 1974 | New York | Sixth Special Session of the General Assembly of the United Nations |
| 9-10 June 1974 | Washington | Group of 24, Seventh Ministerial Meeting |
| 10-28 June 1974 | Mexico City | UNCTAD, Trade and Development Board, Working Group on the Charter of the Economic Rights and Duties of States, Fourth Session |
| 12-13 June 1974 | Washington | Committee of 20, Sixth Meeting |
| 23-24 September 1974 | Addis Ababa | Follow-up Committee on Industrialization in Africa, First Meeting, Preparatory Meeting for UNIDO II |
| 28 September 1974 | Washington | Group of 24, Eighth Ministerial Meeting |
| 2 October 1974 | Washington | Development Committee, First Meeting |
| 3 October 1974 | Washington | Interim Committee, First Meeting |
| 30 October 1974 | Bangkok | Meeting of Ministers of Industry of Developing Countries in Asia and the Pacific Region, Preparatory Meeting for UNIDO II |
| 25-29 November 1974 | Mexico | Latin American Conference on Industrialization, Preparatory Meeting for UNIDO II |
| 25 November-<br>9 December 1974 | New York | Group of 77 at the United Nations General Assembly, Twenty-Ninth Regular Session, Second Committee |
| 5-11 December 1974 | Vienna | First Ministerial Meeting of the Group of 77 in Preparation for UNIDO II |
| 12 December 1974 | New York | Twenty-Ninth Regular Session of the General Assembly of the United Nations, Adoption of the Charter on Economic Rights and Duties of States |
| 13-14 January 1975 | Washington | Group of 24, Ninth Ministerial Meeting |
| 15-16 January 1975 | Washington | Interim Committee, Second Meeting |
| 17 January 1975 | Washington | Development Committee, Second Meeting |
| 22 January 1975 | Vienna | Drafting Group of the Group of 77, Preparations for UNIDO II |
| 15-18 February 1975 | Algiers | Second Ministerial Meeting of the Group of 77 in Preparation for UNIDO II |

219

| Date | Place | Title of meeting |
|---|---|---|
| 12-26 March 1975 | Lima | Group of 77 at UNIDO II |
| 12-26 March 1975 | Lima | UNIDO, Second General Conference |
| 13 March-<br>22 December 1975 | Geneva | Preparatory Committee for the Manila Ministerial Meeting |
| 7-15 April 1975 | Paris | First Preparatory Meeting for CIEC |
| 8-9 June 1975 | Paris | Group of 24, Tenth Ministerial Meeting |
| 10-11 June 1975 | Paris | Interim Committee, Third Meeting |
| 12-13 June 1975 | Paris | Development Committee, Third Meeting |
| 18-29 August 1975 | New York | Group of 77 at the ECOSOC Preparatory Committee for the Special Session of the General Assembly Devoted to Development and International Economic Co-operation |
| 30 August 1975 | Washington | Group of 24, Eleventh Ministerial Meeting |
| 31 August 1975 | Washington | Interim Committee, Fourth Meeting |
| 1-15 September 1975 | New York | Group of 77 in the Ad Hoc Committee of the Seventh Special Session of the General Assembly of the United Nations |
| 1-16 September 1975 | New York | Seventh Special Session of the General Assembly of the United Nations |
| 3-4 September 1975 | Washington | Development Committee, Fourth Meeting |
| 2 October 1975 | Geneva | UNCTAD, Trade and Development Board |
| 13-16 October 1975 | Paris | Second Preparatory Meeting for CIEC |
| 24-29 November 1975 | Algiers | Fourth Conference of Trade Ministers of OAU Member Countries, Preparatory Meeting for the Manila Ministerial Meeting |
| 15 December 1975 | New York | Thirtieth Session of the General Assembly of the United Nations, Resolution on CIEC |
| 16-19 December 1975 | Paris | Opening Ministerial Meeting of the Conference on International Economic Co-operation |
| 6 January 1976 | Kingston | Group of 24, Twelfth Ministerial Meeting |
| 7-8 January 1976 | Kingston | Interim Committee, Fifth Meeting |
| 9 January 1976 | Kingston | Development Committee, Fifth Meeting |
| 12-15 January 1976 | Caracas | Latin American Council of the Latin American Economic System (SELA), First Extraordinary Meeting, Preparatory for the Manila Ministerial Meeting |
| 19-21 January 1976 | Jakarta | Third Ministerial Meeting of the Asian Group of the Group of 77, Preparatory Meeting for the Manila Ministerial Meeting |

| Date | Place | Title of meeting |
|------|-------|------------------|
| 26-27 January 1976 | Paris | Meeting of the Co-chairpersons of CIEC |
| 26-31 January 1976 | Manila | Senior Officials Meeting, Preparatory for the Manila Ministerial Meeting |
| 2-7 February 1976 | Manila | Third Ministerial Meeting of the Group of 77 |
| 23 April 1976 | Geneva | Working Group on Institutional Matters |
| 27 April 1976 | Geneva | Working Group of the Group of 77 – Manila Decision No. 2 |
| 28 April 1976 | Paris | Group of 19 |
| 28 April 1976 | Geneva | Working Group on Membership |
| 5-31 May 1976 | Nairobi | Group of 77 at UNCTAD IV |
| 5-31 May 1976 | Nairobi | UNCTAD, Fourth Session |
| 9 June 1976 | Paris | Group of 19 |
| 8-10 July 1976 | Paris | Meeting of Senior Officials of CIEC |
| 12-16 July 1976 | Geneva | Group of Governmental Experts, First Preparatory Meeting for the Mexico Conference on ECDC |
| 17 July 1976 | Paris | Group of 19 |
| 9-11 September 1976 | Mexico City | Group of Governmental Experts, Second Preparatory Meeting for the Mexico Conference on ECDC |
| 11 September 1976 | Mexico City | Meeting of Heads of Delegations on Organizational Matters, Preparatory Meeting for the Mexico Conference on ECDC |
| 11 September 1976 | Paris | Meeting of Co-chairpersons of CIEC |
| 13-22 September 1976 | Mexico City | Conference on Economic Co-operation among Developing Countries |
| 1-2 October 1976 | Manila | Group of 24, Thirteenth Ministerial Meeting |
| 2 October 1976 | Manila | Interim Committee, Sixth Meeting |
| 3 October 1976 | Manila | Development Committee, Sixth Meeting |
| 6 October 1976 | Manila | Development Committee, Seventh Meeting |
| 6 October 1976 | Manila | Interim Committee, Seventh Meeting |
| 19 November 1976 | New York | Thirty-First Session of the General Assembly of the United Nations, Resolution on CIEC |
| 16 December 1976 | New York | Group of 77 in the United Nations |
| 26 April 1977 | Washington | Group of 24, Fourteenth Ministerial Meeting |
| 27 April 1977 | Washington | Development Committee, Eighth Meeting |
| 28-29 April 1977 | Washington | Interim Committee, Eighth Meeting |

| Date | Place | Title of meeting |
|---|---|---|
| 5 May 1977 | Paris | Group of 19 |
| 30 May-2 June 1977 | Paris | Concluding Ministerial Meeting of the Conference on International Economic Co-operation |
| 31 May 1977 | Paris | Group of 19 |
| 23 September 1977 | Washington | Group of 24, Fifteenth Ministerial Meeting |
| 24 September 1977 | Washington | Interim Committee, Ninth Meeting |
| 25 September 1977 | Washington | Development Committee, Ninth Meeting |
| 29 September 1977 | New York | Ministers for Foreign Affairs of the Group of 77, First Meeting |
| 21 April- 15 December 1978 | Geneva | Preparatory Committee for the Arusha Ministerial Meeting |
| 28 April 1978 | Mexico City | Group of 24, Sixteenth Ministerial Meeting |
| 29-30 April 1978 | Mexico City | Interim Committee, Tenth Meeting |
| 17 September 1978 | Geneva | UNCTAD, Trade and Development Board |
| 22 September 1978 | Washington | Group of 24, Seventeenth Ministerial Meeting |
| 24 September 1978 | Washington | Interim Committee, Eleventh Meeting |
| 27 September 1978 | Washington | Development Committee, Tenth Meeting |
| 27 September 1978 | Washington | Development Committee, Eleventh Meeting |
| 29 September 1978 | New York | Ministers for Foreign Affairs of the Group of 77, Second Meeting |
| 15-17 January 1979 | Colombo | Fourth Ministerial Meeting of the Asian Group of the Group of 77, Preparatory Meeting for the Arusha Ministerial Meeting |
| 15-19 January 1979 | Caracas | Latin American Co-ordination Meeting for the IVth Ministerial Meeting of the Group of 77 in Arusha with a View to UNCTAD V |
| 30 January- 1 February 1979 | Addis Ababa | Conference of African Trade Ministers in Preparation of the Fifth Session of UNCTAD |
| 6-15 February 1979 | Arusha | Senior Officials Meeting, Preparatory Meeting for the Arusha Ministerial Meeting |
| 12-16 February 1979 | Arusha | Fourth Ministerial Meeting of the Group of 77 |
| 6 March 1979 | Washington | Group of 24, Eighteenth Ministerial Meeting |
| 7 March 1979 | Washington | Interim Committee, Twelfth Meeting |
| 7 May-3 June 1979 | Manila | Group of 77 at UNCTAD V |

| Date | Place | Title of meeting |
|---|---|---|
| 7 May-3 June 1979 | Manila | UNCTAD, Fifth Session |
| 20 July-<br>25 September 1979 | Geneva | Committee of 21 of the Group of 77 |
| 10-14 September<br>1979 | Cali | Second Latin American Conference on Industrialization, Preparatory Meeting for UNIDO III |
| 27-29 September 1979 | New York | Ministers for Foreign Affairs of the Group of 77, Third Meeting |
| 28 September 1979 | Belgrade | Group of 24, Nineteenth Ministerial Meeting |
| 29 September 1979 | Belgrade | Ministers of Finance or Economy of the Group of 77, First Meeting |
| 30 September 1979 | Belgrade | Development Committee, Twelfth Meeting |
| 1 October 1979 | Belgrade | Interim Committee, Thirteenth Meeting |
| 17-20 October 1979 | Addis Ababa | Fifth Conference of African Ministers of Industry, Preparatory Meeting for UNIDO III |
| 22-23 October 1979 | Bangkok | ESCAP Preparatory Meetings for the Third General-Conference of UNIDO, Senior Officials Meeting |
| 22-26 October 1979 | Addis Ababa | African Group of Experts, Preparatory Meeting for UNIDO III |
| 25-26 October 1979 | Bangkok | ESCAP Preparatory Meetings for the Third General Conference of UNIDO, Meetings of Ministers of Industry |
| 16-20 November 1979 | Algiers | Fifth Conference on Industrial Development for Arab States, Preparatory Meeting for UNIDO III |
| 26-30 November 1979 | Montevideo | Regional Meeting of Experts on Certain Issues within the Programme on Economic Co-operation among Developing Countries |
| 7-18 December 1979 | Addis Ababa | Joint OAU/ECA/UNCTAD African Regional Meeting on Economic Co-operation among Developing Countries |
| 14 December 1979 | Vienna | Task Force of the Group of 77, Preparations for UNIDO III |
| 15-16 December 1979 | Havana | African Group of the Group of 77, Preparatory Meeting for UNIDO III |
| 17-22 December<br>1979 | Havana | Third Ministerial Meeting of the Group of 77 in Preparation for UNIDO III |
| 7-15 January 1980 | Manila | Meeting of Governmental Experts of Developing Countries of the Asian Region |
| 21 January-<br>9 February 1980 | New Delhi | Group of 77 at UNIDO III |

| Date | Place | Title of meeting |
|---|---|---|
| 21 January-<br>9 February 1980 | New Delhi | UNIDO, Third General Conference |
| 11-14 March 1980 | New York | Ministerial Meeting of the Group of 77 |
| 17 March-<br>8 April 1980 | Geneva | Preparatory Meeting of Governmental Experts of Developing Countries on Economic Co-operation among Developing Countries |
| 24 April 1980 | Hamburg | Group of 24, Twentieth Ministerial Meeting |
| 24 April 1980 | Hamburg | Development Committee, Thirteenth Meeting |
| 25 April 1980 | Hamburg | Interim Committee, Fourteenth Meeting |
| 3-7 June 1980 | Vienna | Meeting of the Ad Hoc Intergovernmental Group of the Group of 77 on Economic Co-operation among Developing Countries in Continuation of the Ministerial Meeting of the Group of 77 Held in New York in March 1980 |
| 25-28 June 1980 | Abu Dhabi | Meeting of Experts of Developing Countries on the Reform of the International Monetary System |
| 21-22 August 1980 | New York | Ministerial Meeting of the Group of 77 |
| 27 September 1980 | Washington | Group of 24, Twenty-First Meeting |
| 28 September 1980 | Washington | Interim Committee, Fifteenth Meeting |
| 29 September 1980 | Washington | Development Committee, Fourteenth Meeting |
| 29-30 September 1980 | New York | Ministers for Foreign Affairs of the Group of 77, Fourth Meeting |
| 1 October 1980 | New York | Group of 77 at the Thirty-Fifth Session of the General Assembly |

# INDEX

# INDEX

operation among Developing Countries; Working Group of 30 on Economic Co-operation among Developing Countries

Economic and Social Commission for Asia and the Pacific, 37, 90-91

Eleventh Special Session of the United Nations General Assembly, 8, 54, 81, 82, 83, 85, 98

Equal geographical distribution *see* Equitable geographical distribution

Equitable geographical distribution, 11-12, 20, 32, 35, 36, 37, 39, 41, 43, 59, 70, 87, 92, 94, 111, 120-121, 126

**F**

Food and Agriculture Organization, 27

**G**

General Agreement on Tariffs and Trade, 86

Geographical distribution *see* Equitable geographical distribution

Global conferences 27, 84, 86, 98

Global negotiations, 22, 50, 51, 54, 68, 75, 82-86, 98
*See also* Group of 77 in the United Nations, New York

Goodwill missions, 4, 43

Group A, 11, 12, 14, 21, 108, 109-110
*See also* African States Group; Asian States Group; Asian and African States Group

Group B, 11, 12, 17, 21, 22, 23, 36, 41, 43, 44, 51, 52, 55, 57, 58, 90, 91, 108, 109-110
*See also* Western European and Other States Group

Group C, 11, 12, 14, 21, 108, 109-110
*See also* Latin American States Group

Group D, 11, 12, 13, 17, 21, 23, 36, 41, 43, 44, 51, 52, 57, 58, 90, 91, 108, 109-110
*See also* Eastern European States Group

Group of Deputies, 28, 61, 64, 67, 93, 94, 95
Bureau, 28, 61
chairperson, 28, 61, 68, 95
*See also* Group of 24

Group of 9, 62, 64, 93
*See also* Group of 24

Group of 19, 6, 29, 51, 69-74, 95
co-ordination with Group of 77, 71-72
difficulties, 72-73
members, 127
question of representation, 70

Supporting Team, 50-51, 71, 95

Group of 77
bargaining strength, 8-9, 10, 18
chronology of meetings, Annex III
constituting parts, 12, 15, 16, 37
co-ordination, 52, 53-54, 59, 71-72
decision-making, 16-18
membership, 14-16, 18-19, 22-23, 24, 103
ministerial-level meetings, 30
number of meetings, 13-14, 96, 108, 112, Annex III
organization, 28, 83-85, Part II
origin, 1-3, 12, 14
purpose and objectives, 3-10, Annex II-A, Annex II-B
rules of procedure, 16, 35
strains within the Group, 9-10
structure, 28, 83-85, Part II
unity, 2, 9-10, 18, 29, 38
*See also* African Group; Asian Group; Latin American Group; Consensus; Regional groups; Resources of the Group of 77; New International Economic Order

Group of 77 in the United Nations, New York, 28, 49-50, 73, 74-86, 97, 99
*ad hoc* working groups, 28, 77, 97
and the Charter of Economic Rights and Duties of States, 75-76
and the Seventh Special Session, 76
and the Sixth Special Session, 75, 96
bureau, 77, 97
co-ordinator, 77, 78, 80, 84, 128
institutionalization, 49-54, 80, 84
number of meetings, 77, 108, 112
plenary, 28, 77
sponsorship of resolutions, 74, 79
*See also* Meetings of Ministers for Foreign Affairs; Ministerial Meetings at the United Nations in New York; Co-ordinator; Group of 27, Regional groups; Resources of the Group of 77; United Nations

Group of 77 in UNCTAD, 28, 29-54
*ad hoc* task forces, 45, 88
*ad hoc* working groups 28, 36, 45, 46, 47
Co-ordinating Committee, 29-30, 47, 86, 112, 116
co-ordinator, 46-47, 122
informal Bureau, 28, 47
liaison with UNCTAD Secretariat, 46
number of meetings, 45, 108, 112
plenary, 28, 31, 45
preparations of UNCTAD sessions, 29-30, 31, 38-44
regional co-ordinators, 28, 43, 46, 47, 88
regular organizational infrastructure, 44-47

230